To Roger,

with best wishes.

Iordi

Leadership Development in a Global World

The Palgrave Macmillan IESE Business Collection is designed to provide authoritative insights and comprehensive advices on specific management topics. The books are based on rigorous research produced by IESE Business School professors, covering new concepts within traditions management areas (Strategy, Leadership, Managerial Economics), as well as emerging areas of enquiry. The collection seeks to broaden the knowledge of the business field through the ongoing release of titles with a humanistic focus in mind.

Books available in the series:

Melé, Domènec *Management Ethics* 9780230246300

Done, Adrian *Global Trends* 9780230284869

Estrada, Javier *The Essential Financial Toolkit* 9780230283596

Canals, Jordi *The Future of Leadership Development* 9780230279285

Leadership Development in a Global World

The Role of Companies and Business Schools

Edited by

JORDI CANALS
*Dean and Professor of General Management,
IESE Business School*

First published 2012 by
PALGRAVE MACMILLAN

Palgrave Macmillan in the UK is an imprint of Macmillan Publishers Limited,
registered in England, company number 785998, of Houndmills, Basingstoke,
Hampshire RG21 6XS.

Palgrave Macmillan in the US is a division of St Martin's Press LLC,
175 Fifth Avenue, New York, NY 10010.

Palgrave Macmillan is the global academic imprint of the above companies
and has companies and representatives throughout the world.

Palgrave® and Macmillan® are registered trademarks in the United States,
the United Kingdom, Europe and other countries.

ISBN 978–0–230–35513–2

This book is printed on paper suitable for recycling and made from fully
managed and sustained forest sources. Logging, pulping and manufacturing
processes are expected to conform to the environmental regulations of the
country of origin.

A catalogue record for this book is available from the British Library.

A catalog record for this book is available from the Library of Congress.

10 9 8 7 6 5 4 3 2 1
21 20 19 18 17 16 15 14 13 12

Printed and bound in Great Britain by
CPI Antony Rowe, Chippenham and Eastbourne

Contents

List of Figures and Tables

Figures

Tables

Preface and Acknowledgments

Throughout the twentieth century, most Western companies with international activities were still operating in homogeneous markets, employing people with similar values. With strong economic growth in China, India, Russia, Brazil, Mexico or Turkey, among others, multinational companies started to operate in those countries more actively, profiting from trade and foreign investment liberalization. Over the past few years, this trend has accelerated, only punctuated by a fall in international trade and investment after the 2008 financial crisis.

This new business context is essentially different from the dominant one just a decade ago. Companies in a variety of industries are generating a substantial share of their revenues in new growth markets. Their business potential looks weak in mature economies—their home markets—and strong in the new markets. As a result, the need to develop local leaders in growth markets is more acute. Nevertheless, as companies try to cope better with globalization, senior managers need to think how to grow the next generation of global leaders who could manage business units locally, regionally or globally, across cultures and contexts, and eventually have overall responsibilities for the whole company, not just for a division or a subsidiary.

Companies that want to succeed in tackling these challenges need to think deeply about how to speed up talent development in an integrated global economy. Good leadership is indispensable in any company. The need for quality leadership in growth markets is crucial to generate sustainable success. These issues are more pressing as we see local champions in those growth markets expanding globally and increasing their capacity to attract the best local talent.

Many large Western international companies are still managed from headquarters, far away from growth markets, not only in terms of physical distance, but in the cultural understanding of those countries, and their cultures and values. Still few Western companies have senior managers originally from growth markets sitting on the board of directors or the board of management, or having global responsibilities within their organizations. Many of them still rely on the work of expatriate executives to run foreign operations.

International companies also have a tough time in recruiting local young talent in growth markets. Talented people increasingly want to work with some growing local champions. Moreover, the levels of loyalty and commitment of those young people to Western companies operating in growth markets seem to be lower than in mature markets. Even if the numbers are smaller, Asian companies operating in Europe and North America experience the same pain.

Integration is also another challenge for companies that do well in recruiting local talent. Integrating local professionals into a global company and leveraging their unique knowledge and expertise is always complex. In a nutshell, what happens is that the learning that occurs at the local level is seldom transferred to other parts of the firm.

Increasing globalization, the economic shift to Asia and the demographic and social changes that it brings about, require a different type of leadership in the business world. International business leaders need to think beyond market penetration and off-shoring in growing markets; they also need to develop a long-term business strategy that includes a talent development strategy fully aligned with those new realities. Otherwise, their efforts in emerging markets may end up in failure.

This book presents a collection of papers that deal with the topic of global leadership development. The origin of most of the papers is the 2011 International Conference on "Global Leadership Development in an Integrated World: Implications for Companies and Business Schools," held at IESE (Barcelona Campus) on 7–8 April, 2011. The audience consisted of CEOs, HR managers and business school deans, faculty and administrators. The discussions around the presentations were extremely engaging and insightful.

The authors of the chapters are well-known scholars and business schools' deans who come from different backgrounds. Perhaps one of the salient qualities of this book is the variety of perspectives from which authors try to tackle the challenge of leadership development in a global economy. The different chapters cover organizational, economic and sociological perspectives of leadership development, and include important contributions to the role of business schools in this process.

This book is organized around three sections. Part 1 is titled "Developing Leadership Capabilities in a Global World." The chapters in this section present and analyze different capabilities that leaders need to develop in an integrated global economy. They are related with the changes in the business context and the complexity that corporate strategy adopts in a global world. One of the chapters also deals with how to organize leadership development programs and link them up with corporate needs. By using different perspectives, authors provide some useful categories and concepts to think about leadership development in a global world.

Part 2 is "Leadership Development in a Global Context: The Contribution of Business Schools." The chapters in this section also analyze and discuss leadership competencies and reflect upon them from the business schools' angle. They provide both a historical perspective on leadership development at business schools and an insightful look into the future, by highlighting some key issues that business schools should address to remain relevant for global companies over the next years.

Part 3 is "Leadership Development, Globalization and Cross-Cultural Issues." One of the unique dimensions of leadership development in a global world is the increasing role of cultural factors both in globalization and leadership. These go beyond the debate on values and step into issues of leadership effectiveness, the functionality of management teams, team work across countries, talent development or corporate governance. Understanding these issues and how they may have an impact on leadership development remain complex questions. The authors focus on some of the key areas and offer useful and innovative reflections.

I am very grateful to the chapter contributors. They have produced a rich and very useful work. If this book were to have an impact, it would be due to the fact that the authors are pre-eminent scholars in their subject areas and some have many years of experience in leadership development as business school deans.

At the IESE 2011 Conference, it was a real privilege to count on CEOs and senior HR managers whose contribution was superb: Juan I. Apoita (BBVA), Xavier Coll (CaixaBank), Christian Finckh (Allianz), Patricia Francis (International Trade Center), Laurent Freixe (Nestlé), Antonio Gallart (Gas Natural Fenosa), Francisco Fernandez de Ybarra (Citi), Denise Kingsmill (British Airways), Bruno di Leo (IBM), Tim MacNicholas (Siemens), Hans Ulrich Maerki (ABB), Bernardo Quinn (Telefonica), April Samulevicz (Zurich), Christine Scheffler (Bertelsmann), Martin Sorrell (WPP), Kees Storm (Unilever), Didier Tisserand (L'Oreal) and Gildo Zegna (Ermenegildo Zegna). Aaron Heslehurst (BBC) and Adrian Wooldridge (The Economist) did a brilliant job in leading some of the sessions and stimulating the discussions. I am very grateful to them all: counting on their contribution was a real pleasure and a great learning opportunity for all of us.

In the organization of the conference, I was privileged to have the support of IESE colleagues including Luis Arias, Giuseppe Auricchio, César Beltrán, Marta Elvira, Alex Herrera, Pedro Nueno, M. Julia Prats, Mireia Rius, Carlos Sánchez-Runde, Pedro Videla and Eric Weber. The IESE Alumni and Institutional Development team did a great job in organizing the conference and making it an excellent event for participants and speakers.

Eleanor Davey-Corrigan of Palgrave Macmillan has been very supportive of this work. Hannah Fox and Mritunjai Sahai helped me along the editorial process with many useful ideas and suggestions.

Assumpció Cabré, Miriam Freixa, Teresa Planell and Ana Vericat did a wonderful job both before and during the conference, while keeping up with their regular duties at IESE. Without their help and commitment the conference and this book would not have been possible. I am very grateful for their outstanding support.

Jordi Canals
March 2012

About the Authors

Robert F. Bruner
Dean and Charles Abbott Professor of Business Administration, Darden Graduate School of Business, University of Virginia

Jordi Canals
Dean and Professor of General Management, IESE Business School, University of Navarra

Robert M. Conroy
J. Harvey Wilkinson Professor of Business Administration, Darden Graduate School of Business, University of Virginia

Anabella Davila
Professor of Business Administration, EGADE, Tecnológico de Monterrey

Marta M. Elvira
Professor of Managing People in Organizations, IESE Business School, University of Navarra

Pankaj Ghemawat
Anselmo Rubiralta Professor of Global Strategy, IESE Business School, University of Navarra

Matt Golosinski
Director of Research, INSEAD

Dipak Jain
Dean and INSEAD Chaired Professor of Marketing, INSEAD

Yih-teen Lee
Associate Professor of Managing People in Organizations, IESE Business School, University of Navarra

Randall Morck
Jarislowsky Distinguished Chair in Finance and Distinguished University Professor, University of Alberta

Luciara Nardon
Assistant Professor of International Business, Sprott School of Business, Carleton University

Nitin Nohria
Dean and George F. Baker Professor of Administration, Harvard Business School

Pedro Nueno
José F. Bertran Professor of Entrepreneurship, IESE Business School, University of Navarra, and President, CEIBS

Carlos Sánchez-Runde
Professor of Managing People in Organizations, IESE Business School, University of Navarra

Scott A. Snell
E. Thayer Bigelow Professor of Business Administration, Darden Graduate School of Business, University of Virginia

Edward A. Snyder
Dean and William S. Beinecke Professor of Economics and Management, Yale School of Management

Richard M. Steers
Professor of Organization and Management, Lundquist College of Business, University of Oregon

Bernard Yeung
Stephen Riady Distinguished Professor and Dean, National University of Singapore Business School

PART 1

Developing Leadership Capabilities in a Global World

CHAPTER 1.1

The Development of General Management Capabilities in a Global World

ROBERT F. BRUNER, Dean and Charles Abbott Professor of Business Administration, Darden Graduate School of Business, University of Virginia, **ROBERT M. CONROY,** J. Harvey Wilkinson Professor of Business Administration, Darden Graduate School of Business, University of Virginia, and **SCOTT A. SNELL,** E. Thayer Bigelow Professor of Business Administration, Darden Graduate School of Business, University of Virginia

Introduction

Many of the graduates of today's business schools are well prepared to excel in applying the *functional* knowledge and skill they have acquired. The world needs people who can do this. Yet the business profession expresses a growing need for general managers and leaders, people who can knit together the work of many technicians, who take an enterprise point of view, and who create a whole that is greater than the sum of the parts. As business grows more global in form and content, the need for leaders who can synthesize activities across borders grows more urgent. The gap between what schools produce and what business needs is at the heart of a chorus of criticism of business education.

This chapter lays out some of the work we have undertaken at the Darden Graduate School of Business Administration to gauge the dimensions of this unfilled need, and the ways in which we can continuously improve our MBA program to meet the requirements of our students and global partners. In other words, we looked at both the "what" question of MBA learning, as well as the "how" question of program delivery. The process and results are relevant to other business schools as well to corporate executives who are concerned with developing the next generation of business leaders.

The "what" question: Competencies B-schools must build for global business

The recent AACSB report, *The Globalization of Management Education* (Bruner *et al.*, 2011) challenged business schools' foundational attitudes about the education of business professionals. Business today is not perfectly globalized; nor does it remain localized. Rather, in the terms of Pankaj Ghemawat (2007), it is "semi-globalized," meaning that the effective business leader must understand both global forces and local contexts. And business schools should aim to produce graduates who are globally confident and competent. Today we graduate students who master the technicalities of working across borders and yet fail to listen, judge, and act effectively. There is more to global effectiveness than technical mastery: the AACSB report argues that schools should aim to prepare their graduates more deeply.

The ultimate ends of management education should include the development of competencies—the knowledge, skills, and attributes (KSAs) that distinguish successful managers and leaders. We know that, for decades, schools have focussed on functional knowledge. The "*know what*" factor in learning; the "what do you know"—do you know this formula, do you know these definitions, can you explain these relationships? But we also know that effective management relies on skills—the "*know how*" factor of learning; the ability to do things or more aptly, to get things done. And the third factor, perhaps more intangible but potentially more foundational, would be personal attributes. These are qualities of who you are—the "*care why*" factor imbedded in values, attitudes, and experiences that define who you are as a person. Why do you do things the way you do?

Ironically, these are not particularly new ideas to most global corporations. The notion of competencies grew in popularity with the publication in 1973 of a paper by David McClelland (1973) titled "Testing for Competence Rather Than for Intelligence." Since then, experts in the area of leadership development have emphasized the importance of competency-based approaches to learning, development, and career management (McCall and Hollenbeck, 2002), and, generally speaking, corporate leadership development programs have followed suit. Talent management systems focus on the KSAs required for success (Price and Turnbull, 2007; Wright, Snell and Dyer, 2005), and more directly targeted to business schools, corporate recruiting and selection criteria for MBA students tend to privilege competency-based criteria that extend beyond technical knowledge alone.

This really suggests that business schools have an opportunity to achieve better alignment with our corporate partners by focussing on the *whole individual*—people who are truly well-rounded, not merely functional technicians of business; but people who have a broader set of skill-based competencies and personal attributes to succeed in a global environment.

The response of business educators to these concerns has too often been to target the usual suspects of functional expertise in management education. Surely, students need to master business issues and the functional tools that apply. However, students also need an orientation toward getting results, not merely analysis; the capacity to collaborate, to contribute to teams, and to get the most out of those teams that span cultures and differences in ethnicity—the ability to build relationships; the capacity to communicate very effectively, to listen well; the capacity to judge well in the face of ambiguity that derives from the complexity and dynamics of a global marketplace; and the capacity to think in terms of the entire enterprise and the linkages among functional specialties. We need to build in our students the capacity to tolerate risk—and the entrepreneurial initiative that it implies. We need to nurture in our students their qualities of integrity and honesty, the ability to inspire trust in those with whom they work. Too often business schools turn out students who are narrowly trained in areas of functional expertise and don't understand the linkages across the fields of expertise.

We emphasize this long list to say that the challenges of managing in a complex global environment require graduates who are more than technicians; they must be leaders. In this context, how should business schools respond?

The "how" question: Our development model

The model of human resource development as seen from business schools has to adapt. This goes beyond what we teach to how we teach it. Henry Mintzberg (2004) goes so far as to say that business schools misconstrue management and so teach it in the wrong way.

At the heart of the criticisms is that much of business education centers on traditional classroom instruction focussed on delivering technical knowledge. And one might say that there is nothing wrong with that. Technical and functional knowledge will always be a primary contribution provided by management educators. However, by contrast, the best corporate development programs assess and develop their employees using a broad array of methods that include formal training, but also incorporate other experience-based methods that are real-world and real-time (Ready and Conger, 2007).

Not surprisingly, as Pankaj Ghemawat ably discusses in a related chapter, there is a gap between what schools say they do and what they actually deliver. The AACSB report provides further insights from its survey that contrast the curriculum and missions of business schools.

Functional and technical education are quickly commoditized, particularly those aspects that involve the kind of learning you can do sitting at a computer and working through trial and error processes—how to get the two sides of a balance sheet to balance, how to price a product, how to define terms, etc. That is rapidly gravitating to the Internet and to for-profit providers (Christensen, 2008) and (Christensen *et al.*, 2002). Perhaps that is as it should be. But if we hope to differentiate ourselves by turning out the kind of professional that can successfully manage in a complex and dynamic global environment, then business schools frankly need to do more (Kedia and Englis, 2011) and they need to do things differently.

But the news isn't all bad. The AASCB report gives nine in-depth case studies of what leading business schools have been doing to drive innovation. Contrary to the conventional view of business schools as lacking innovation, the case studies document a wave of experimentation. These cases suggest a shift away from what Khurana (2007) referred to as a "rules-plus-analytics" model of education toward a "principles-plus-implementation" focus on development of managers. This is a very different mindset.

It is an exciting moment in the field of management education to watch its development and to think about serving the needs of the business profession. Surely, some of the other 13,000 institutions of management education in the world are coming along in this direction. But the forces of globalization, technological change, and demographic shifts in the context of the recent global financial crisis are driving immense change in business schools right now.

Our approach: The program concept team

At Darden our mission is "to improve society by developing principled leaders for the world of practical affairs." We are rapidly gravitating toward a new model that addresses the classic criticisms of management education, a model that focusses on management *development*, rather than mere training. A critical driver here has been globalization. More than anything, globalization has placed a higher premium on people who can knit together the work of many technicians, who take an enterprise point of view, and who create a whole that is greater than the sum of the parts. In parenting, raising one child takes a certain set of capabilities. Raising three or more children requires the same basic set of capabilities but also requires more breadth since each child is the same yet unique in his or her own way. Globalization is like going from one child to three children. It is this realization that motivated us to take a comprehensive look at our programs.

In 2008, we created a Program Concept Team (PCT) of faculty and staff members to facilitate a comprehensive review of the Darden MBA program, and to bring to the school new concept designs and specific recommendations for improvement and innovation. Over an eighteen-month period, the PCT engaged students, corporate partners, alumni, faculty, and staff in a series of focus groups, interviews, surveys, and other forums in order to bring to light the most promising levers for change. The PCT asked, "What is the value proposition of management education for each of these stakeholders and how were we delivering against it?"

The PCT took an "outside-in" approach, grounding its work in the data gathered from our key stakeholders—this was in contrast to the inward-looking "inside-out" approach for which academia is famous. The approach purposefully followed the principles of design innovation: moving from exploration and pattern finding; to concept develop and strategy, to prototyping and piloting initiatives. At each stage, the PCT brought the data to the larger Darden community in order to ensure a continuous dialogue.

First, the PCT mapped the students' experience, their highs and lows in stress and satisfaction, and particularly focussed on what students were able to demonstrate upon leaving business school. The mapping allowed us to assess the current state of Darden's infrastructure for delivering the educational experience.

Second, this task force delved into the data gathered from corporate recruiters, learning among other things, that companies expect competency in functional knowledge/technical expertise. The recruiters reinforce the idea that a focus on competencies is increasingly seen as a basic expectation. Recruiters seek out MBA graduates who have a broader set of competencies, and who have a more deeply aligned relationship with the faculty.

Third, the PCT examined the MBA in context, the shifting ground of education globally, and the influence of demographic, technological, and cultural shifts. The faculty formed working groups to benchmark other schools and to focus more deeply on implications for governance, culture, careers, and competencies.

Fourth, the task force synthesized all the data and findings, to look for patterns and trends that integrated the needs and interests of stakeholders. Through a series of day-long workshops, the school identified the most promising themes for innovation, and subsequently devised a strategic concept for transformation.

Toward a management development concept

The transformation plan can be summarized in Figure 1, depicting the key elements of an expression of our strategic intent to orient our programs toward management *development* and away from mere management *training*. Importantly, this shift does not abandon the core tenets of our program, such as a case-teaching approach that emphasizes a high engagement culture, student-centered learning, and an enterprise perspective. We were motivated by three premises: (a) the requirements for managerial success are more

Figure 1: Toward a Management Development Concept

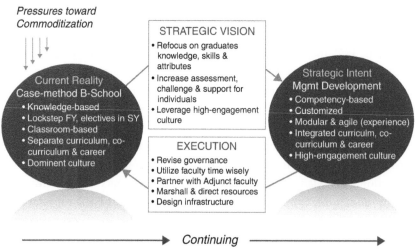

complex; the standard of high performance is rising; (b) it is necessary to be more explicit about how to use the *entire* program experience to deliver the learning; learning occurs not only in class but also in extracurricular activities, the career search, and in engagement with society; and (c) students must take greater ownership and navigate their individual course through the program.

The strategic intent of this shift in concept rests on five design pillars: (1) competency-based, (2) customized, (3) modular and agile to enhance experience-based learning, (4) integrated across the curriculum as well as co-curricular and career-oriented activities, and (5) leveraging a high engagement culture.

Competency-based to develop the whole person. As noted earlier, the next level to which management education must move is to focus on a broader set of competencies. Simply stated, the requirements for success are more complex, and the dynamics of global business require that students learn how to learn rapidly.

Customized to charter a personalized course. Management development is necessarily more customized to the company, and to the individual. One size doesn't fit all. We found from our work at Darden that there are (at least) four different student profiles; students who come from different places and are approaching their careers in different ways. Students are challenged with trying to navigate all of the opportunities they have to build a competency portfolio for their career goals. A competency-based approach to the program needs to design in mechanisms for self-assessment, planning, challenge/learning, and feedback/coaching. If we are to create a learning experience that meets all of their needs, the program is must become more student-focussed.

Modular and agile to learn from experience. Learning doesn't always occur in standardized blocks of time. For example, the reactions, concerns, and questions that students (and faculty) had to the Wall Street meltdown showed us that we need to respond real-time to learning opportunities. Other concentrated learning opportunities are designed to help students learn "where they are." Increasingly, these opportunities were seen as being outside the traditional classroom, including field work and experiential projects that reinforce the ideas of learning by doing. This is especially true with regard to developing the ability to manage in a global environment. As every parent knows, no one can tell you what it is like to raise children. You need to experience it yourself and be able to learn and adapt as you go along.

Integrative to synthesize learning. Although Darden has a tradition of focussing on general management, at its core, management development is intensely integrative. It is more than breaking down the silos of a functional orientation. That's a start, but our challenge is to combine what happens in the classroom, in clubs, in briefings, in global business experiences, in business projects, and the recruiting experience of students to create a synthesized learning experience. The synthesis also includes learning cumulatively over time through a sequence of experiences. From the standpoint of what a school needs to provide, it must present an incredibly challenging experience to students.

High engagement culture for collaborative learning. Management development follows the principles of adult learning, or andragogy (as opposed to pedagogy) (Knowles, Holton and Swanson, 2005). We seek to leverage a culture based on high engagement and collaborative learning. Students learn best from one another when they own the learning process, focus on problem-solving, and extract aspects that are particularly relevant to them, reinforced by lessons of experience, and pointed toward a decision based on reasoned principles.

Implementing the conceptual model: Three key processes

One of our strongest convictions is that a management development approach needs to be seen as continued evolution. It is a linked set of processes, rather than a checklist of one-time decisions. We focus on three processes:

1. *Competency Identification and Refinement*: How do we as educators and scholars of business engage in an ongoing conversation about the changing challenges of management and in that context define what success looks like?

2. *Program Design*: How do we continually update the program offerings to address these competencies, seeking continuous improvement and innovation, in program delivery?

3. *Student Development*: How do we help students plot a course through the program and navigate their learning and development?

The latter two are familiar for most schools, including Darden, for whom there are elements of those processes already in place. We review and update our programs; and most schools offer some required curriculum, offering guidance on course selection based on career goals. However, the first may be new—or it may be making explicit and formal debates that were at best implicit and informal. However, regardless whether it is new or just making it explicit and formal, it will have a dramatic impact on how we view and implement the latter two items. As such the first item is a critical input to the whole process.

Process 1: Competency identification and refinement

What should our students learn, to succeed in "the world of practical affairs"? One of the major challenges of any leading MBA program is to identify what students should master during their time in a program. The goal of the PCT was to inform this identification process for the Darden MBA full-time program. We focussed on our mission to develop "principled leaders in the world of practical affairs." And we also engaged in comprehensive discussions with our key stakeholders: students, faculty, alumni, and corporate partners.

At the outset, we should note that the real learning from our attempts to develop an initial list of competencies was how complex is the process itself. It is critical to understanding what constitutes managerial success, how that may be changing as the world of business evolves, and how to translate that into a compact set of competencies that would be meaningful to students, faculty and employers. We also learned that the process itself is valuable, demanding real clarity in thinking about business, management, and education. Figure 2 summarizes how we viewed the competency refinement process.

Observation/Benchmarking. The PCT examined a large number of competency models developed by different organizations. First we examined in detail the competency models for a total of 19 different firms for which we were able to obtain information.

Review. We also reviewed the work of subject matter experts (SMEs) (see Andrews and Tyson, 2004; Pink, 2006; Ghemawat, 2007), state-of-the-art thinking, and emerging research, as a comparison to the corporate data. Corporate models may tell us what is important to them today, whereas SMEs may give us insight to what is important for tomorrow (e.g., critical thinking).

In addition we examined several studies of competency models. The first was from the Center for Advanced HR studies at Cornell, "Summary

Figure 2: Competency refinement process: What does success look like?

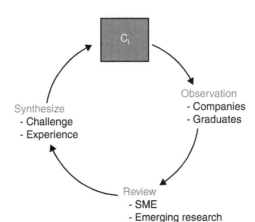

of Best Practices Findings: Leadership Development" (Sovina, Wherry and Stepp, n.d.). This examined the competencies used by 17 firms in different industries. Another study of 80 Indian and multinational firms was done by Asha Bhandarker (Bhandarker, 2008). Finally, we reviewed the leadership competencies discussed by Javidan and Dastmalchian (Javidan and Dastmalchian, 2009).

In addition to the above we studied the Harris/WSJ survey of MBA recruiters and some of the popular literature on competencies for success. The final source used was an article by Nigel Andrews and Laura Tyson (2004), then Dean of London Business School, who interviewed over 100 executives from global companies on the desirable attributes in MBA graduates. In this article the authors argue strongly for business education to adopt a more competency-driven model of education. Their major point is that business education is and has been mainly focussed on the transfer of knowledge under the assumption that the keys to managerial success were functional expertise. While this is still important, it is not the only thing that matters. We need to move away from a model of knowledge acquisition to one that emphasizes practical knowledge and experiential learning. To do this, Andrews and Tyson offer a version of the knowledge, skills, and attributes (KSA) model for competencies in manner similar to what we are proposing.

Synthesis. Finally, we cross-referenced the list of competencies that was generated from the corporate data with the terminology that is currently being used at Darden. While there are differences across all of the data examined, there was extensive overlap and commonality. During the spring 2009 meeting of the Darden Corporate Advisory Board (CAB) (with representatives of some 30 firms among Darden's most valued partners) the members provided a set of attributes that they would like to see in MBA graduates. In a survey, we asked the CAB members to tell us which competencies were most important for making an initial hiring decision, which were most important over the course of someone's career, and how well Darden delivered on these competencies.

One interesting observation on the set of competencies we identified is that does not seem to be a "different" set of competencies that relate to globalization but rather that some matter more. Clearly adaptability, a tolerance of ambiguity, and the ability to learn quickly are always important but in a global environment these stand out as competencies that matter.

Importantly, although this list reflects the synthesis of work we have done, we have concluded that arriving at a final list should not be the goal of a competency refinement process. Rather developing an mechanism for continually engaging in a conversation about what "success looks like" and what our students should learn while in the program may be one of the most valuable school-wide initiatives to engender continuous improvement and innovation.

This process, more than the list, is what defines a competency-based approach to MBA education. We believe that this process may be important to business schools as a whole, and particularly useful for connecting the academicians with corporate partners. While the precise focus of each program may differ, all programs, the full-time MBA program, and the executive format programs should all be shaped by a view of what constitutes managerial success, both today and tomorrow.

Process 2: Program (re)design

The second key process for a competency-based approach is the process of designing (or continuously redesigning) the program. To be clear, this extends beyond curriculum discussions alone. Traditional MBA programs typically do not address the full range of skills and attributes necessary for managerial success over a person's career, nor do they explicitly address the roles that each element of the program can play. By contrast, a management development (competency-based) approach more closely mirrors the best corporate leadership development and talent management programs. These create and promote a broad set of learning opportunities—experiences, assignments, and challenges required to acquire, refine, and improve on a set of competencies important for being a successful manager.

Of course, in any program design, there are several tradeoffs that need to be reconciled. One is the duality of near-term versus long-term learning. We would suggest that while our intent is to provide clear value for early and long-term career success, the ultimate goal at business schools may be to help our students "learn how to learn." The concept of learning agility implies that, while specifics may change, we hope to give our students the tools to adapt as the specific situation changes. In a global context this must extend to the capability of identifying and dealing with cultural differences. Learning agility is critical in this context.

The matrix in Figure 3 illustrates how the Program Design Process can map existing program activities on to a competency framework. Knowledge, skills, and attributes can be arrayed horizontally across the top, with

Figure 3: Program design process

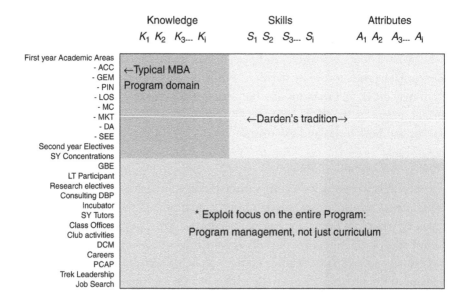

program activities vertically along the side. The typical MBA program focusses mainly on the area of the matrix at the top left knowledge delivered in the classroom. Please note: Functional knowledge is, and always will be, a primary contribution provided by MBA programs, but the most successful MBA programs of the future must also produce graduates who have competencies that extend beyond that.

Darden's tradition has been to focus on a wider range of KSAs, including the area in the top right: what you know, what you can do, and who you are. However, this focus has emphasized the classroom experience, to the exclusion of co-curricular/career-related activities that are often viewed as competing for time with classroom learning.

Andrews and Tyson (2004) have noted the difference between knowledge-based classroom learning and skills-based experiential learning:

> These are not simply different in content. They are different in essence. We can teach knowledge, but we need to train people in skills, and we can only develop attributes. This changes not only the "what" of management education, but also the "how" and "who" of the process.

We have leveraged our strength in collaborative learning, casework, high engagement culture, etc. But the kind of customized experiential learning approach we are discussing here requires a more customized, modular, flexible, agile, and experience-based approach to learning.

A competency-based approach reinforces the notion of a "program focus" that integrates curricular, co-curricular, and career-related learning experiences, drawing on each to help develop and reinforce the chosen competencies. This is particularly true for the skills and attributes that need to be practiced to be learned. The next step is to identify how each activity contributes to the competency based model.

Figure 4 illustrates the program design process. The mapping allows us to analyze two related elements of program design. First, we can look at a vertical slice of matrix to analyze one competency (e.g., decision-making) and all the program elements that help to develop it. Second, we can look at a horizontal slice of the matrix to analyze one program element (e.g., club activities) and all the competencies that it helps develop. The circles in each cell can visually display an assessment of whether the program area covers the competency well, partially or inadequately. This mapping process allows us to

Figure 4: Program design process: A deeper perspective

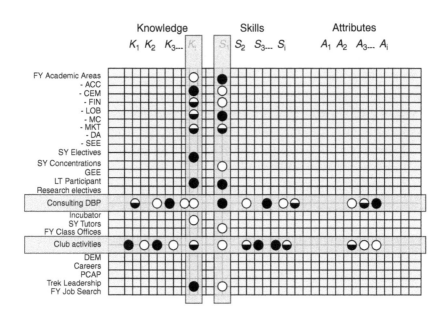

identify gaps and to guide students to the best combination of activities that meet their individual development needs.

Process 3: Student development process

The third key process in a competency-based approach is the student development process that focusses on experience-based learning. While the prior two processes are single, institution-wide processes, the student development process is one that each individual student needs to personalize, with the school providing the basic design and tools to assist them. At the most elemental level, this process reflects a talent-management cycle of: (1) assessment and planning, (2) challenge and learning-by-doing, and (3) support, coaching, and feedback.

Up close the process is more detailed for the individual student and more complex for the institution because the number of variations across all students can be quite large. How does *each* student plot a course through the program and navigate the terrain? However, the basic development process is clear. Based on the work of Groysberg and Cowen (2007), there are three key components for developmental experiences to be of value: assessment, challenge, and support. As Figure 5 suggests, these components influence one another.

Assessment and planning. The first step is to assess an individual's current performance for a set of competencies against some benchmark or desired level of competency. The second issue is determining a benchmark. Questions such as whether the benchmark is absolute or relative would need to be addressed. Once a set of competencies is selected and benchmarks are set, we must address the mechanisms to measure performance. We start with an advantage. Darden's admissions process evaluates the students' ability to succeed in the classroom along many dimensions, some of which could provide a starting point. However, we will need to adopt mechanisms such as 360-degree feedback to measure performance. The goal here is to identify areas and set targets for improvements. Once individuals can identify these, it is easier to plan and motivate change and learning. The key here is to identify a set of developmental goals. Currently, we do not do this in any formal way.

Assessment is an ongoing process. A strong feedback component is needed in order to maintain motivation. One question for any school is who can best perform this important component of the overall experience: faculty, staff, or outside experts?

Challenge and learning by doing. Groysberg and Cowen's (2007) research shows that the key to development is to challenge individuals by placing them

Figure 5: Components of a development experience

in situations where their current skills or perspectives are inadequate for addressing the challenge. Familiar situations only encourage individuals to fall back on past behaviors or assumptions. The questions for Darden were: Should we do this? Do we currently do this? And if we want to but don't, how do we do it? The goal here is to get individuals to operate outside their comfort zone. Can we create mechanisms to help students select activities (classes and co-curricular activities) that create this discomfort?

Support coaching and feedback. This is an essential element. What structures are in place to provide support and encouragement? Without encouragement and support the stress induced by placing individuals in challenging situations will result in a negative attitude and only induce individuals to follow old patterns in which they feel comfortable.

These features can be incorporated into the student development process over the two years of a typical MBA program. A true management development model would incorporate the upfront assessment with feedback, coaching, and planning. Throughout the first year of the program there would be feedback and reevaluation of the student's progress and needs. Figure 6

Figure 6: Student development process: How do students navigate their learning?

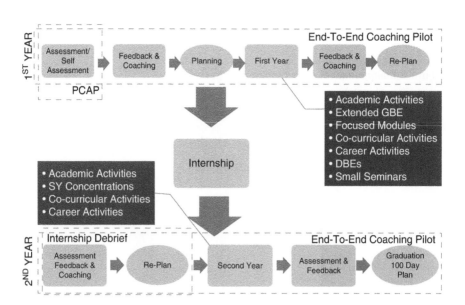

depicts the student development process. Based on the experiences during the summer internship, students would once again use assessment, feedback, and coaching to plan their activities in the second year.

Globalization and the management development approach

We began this chapter with an acknowledgment that globalization is perhaps the major force of change in management education. Our program development work at Darden suggests a range of considerations for educators as they strive to adapt to the implications of globalization. These include:

1. Competency Identification and Refinement. The framework of knowledge–skills–attributes offers a basis for assessing the completeness of the preparation of students to be globally confident and competent as managers. Perhaps most importantly, globalization will force a reconsideration of priorities of topics. The CAGE framework of Pankaj Ghemawat (2007), for instance, can test the suitability of knowledge and skills for a globally prepared graduate.

2. Program (Re)Design. The ideal global competencies can be added to the process framework shown in Figures 3 and 4.

3. Student Development Process. Student assessment and the engagement of students in the process of planning his or her developmental experience should now embrace the global competencies. Challenging students to extend the boundaries of their comfort zones is naturally promoted by foreign immersion experiences and field projects away from home.

In short, our three-part process can be adapted to respond to the special demands for management development in an increasingly global business environment.

Conclusion and implications for business leaders

About half of the worldwide expenditure on management education is showered upon educational activities *within* business enterprises themselves. As businesses seek to improve and accelerate the development of global leadership within their walls, they are experimenting actively with alternative approaches. Business schools should do so too.

Darden's experience illustrates the intensity of reflective process and transformation necessary to define a new approach. Several important elements suggest the extent of this intensity:

- Shift from a focus on management training to a focus on management *development*.

- Enlargement of the scope of the development aspiration from mere knowledge ("know what"), to include skills ("know how"), and attributes ("care why").

- An inclusive effort that reaches out to a large cross-section of stakeholders of the enterprise, rather than focussing inwardly in the classic secretive "skunkworks" model.

- Being fact-based: studying patterns in fresh data about the learning needs of students, rather than simply relying on ungrounded opinions.

- Emerging into a new framework for learning that is:

  o Competency-based.

  o Personalized to the student.

  o Integrative across specialties.

  o Highly engaging, modular, and agile.

We are not arguing that our transformational effort is applicable in its particulars to all enterprises. Tailoring will be warranted to suit the culture, administrative practices, and needs in different institutions. But we do argue that the transformational effort must be intensive to overcome the natural inertia of organizations and the human instinct to resist change and uncertainty.

Such an effort is only a beginning. It must be sustained through time in a continuous improvement effort simply because the best practices of management are constantly evolving as are the knowledge, skills, and attributes demanded by a profession that must manage in an increasingly complex global environment. A pre-eminent force of change is the globalization of business, which is changing assumptions about the proper mix of knowledge, skills, and attributes toward which we should strive for our students. Related to this is the question of the relevant scope of awareness that educators should seek to instill in their students and in executives: the AACSB task force report affirms the vital importance of instilling an awareness of the environment that is not merely local, national, or regional, but truly global in scope.

Table 1: Sample of competencies by firms

Attribute	Count	Global Energy generation business	Global Petroleum Business	French Nuclear Energy Firm	Telecommunications	Financial Services	Retailer	Government	Financial Services (Insurance)	Communications Manufacturer (Defense)	Consulting/Computer services	Defense Manufacturer	Consumer Goods	Middle Market Investment Bank	Small Private Equity Firm	Financial Services	Property and Life Insurance (Financial Services)	Owns and manages Government's direct investments	Aircraft Engines, Air Conditioning, & Elevators	Electrical Appliances
Ability to manage information	1											1								
Accountability	6	1	1	1	1	1							1							
Adaptability	7					1	1	1	1		1				1				1	
Analytical thinking	13				1	1	1	1	1	1	1	1			1		1	1	1	1
Builds interdependent partnering	1																1			
Builds trust	1																1			
Business Acumen	3		1	1										1						
Business Judgment (acumen)	7	1						1	1		1				1		1		1	

continued

Table 1: Continued

Company-->	Global Energy generation business	Global Petroleum Business	French Nuclear Energy Firm	Telecommunications	Financial Services	Retailer	Government	Financial Services (Insurance)	Communications Manufacturer (Defense)	Consulting/Computer services	Defense Manufacturer	Consumer Goods	Middle Market Investment Bank	Small Private Equity Firm	Financial Services	Property and Life Insurance (Financial Services)	Owns and manages Government's direct investments	Aircraft Engines, Air Conditioning, & Elevators	Electrical Appliances
Champions Change	12	1	1		1	1	1	1	1	1	1		1	1				1		
Collaborative	1											1								
Communication Skills	11	1	1	1	1	1			1	1	1			1		1			1	
Confidence	1												1							
Continuous improvement	2									1			1							
Courage	4									1	1		1				1			
Creates an achievement environment	4								1	1	1						1			
Creates Teaching Opportunities	2							1		1										
Customertcleint Focused	13	1	1		1	1		1	1	1	1			1		1	1		1	1
Decision Making skills	2											1				1				
Decisiveness	3						1									1		1		

	Count
Develops Self and Others (Learning)	15
Develops Talent (Coaching)	4
Engaging talent	2
Enterprise Perspective	1
Financial Acumen	2
Forward Thinking	2
Functional excellence	1
Global Acumen	3
Have a compelling "employee value"	1
Industry knowledge	3
Influence edge	6
Innovative	12
Integrity/Honesty	13
Interpersonal skills	1
Inspires trust	3
Leading/Coaching	3

continued

Table 1: Continued

Company-->		Global Energy generation business	Global Petroleum Business	French Nuclear Energy Firm	Telecommunications	Financial Services	Retailer	Government	Financial Services (Insurance)	Communications Manufacturer (Defense)	Consulting/Computer services	Defense Manufacturer	Consumer Goods	Middle Market Investment Bank	Small Private Equity Firm	Financial Services	Property and Life Insurance (Financial Services)	Owns and manages Government's direct investments	Aircraft Engines, Air Conditioning, & Elevators	Electrical Appliances
Listening	4					1		1			1								1	
Motivates others	2					1	1													
Negotiating skills	5					1	1					1		1	1					
Networking builds relationships	3					1				1				1						
Organizational knowledge	2	1	1																	
Passion	2											1						1		
Performance Oriented	2									1		1								
Planning and Organizing	5				1	1			1	1		1								
Prioritizes	1								1											

Problem Solving	6			1				1		1			1	1			1		
Results Oriented	15	1	1	1	1	1	1	1	1	1	1	1	1	1			1	1	1
Self Awareness	2						1							1			1	1	
Self Management	1								1										
Strategic Perspective	13	1	1	1	1	1	1	1	1	1	1	1					1	1	
Synthesize data	1									1									
Takes risks	2				1	1													
Team Player	14	1	1	1	1	1	1	1	1	1	1	1	1	1			1		
Technology Savvy	4	1	1				1		1										
Thinking Skills	2		1						1										
Treat people with dignity & respect	1								1										
Values differences (Diversity)	2						1		1					1			1		
Vision	7			1	1	1	1		1		1	1		1			1		

Table 2: Frequency of competency descriptors—a study of 19 firms

	Count		
Develops self and others (Learning)	15	Networking builds relationships	3
Results oriented	15	Continuous improvement	2
Team player	14	Creates teaching opportunities	2
Analytical thinking	13	Decision making skills	2
Customer/client focussed	13	Engaging talent	2
Integrity/honesty	13	Financial acumen	2
Strategic perspective	13	Forward thinking	2
Champions change	12	Motivates others	2
Innovative	12	Organizational knowledge	2
Communication skills	11	Passion	2
Adaptability	7	Performance oriented	2
Business judgment (acumen)	7	Self-awareness	2
Vision	7	Takes risks	2
Accountability	6	Thinking skills	2
Influence edge	6	Values differences (Diversity)	2
Problem solving	6	Ability to manage information	1
Negotiating skills	5	Builds interdependent partnering	1
Planning and organizing	5	Builds trust	1
Courage	4	Collaborative	1
Creates an achievement environment	4	Confidence	1
Develops talent (Coaching)	4	Enterprise perspective	1
Listening	4	Functional excellence	1
Technology savvy	4	Have a compelling "employee value"	1
Business acumen	3	Interpersonal skills	1
Decisiveness	3	Prioritizes	1
Global acumen	3	Self-management	1
Industry knowledge	3	Synthesize data	1
Inspires trust	3	Treats people with dignity & respect	1
Leading/coaching	3		

Table 3: Summary of competency descriptors

	COMPETENCIES OF GLOBAL LEADERSHIP	
Academic areas	**Collaborative / team player**	**Results orientation**
Accounting	Networking/Build Relationships	Accountability
Global Finance	Value differences/diverse cultures	Priorities
Global Macroeconomics	**Communication & Interpersonal skills**	Project Management
Competitive Microeconomics	Listening and observation	Bias for action
Decision Sciences	Empathy	Decisiveness
Global Marketing/Brand	Negotiation skills	**Confidence**
Sales/Account Management	Presentation Skills	Courage
Operations Management	**Develop self and others**	Risk tolerance
Corporate Governance	Motivation	**Integrity/Honesty**
Strategic Management	Managing performance	Inspire trust
Ethics	Self awareness	**Learning agility**
Entrepreneurship	Develop talent (coaching)	Adaptability
General Management	Giving/receiving feedback	Champions/drivers of change
Management Communication	**Business analysis and judgment**	**Curiosity and creativity**
Leadership in Organizations	Dealing with ambiguity	Innovative
Human Resources Management	Ability to make the complex simple	**Perseverance and Tenacity**
	Reward thinking	Hard working
Business Issues	Pattern recognition	Passionate and persuasive
Globalization	Analysis	Demands excellence
Diversity	**Enterprise perspective**	Boundless energy
Sustainability	Customer/client focused	Desire to make a difference
Innovation	Strategic perspective	High intensity
	Vision	**Social awareness**
	General management perspective	Social responsibility
		Global awareness&perspective
		Sensitivity to other cultures

REFERENCES

Andrews, N. and Tyson, L. D. (2004) "The Upwardly Global MBA." *Strategy + Business* 36 (Fall): 1–10.

Bhandarker, A. (2008) *Shaping Business Leaders: What Business Schools Don't Do* (Thousand Oaks, CA: Sage Publications).

Bruner, R. F., De Meyer, A., Ghemawat, P., Gómez, J., Lenway, S., Rao, M., Snyder, E., Tapie, P. and Teegen, K. (2011) *Globalization of Management Education: Changing*

International Structure, Adaptive Strategies, and the Impact on Institutions (Tampa, FL: Association for the Advancement of Collegiate Schools of Business).

Christensen, C. M. (2008) "Disruptive Innovation and Catalytic Change in Higher Education." *Forum for the Future of Higher Education, 2007* (Aspen Symposium).

Christensen, C. M., Aaron, S. and Clark, W. (2002) "Disruption in Education." In *The Internet & the University*, ed. Maureen Devlin (Forum for the Future of Higher Education and EDUCAUSE): 19–44.

Ghemawat, P. (2007) *Redefining Global Strategy: Crossing Borders in a World Where Differences Still Matter* (Cambridge, MA: Harvard Business Publishing).

Groysberg, B. and Cowen, A. (2007) *Developing Leaders* (Boston, MA: Harvard Business School-HBS Case No. 407-015).

Javidan, M. and Dastmalchian, A. (2009) "Managerial Implications of the GLOBE Project: A Study of 62 Societies." *Asia Pacific Journal of Human Resources* 47: 41–58.

Kedia, B. L.and Englis, P. D. (2011)_ "Transforming Business Education to Produce Global Managers." *Business Horizons* 54.4: 325–331.

Khurana, R. (2007) *From Higher Aims to Hired Hands: The Social Transformation of American Business Schools and the Unfulfilled Promise of Management as a Profession* (Princeton, NJ: Princeton University Press).

Knowles, M., Holton III, E. F. and Swanson, R. A. (2005) *The Adult Learner: The Definitive Classic in Adult Education and Human Resource Development*, 6th edn (Burlington, MA: Elsevier).

McCall, M. W. and Hollenbeck, G. P. (2002) *Developing Global Executives* (Boston, MA: Harvard Business School Press).

McClelland, D. C. (1973) "Testing for Competence rather than for Intelligence." *American Psychologist* 28: 1–14.

Mintzberg, H. (2004) *Managers Not MBAs: A Hard Look at the Soft Practice of Managing and Management Development* (San Francisco, CA: Berrett Koehler).

Pink, D. (2006) *A Whole New Mind* (New York, NY: Penguin Group).

Price, C. and Turnbull, D. (2007) "The Organizational Challenges of Global Trends: A McKinsey Global Survey." *McKinsey Quarterly* (May).

Ready, D. A. and Conger, J. A. (2007) "Make your Company a Talent Factory." *Harvard Business Review* (June).

Sovina, J., Wherry, M. L. and Stepp, P. L. (n.d.) "Summary of Best Practices Findings: Leadership Development." Working Paper.

Wright, P. M., Snell, S. A. and Dyer, L. (2005) "New Models of Strategic HRM in a Global Context." *International Journal of Human Resource Management* 16.6: 875.

Rethinking Global Leadership Development: Designing New Paradigms

JORDI CANALS, Dean and Professor of General Management, IESE Business School, University of Navarra

A changing context

In the twentieth century, the company became one of the most successful social innovations, and management emerged as an essential pillar for economic growth and social progress. The application of management models and techniques to the corporate world had a positive impact by improving firms' output, productivity, product innovation and variety. The implementation of some of those models after the Second World War brought about formidable GDP growth in Western Europe, North America and Japan.

In those models, management was considered to be a rational science consisting of a set of techniques that helped improve the resource allocation problem. In this context, management and management development were, essentially, domestic affairs.

Executive education and management development started to grow in the 1960s. The driving force was that senior executives realized they needed to become familiar with the models and tools associated with modern management. In many business schools, executives programs were centered on the basic business disciplines—production, finance or marketing, among others.

The oil crisis and the turmoil in the international financial system in the 1970s brought a sense of realism to management. Uncertainty became the dominant attribute of the business context. The future could not be predicted, and the assumptions of rationality and stability did not hold any more. In the early 1980s, economic stagnation in the US and Western Europe provided a fertile ground to reflect upon the importance of leadership in society, both in government and the private sector. The challenge of leading a company successfully in the 1990s was not only a question of applying principles of scientific management, but also of understanding the firm's challenges, deciding about the firm's future direction, and mobilizing people and resources to achieve that goal.

Nevertheless, in the early 1990s, Western companies were still operating essentially in homogeneous markets and regions, employing people who shared similar cultures, values and behaviors. The integration of the world economy started to speed up in the mid-1990s with high-growth countries like China, India, Russia, Brazil or Turkey, among others. Multinational companies started to operate in those countries more actively, profiting from trade growth and foreign investment liberalization. We have seen a steady acceleration of this trend over recent years, only punctuated by a fall in international trade and investment right after the 2008 financial crisis.

This new business context is essentially different from the one that was dominant just a decade ago. Companies in a variety of industries, such as BASF, Nestlé, Novartis, Unilever or Siemens, are generating a substantial share of their revenues and profits in new growth markets. Firms' growth prospects are weak in mature economies—their home markets—and strong in those new markets. As a result, their investment and the need to develop local leaders is growing quicker in those countries than in their own home countries.

These changes bring about new challenges for companies and business leaders. It is not only a matter of developing leaders in those countries. It is also about growing global leaders who can manage across cultures and complex contexts. Those challenges do not change radically many of the basic functions of leaders, but they do change some of the activities that they do, how they do them and the capabilities they need to develop them.

The CEO of a large US company recently told the author that his firm in the United States was different from his company in Asia. It was the same company, indeed. It also sold the same products in both continents. Strategies and the organization in those two regions were only slightly divergent. But the main difference was that the culture and the ways of doing things were not the same, and the challenge of developing local managers required different approaches in each region. This is an observation I have heard many times from senior executives in international companies. In this chapter I try to discuss some of these differences around leadership development and how companies can deal with them. I argue that increasing globalization, the economic shift to Asia, and the demographic, cultural and social changes that globalization brings about, require a different type of leadership in the business world.

This chapter is organized in the following way. In the next section, I will introduce the notions of global leadership and global leaders, as well as the tasks they should undertake and the capabilities they need to develop. In the third section, I will review different models of leadership development and will present a more comprehensive model. Then I discuss the role of business schools in tackling the challenge of global leadership development. Finally, the role of CEOs and senior managers in helping develop the new generation of global leaders will be outlined.

What do global leaders do? What attributes and capabilities do they need?

We understand that global leaders are senior managers who not only have technical responsibilities, but also some functions that involve direct participation in overall business decisions in an international context. We make the assumption that leaders and managers are somewhat different (Kotter, 1990). The differential role of leaders is to provide a meaning for the people working in a firm (Nohria and Khurana 2010b; Podolny, Khurana and Besharov, 2010) and shape the direction of an organization (Kanter, 2010; Tichy and Cohen, 1997).

For many years, global leadership concepts borrowed from and extended traditional definitions of leadership (Yeung and Ready, 1995; Osland, Taylor and Mendenhall, 2009). But some researchers realized that concepts in both contexts meant different things. As Adler (2001: 77) describes well,

> Global leaders, unlike domestic leaders, address people worldwide. Global leadership theory, unlike its domestic counterpart, is concerned with the interaction of people and ideas across cultures, rather than with the efficacy of particular leadership styles within the leader's home country or with the comparison of leadership approaches among leaders from various countries.

Global leadership may seem a special category of global talent. And leadership development may be considered a special field within global talent management. Tarique and Schuller (2010: 124) present a framework for global talent management that stems from the need that international companies have to improve their talent development in a more global world. They define global talent management as

> systematically utilizing IHRM activities ... to attract, develop and retain individuals with high levels of human capital (e.g., competency, personality, motivation) consistent with the strategic directions of the multinational enterprise in a dynamic, highly competitive, and global environment.

The special nature of leadership and the complex challenge of leadership development make it different from pure talent development, but some concepts around talent development are also useful here.

There are three significant questions that arise when observing global leaders. The first is the difference between global and domestic leaders. The second is whether there are some universal patterns in what global leaders do. The third is whether there are universal traits in the competencies that global leaders need to have in order to carry out their functions in the best possible way. These are important considerations when thinking about leadership development. I will try to address them in the following sections.

Global leaders: Are they different?

Global leaders carry out some basic functions and activities within an organization that share many qualities with business leaders in domestic firms. McCall and Hollenbeck (2002) define global leaders as those who do global work; and global work has two dimensions: business complexity and cultural complexity. They assume that what global leaders do is the same as local leaders, which, as we discuss above, is not always the case; they also argue that what separates them from local leaders is not what they do, but how they do things.

The defining qualities of a global leader come from the leader's participation in overall business decisions and the fact that those decisions take place in an international context. Global leaders make things happen in an international context, contribute to moving an organization from stage A to stage B, and mobilize people and resources for this purpose. What is different about them is the sheer complexity and additional uncertainty that working across borders bring to the job of a senior manager. This complexity arises from a variety of factors: diversity of cultures, societies and individuals; heterogeneity of companies, clients and suppliers; different governments and policies; diversity of colleagues, employees and managers; greater uncertainty; an increased interdependency among units, businesses and countries involved; and feedback effects and learning processes stemming from operating in a more diverse context.

It may seem that the main factors separating domestic leadership from global leadership are cross-cultural issues. These are important, but not the only factors. Global economic factors, social factors and behavioral factors must also be considered alongside cultural differences. These factors create a different type of context for companies operating internationally, one that is more interdependent, uncertain and ambiguous; and this context has an impact both on the definition and expectations of what leaders do and what their capabilities should be.

Leadership requires the ability to make the right decisions at the right time and place. Decision-making always deals with uncertainty, which, in the context of global business, increases very quickly. In this context, cross-cultural factors per se are not the only major difference between local and global leadership. It is the way that additional complexity, uncertainty, diversity and heterogeneity enter into the decision-making process that makes global leadership different.

Some general patterns in what leaders do: Are there universal models?

There is a hot debate on whether leadership and leadership qualities can have universal validity. One school of thought considers that leadership and the main leadership traits are valid across cultures (e.g., Bass, 1995). Other authors do not delve into this issue, but assume the hypothesis that the main tasks that leaders carry out can be generalized across cultures (e.g., Kanter, 2010). Finally, some authors think that leadership is not universal: it consists of traits that are culturally embedded, and what really matters is the work of local leaders getting things done, and not so much that of global leaders. Sánchez-Runde, Nardon and Steers (2011) offer a good discussion of the different perspectives. Moreover, leadership development in growing economies is more complex than in domestic markets (see Ready, Hill and Conger, 2008).

While it is obvious that cultural biases and roots have a very important role in defining leadership and what leaders do, and that personal leadership styles are more accepted in some countries than others, my experience in dealing with international companies and international executive development programs suggests that many of the broad tasks of leaders are valid across cultures. The capabilities needed to achieve them may have a different importance depending on the location. In some countries leaders need to lean more on some of them, while in others the qualities in need may be slightly different.

With the goal of helping tackle this challenge, I introduce a framework that combines classic leadership tasks with functions that global leaders need to carry out in a global context. In this model I distinguish major tasks for global leaders that seem important irrespective of the home country of their firms (see Table 4).

The first task is the definition of the mission and values of the firm, and the meaning that they offer. This is a key task for leaders, which becomes more relevant when organizations are dispersed in different countries and continents, and the different firm's units need to stick together. The firm's mission provides meaning (Poldonyi, Khurana and Besharov, 2010; Nohria and Khurana, 2010b) by describing the impact the organization wants to have. It offers an anchor to people's expectations on what the firm is and tries to achieve.

The second task is to develop a point of view about the future of the firm. This does not require a fixed strategic plan, but involves creating a map that provides a sense of direction for the company, irrespective of the geographies it operates in, and a wider context and perspective (Tichy and Cohen, 1997). It should also explain in a simple way how the company tries to create economic value in the long term. In a global context, uncertainty and complexity increase, and having a compass in terms of long-term orientation is extremely important.

The third task is integration across business, functions and geographies: helping the organization come together and work together as a team (Kanter,

Table 4: Tasks and responsibilities

Mission and values

Point of view about the future

Integration

Meet standards and expectations

Leadership development

2010). Cross-disciplinary teams that understand differences and are able to work with people from different countries are more important in global firms than in domestic ones.

The fourth task is delivery: meeting the standards and expectations that stakeholders have about the firm and its senior leadership, including financial and non-financial performance, and sticking to the standards of conduct of responsible companies.

The fifth task is to make sure that there is a culture of people and leadership development within the firm, a concern for growing talent internally, a carefully designed plan for high potentials to take up new responsibilities and a concern for developing the next team of top leaders.

In some companies, their leaders may put more emphasis on some of those dimensions. The experience in leadership development in dozens of companies in Europe, the US, Latin America, Africa and Asia, irrespective of the location of the home country, shows that those tasks are key challenges that leaders need to tackle in an effective way.

What capabilities and attributes do global leaders need to have and develop?
A brief introduction to different paradigms
The professional and personal qualities that leaders need to develop in their job stem from the functions that they should perform. Both within formal corporate development programs and in executive programs at business schools we should not forget the goal of leadership development: education and development for a better professional performance as leaders, which also includes personal development. For this reason, it is important to understand what leaders do—which we explored in the previous section—and how they can improve the qualities that they need to do those tasks.

There are different typologies of capabilities and skills that global leaders need to develop or acquire. Osland, Taylor and Mendenhall (2009) provide a useful description of the different paradigms about global leaders' capabilities by distinguishing two major streams of research. The first paradigm emphasizes the notion of the global mindset: a cognitive structure that articulates a special understanding of complexity and an openness to the others and the world (Levy *et al.*, 2007). Other authors describe a global mindset as the expert mind that a global leader needs to develop to be effective (Osland and Bird, 2006). Although the global mindset seems a simple concept to define, and rather intuitive, its articulation needs to be developed deeper, and the standards of what a good global mindset is remain elusive.

The second paradigm highlights some key global leadership competencies, as opposed to a global mindset. Instead of describing a global mindset, authors following this approach simply consider the right set of competencies needed to be an effective global leader (Adler, 2001; McCall and Hollenbeck, 2002; Gundling, Hogan and Cvitkovich, 2011). We will highlight some of them. Jokinen (2005) presents an integrated framework of global leadership, made up of three layers of competencies. The first is a fundamental core, including self-awareness, personal transformation and inquisitiveness. The second layer is a set of capabilities that helps leaders approach problems, and includes qualities such as optimism, self-control, empathy, motivation and the acceptance of complexity. The third layer is behavioral and includes skills and knowledge that lead to action; it involves social skills, networking skills and knowledge.

Osland (2008) proposes the pyramid model of global competencies, which includes five different levels of capabilities. Level 1, the foundation level, incorporates global knowledge in a variety of forms: know what, know who, know how, know when and know why. Level 2 includes some threshold traits: integrity, humility, inquisitiveness and resilience. Level 3 is composed of attitudes that help global leaders see and interpret the world, and includes a global mindset, cognitive complexity and cosmopolitanism. Level 4 concerns the interpersonal skills necessary to work across cultures: communication to develop trust and work in multi-cultural teams. Finally, Level 5 involves systems skills, or meta-skills necessary for global work, such as building communities, ethical behavior, creating a vision or leading change.

Javidan *et al.* (2006) describe some basic capabilities needed for global leaders: intellectual capital, which includes global business savvy and cognitive complexity; psychological capital, which includes diversity, self-knowledge and spirit of adventure; and social capital, which includes empathy, interpersonal skills and diversity. This is a brief articulation of different capabilities and knowledge that global leaders need to have.

These models provide some important building blocks necessary for developing global leaders' capabilities, but their main problem is that the different blocks are not deeply connected.

An integrated framework on global leaders' competencies

I present a framework organized around what a global leader is and what he or she does in the real world: a person who knows, who does things, and who becomes a more balanced person through leadership. The key dimensions in this comprehensive framework are knowledge, capabilities and attitudes (Perese Lopez, 1993; Khurana and Noria, 2010b). Bruner, Conroy and Snell, in Chapter 1 in this book, also provide a very good perspective on this framework. Knowledge includes the facts, notions, models and ideas that global leaders need to have or acquire. Capabilities show the capacity to do things and get things done with people; interpersonal skills can be considered as a special set of capabilities. Attitudes are solid dispositions of the character of a person that shape her conduct and behavior, and establish the foundations of her relations with others. Attitudes stem directly from the classical notion of virtue (Aristotle, 1980 edition), that is, a stable disposition that helps a person behave in a positive way.

The coherence in this framework is provided by its development around the individual person, and what she does. The main difference with the models described in the previous section is that includes both the cognitive side—the global mindset—with the capabilities needed by global leaders.

This model can embrace universal factors. In any culture, knowledge, capabilities and attitudes are of high importance. It is true that some cultures may emphasize some attitudes more than others, but in all of them there is a strong demand for certain attitudes. It may be interesting to note that what sometimes is referred as a cultural difference—for instance, whether leadership is more top-down in some Western countries or more collaborative in some Asian countries; or whether humility and prudence are virtues more cherished by Asian managers than Western managers—is more a matter of style and accumulated practical behavior, rather than substantial differences. It is interesting to note that the theoretical foundation of those virtues—humility, prudence, fairness, temperance—was first developed in the 5th century BC by Aristotle, who opened the way to what became one of the foundational pillars of Western civilization (see Aristotle, *The Nicomachean Ethics*, 1980 edition).

Based on those ideas, we present a model of global leaders' competencies that has four major elements (Figure 7): knowledge, capabilities, interpersonal skills and attitudes. In this model we distinguish basic capabilities—like decision-making, or dealing with complexity—from interpersonal (relational) skills that focus more on how one person deals with others in different contexts. Those competencies are related with major questions (know what, know how, know with and know why) that each leader needs to consider. They are connected with the global leader and her main actions: knowing, doing, working with others and being.

The set of business knowledge competencies includes the basic business functions and a good understanding of the global context (political, economic, cultural). The set of capabilities includes decision-making, analysis and synthesis, problem-solving, action orientation, complexity, uncertainty and implementation.

The set of interpersonal skills includes, among others, personal empathy, communication, team work, cultural sensitivity and appreciation for diversity.

Finally, the set of attitudes includes those that are of the highest value in our relation with others: integrity, self-awareness, self-control, humility, respect, coherence and fairness. These basic attitudes stem from the key classical virtues—personal habits that help us do good, and aim at goodness and excellence: prudence, justice, fortitude and temperance.

We make two assumptions here. The first is that the pillar of attitudes—the being dimension—is the linchpin of the other competencies. Without attitudes, strongly founded on personal virtues, the potential impact of the other competencies will be limited. Attitudes have an effect on the way we work with others (relational skills), how we do things (capabilities) and the way we get to know things (knowledge). The second assumption is that those competencies reinforce each other. The more and better we know, the bigger the positive impact on attitudes. By doing things better or relating with others in a more positive way, we can improve the quality of our personal attitudes. The reason is very simple. Behind attitudes there are some key human virtues (prudence or justice) that are dynamic by nature. The more one practices them, the better and stronger they grow. And, as they grow, capabilities, knowledge and skills also improve.

The organization and design of global leadership development programs

After a relatively stable environment with economic growth in the West since the early 1950s, the oil and financial crisis in the 1970s and early 1980s threw the world economy into a period of stagnation. Companies suffered in the slowdown. Moreover, the stable context that had dominated for several decades had disappeared, and uncertainty—fostered by a period of high interest

Figure 7: Global leaders' competencies

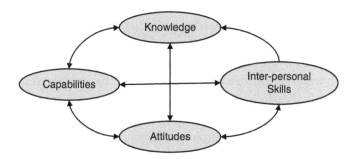

rates, high inflation rate and slow growth—shaped the business context. It is reasonable to understand that, in this context, the importance of leadership, both at the country level and in the corporate world, was in high demand.

Kotter (1990) observed that in the US companies there were strong managers, but few leaders to take their companies into the future. Kotter's observation had a point. The notion that leadership development programs were needed to revitalize some companies started to have an impact in some companies (Conger and Benjamin, 1999). Business schools, like Harvard or Michigan, started to offer new executive programs around leadership. A literature on leadership began to grow (Bennis, 1989). Some new executive development centers, such as the Center for Creative Leadership, and consulting firms started to develop very successful programs, meeting a latent demand in many companies. The example of some corporate universities working on leadership programs was also a driving factor of the new interest in the area; and GE's Executive Center in Crotonville became a global reference.

The new focus on leadership development programs also emerged as a result of new expectations among some companies that were customers of Executive Education programs. Those programs, which had been quite successful after the Second World War, seemed to have lost edge. The roots of this phenomenon were diverse. The first was that some schools kept offering general management programs articulated around classical functional areas; integration across areas, the development of an integrated view of the firm or strategic thinking were not in offer. The effect was not only a limited view of the firm, but also an overlapping with the increasing business knowledge that many managers already had after graduating from college.

Companies also began to realize that the speed of change through education by using some executive programs was not always as effective as they expected in order to bring about changes. For this reason, in the late 1980s, the demand for customized programs started to grow. Initially, many of them were traditional general management programs, slightly adapted to the specifics needs of a company. After a while, many of those programs became totally customized, with specific materials, cases and other tools designed for a company. The focus of these customized programs was not so much to educate executives with general capabilities, knowledge and skills, but to give them a quicker understanding of some problems and challenges, and offer them the tools and models to implement change. In these programs, a classical principle of leadership—effecting change—took a primary role in these educational experiences.

As a natural process, many of those programs were based on small teams, which had to develop projects before, during and after the program. With the application of this model to international companies, it was quite a logical step that those teams quickly became multinational groups of people who had to develop proposals by working with people from other cultures and backgrounds.

GE offers a unique perspective in this respect (Conaty and Charan, 2010). It was not only a pioneer in designing and delivering customized programs, but was also considered a leadership machine, through the daily challenges in the life of senior executives, specific job assignments and projects, and formal programs for executive education and leadership development.

One of the most important experiences in GE's leadership programs was the design of formal programs to help develop leadership competencies, at the knowledge level, the capabilities level and the skills level. GE Programs relied on external consultants and business school professors as well as its top management team spending time with participants and teaching them about their experiences. In a natural way, the programs became a process for sharing the culture and values of the firm, expanding networking opportunities and helping make connections among managers from different business units and geographies.

We can observe that these leadership programs that GE designed became a reference in terms of leadership development, creating a new breed of global managers for GE, and pioneering and putting into practice some principles for developing global leadership. Nevertheless, it is also fair to say that there are very few experiences as successful as GE's in this area. The reason is that GE has developed an integrated model whose pillars are GE's stable top management, its commitment to this effort, substantial financial resources allocated to the project and a good combination of external and internal speakers. It seems reasonable to argue that only companies with similar resources and commitment to leadership development as GE can master the process in a successful way.

Models to organize leadership development

Any leadership development program is based on the assumption that leaders and managers bring with them their professional experience and knowledge, capabilities and skills developed over the years. The main role of a leadership development program is to help acquire new competencies while strengthening the already developed competencies.

After observing the experience of many international companies and their leadership development efforts, one can distinguish three basic models to organize this process: the internal model, the external model and the comprehensive model. There are many varieties around them, but they all keep some of the basic traits.

The first is the **internal model**. In this model, the design and development of the project are done by the business units or divisions, together with the people's division. In some companies, the people's division takes the lead; in others, it is the business unit that takes the lead. Senior managers take care of the development needs of executives, who are guided by mentors through a process of personal discovery and change. Advice, assessment and coaching are widely used tools. Some individual learning actions are also on offer, such as executive programs at business schools. The development process is essentially under the control of senior managers.

The weaknesses of this model are: the development of capabilities is closely associated with the needs and challenges of the firm, and the functions and responsibilities that the executive should take up. But the lack of external inputs and the interaction with managers from other industries may limit the learning process. If the goal of the program is to produce short-term results, long-term capability development may be missing. Finally, the development process of new competencies is limited to the firm's experience and the expertise of senior managers in charge of the project.

The second model is the **customized approach to leadership development**. Since leadership capabilities have to be deployed in very specific contexts, the use of the company and its industry as contexts provide a ground for expanding leadership competencies. This model counts on the help of a business school or external teachers who guide executives through a more formal education process towards the development of knowledge and capabilities.

These programs may be coordinated by HR managers with the support of the CEO. They include some internal initiatives that the company launches to facilitate the discussion of those issues or the application of the program to improve the way the company operates. Those initiatives include business plans, change projects or cross-functional initiatives.

These programs may also include some modules on basic business literacy, so that managers with an experience in some functions—finance, for instance—may quickly develop a good knowledge and judgment about other business areas—like marketing, production or logistics, for instance. Nevertheless, the business literacy part of this program is not its essential ingredient. Leadership development concepts and models are the linchpin of the program.

If these programs are well designed and executed, they usually have a deep impact on executives and their companies. The major challenges that they face are the need to focus on the long term, the definition of goals and their alignment with the strategy and goals of the firm, and the follow-up of the learning outcomes of the program and their application to the firm. The worst thing that may happen with these programs is that they may be well designed and delivered, but there is little alignment between the learning and the strategy and priorities of the firm.

The third is the **comprehensive model**, where there is a continuum of leadership development experiences in the professional career of a manager. In a more or less planned process—some companies do a great job here anticipating the long-term development of young managers—job experiences combine with international assignments, special projects, executive courses at business schools, formal coaching sessions and participation in customized programs.

A key advantage of this model is that it is more eclectic, by using what is good and effective in the other models. The main difference is conceptual: it is the realization that the leadership development needs of a manager are not covered by a few isolated actions, whatever their strength and quality might be. It is a process that spans many years of a professional career, with different needs at different stages. Some of those needs may be covered inside the company. But other needs are more complex and may require external actions, like a customized program or a portfolio of open leadership programs offered to executives from different companies and expertise.

The external perspective that those programs bring to the company is very relevant, and help understand the challenges of the corporate world in a wider context, shifting from the pressing short-term needs towards the long term. In the same way as some companies manage financial investments in a masterful way, other companies manage the investment in leadership development as a very delicate process of wide impact. With this purpose in mind, these companies use all the available possibilities and try to combine them effectively.

This model also offers a more personalized approach. Some people may need formal programs to develop or acquire some competencies. Others may go quicker and work more intensely in other areas. As it happens in other areas of education—in particular, in adult education—personalization is key. Learning involves understanding and framing problems, asking the right questions, getting external perspectives, developing the knowledge and capabilities required and putting them at work. This process calls for an individualized approach, which the comprehensive model approaches better than the others.

Some guidelines for an efficient design of leadership development programs

Executive programs—either customized programs or a portfolio of open executive programs—complement in an effective way the "on the job" learning experience and the special projects that can speed up leadership development. Actually, the internal development initiatives are reinforced when a formal leadership program is designed and implemented. Based on the experience of schools like IESE and others, with a rich tradition in international executive education, I highlight some basic principles for a successful program design.

Consistency. Program design, content and delivery should help participants think long term and develop the capabilities they need. But they also should be well aligned with the firm's mission, as well with its strategy goals and action plans.

Coordination. A successful program needs to have the support and endorsement of the firm's chief executive and the top management team. They need to make sure that the program is coherent with and will help achieve firm's strategy and goals. The CEO should work with the HR team and the business units to ensure that there is learning and coordination in the program across business units and geographies within the firm.

New concepts and ideas. Excellent development programs are based on the conceptualization of ideas, models, knowledge and empirical evidence developed by companies and leaders in the real world. Global leaders need not only best practices, but also knowledge and ideas on how the world works and how it changes. These programs help participants to rethink their approaches to problems, solutions and action plans to face new challenges. The discussion takes place in the context of real business problems in their own companies or in companies in other relevant industries or geographies.

Decision-making and implementation. A good program should focus on decision-making, a pragmatic approach that highlights the choices and trade-offs leaders have to tackle in their careers. These formal programs do not intend to illustrate state-of-the art techniques or approaches, even when they are useful or interesting. Program design aims at raising questions and challenges, and exchanging views about them with other executives. Participants, by using their previous expertise or some newly developed capabilities, need to frame the problems in a different way, rethink approaches to solutions, consider different alternatives to implementing those solutions and calibrate the impact of their decisions, both in the short and the long term.

This principle highlights in a very special way that successful executive programs are not about answers or techniques, but about framing problems, developing a point of view about the future, designing solutions and considering action plans. This set of activities makes a big contrast with the traditional functional-based management programs that dominated the executive landscape until very recently. Even if functions and business literacy are still very important, they are one step in the leadership development process, which a leader needs to take at some point; but this type of program falls short of covering all the development needs of global leaders.

Knowledge, capabilities, interpersonal skills and attitudes. Formal programs should blend in a harmonious way relevant knowledge, capabilities development, interpersonal skills acquisition and reflection on the inner attitudes and the changes required. A well-designed program intended to have a deep impact on companies and their leaders aims at working at the different levels of leadership competencies. The main domain of these programs is both group work and classroom discussion of real problems and challenges, potential solutions, implementation plans and an overall understanding the role that different stakeholders play in this process.

These programs aim at the acquisition of new knowledge and the development of capabilities, skills and attitudes. This is a key advantage of a good formal program: the simultaneous development of different competencies—intellectual, psychological or relational. It is actually a process that resembles in a close way, as in a laboratory, what happens in the real world. The main advantage here is that a participant can calibrate things a bit better, using more diverse points of view, including perspectives from other industries and companies. A program that only focuses on knowledge could be very useful but would not qualify as a leadership development experiment. A program that highlights skills and capabilities but which does not help explore the deeper attitudes will be useful but at the risk of excluding a critical dimension of leaders and an important engine of their capacity to effect change and engage other people. Good formal programs need to consider these dimensions. This is costly in terms of time: those programs cannot be too short if they need to tackle all those dimensions and want to have a transformational impact on people. They do not need to be very long either. Moreover, a distribution of the program delivery over several months, with some days of more formal learning process, tends to be more effective than just immersing in a long program for several months.

Integration. This has two dimensions. The external dimension is that the program should be well integrated with the mission of the firm, its culture and values, its strategy, as well as with the different leadership initiatives that the firm has in place, like assessment, coaching or special assignments and projects. Leadership development is multi-functional, and needs to take advantage of different ways to strengthen it.

The internal dimension of integration relates to the need to help the different modules, topics and methodologies of the program converge towards a more comprehensive model of leadership development. Let us consider the following example. In a good formal program, new knowledge on customers' behavior in an emerging country will connect with some methods and models to assess customers' preferences, will relate with some capabilities to analyze those changing individuals' tastes, will foster new skills to connect with customers in segments that were previously approached in a different way, and individuals' behavior will shed light on some basic attitudes that executives have towards other people's behavior.

We have followed here a train of events, from new knowledge to reflection on deeper personal attitudes. But we can make a similar process starting, for instance, with the challenge of a new capability important to make decisions in high-growth, high-risk countries: framing problems in a context of high uncertainty due to financial constraints. The development of this new capability involves knowing better about market and consumer trends, or the motives of government intervention in certain contexts. This new knowledge helps frame the problem better. And this process not only opens up the senior executive's mind, but also incorporates new experiences about the values and motivations of other people in very different contexts.

It is clear that each one of those dimensions—knowledge, capabilities, interpersonal skills and attitudes–is complex and requires special work and development. But leaders need to use them and develop all of them when facing complex problems, and implement action plans. It is because the real-world demands of leaders are so complex that the formal programs need to provide a context where those competencies can be exercised and trained in a systematic way.

This approach also highlights a difference between business schools that believe in organized integration and those that assume that individuals should make the integration by themselves. Some schools design outstanding programs highlighting specific business function challenges (marketing, technology, operations or finance). When asked about the integration of those issues with the overall orientation of the company, the answer is that leaders will integrate the necessary dimensions in the real world once they have the tools to understand and solve functional problems. This is one way to look at the world of organizations.

Another way is the one followed by schools like IESE, which believe that integration of the different dimensions is important, and that formal programs can help this process in a particular way. It is not an easy task, but one worthy of effort through different methods.

This integrative approach should consider several dimensions. The first is the balance in any program between knowledge, capabilities, interpersonal skills and attitudes. The second is the internal connection of the different business functions with the overall strategy of the firm. The third is the balance between the short-term and the long-term goals and development of the firm. The fourth is the integration of the firm's strategy with the mission, culture and values of the organization. The fifth is the reasonable integration of the different goals and expectations of the firm's stakeholders.

The importance of integration is even greater in international leadership development initiatives. In these programs, participants need to relate the learning process both to the needs of the firm in the local market and the needs of the whole firm. This requires not only an integration of goals and objectives, but also an understanding of the meaning and impact of the different values and ways of doing things throughout the organization.

In this context, the organization of executive programs in different locations around the world—in particular, when they include some specific projects to be developed by international teams—helps executives deal with the complexities of the local and the global. IESE has had an experience of working in both open programs and custom programs, including modules in Europe, the US, Latin America, China, India and Africa. Some of those programs are jointly offered with US schools like Harvard, Stanford or Wharton, and the associated schools that IESE has helped develop in 16 growth countries round the world, including IPADE (Mexico), CEIBS (China), ISE (Brazil), Lagos Business School (Nigeria) and IAE (Argentina), among others. The development of learning experiences in each one of those locations end their organized transfer to other parts of a global company are unique opportunities to foster leadership development and innovation in an international firm.

Commitment. The final principle is commitment. Companies need to devote time and resources to leadership development. Leadership is so important that it should not be neglected, or left to spontaneous forces or initiatives. The top management team needs to consider leadership development as a key priority. CEOs should also understand that leaders at all levels—including themselves—need time to keep learning, reflect on their performance, and understand the changing world around them and the changing expectations and motives that their colleagues around them develop. Leadership development needs time and context, in the same way as lawyers, medical doctors or orchestra conductors need time to reflect and assess their performance, as they invest in new capabilities. Leadership development is not cheap; it requires a commitment of time and effort, and the allocation of financial resources. The investment in leadership development is the most complex one any organization faces. In the same way as a world-class manufacturing firm will not settle with equipment, technology or processes that are not state-of-the-art, leading companies should not settle with leadership development programs that only offer a quick fix. Formal programs need to be coordinated with the other development activities that the company designs, including assessments, coaching and special assignments, among others. But there is no replacement for formal programs that take leadership development seriously in order to have an impact on individuals and the company as a whole.

The role of business schools in global leadership development

How can business schools help companies in global leadership development? For many years, business schools offered executive programs that mainly provided basic functional education—on areas such as marketing, managing people, finance, operations or technology, among others—to middle and senior managers. More recently, some horizontal challenges that firms face, such as globalization, innovation, social media or change, have become the core of executive programs. A key question for business schools is whether they are quick enough to adapt and tackle the new challenges that international companies actually face.

It is important to consider that those challenges are not only related to globalization, but also to some important new trends shaping the business world, such as the complexity of large organizations, the need for effective decision-making processes or the new diversity in the workforce, and not just because of the increasing number of cultures and countries represented in it.

In this process, business schools may focus exclusively on globalization initiatives that may bring the school more in tune with the needs of international companies. This is an important ingredient, but there are others that need deeper consideration. In this respect, we can observe several steps for business schools in reconsidering how they can better serve companies and business leaders over the next years in the fascinating process of speeding up leadership development. These steps are: understand the new context, define a leadership development model, reflect on the nature of the person, rethink program and content design, formulate a coherent strategy for globalization and implement a holistic system.

Understand the new context

Business schools need to understand the challenges that globalization and other changes in the environment are bringing about and the implications that they have for their students and customers, programs, faculty development, strategy and resource allocation. In strategy courses, we encourage managers to think about the future and develop a point of view about it, one that would give some coherence to the different actions and initiatives. Business schools should do the same thing. An informal exploration of some globalization initiatives at business schools shows a wide array of initiatives that push the institution towards a more active engagement with the global economy and its corporate clients. Nevertheless, there is not always a strong sense of coherence and consistency among those actions, or a clear point of view about the future, and on how to serve students or corporate clients.

We are not advocating here for a top-down strategic process that predetermines in a rational way all the steps that the business school will take over the next few years. A good strategic process should also take advantage of new opportunities. But business schools should define what they stand for, what type of institution they want to be and which role they want to play in a more global world.

Define a leadership development model

As we have discussed above, there are different models of leadership development. What is important to understand is that old models of leadership may not be enough to help global leaders and companies tackle some of the challenges that they face.

Some executive programs make certain assumptions. The first is that the program focusses on functional or business areas and that participants will integrate the different issues. The second is that leadership development involves both knowledge and capabilities development; both are in offer in most programs, but not always integrated in a coherent way. In many cases, capabilities development are offered as separate modules whose links with the rest of the program are not always well defined. In a nutshell, those capabilities development modules are nice to have, but they are not always well integrated in the curriculum or connected with the other modules and courses.

Schools need to think again about those issues. In particular, a systematic review of knowledge, capabilities, skills and attitudes needs to be put in place. Moreover, these dimensions should be connected with one another. For example, negotiation capabilities for a senior executive in a multinational company should not be developed irrespective of the cultural issues specific to the countries where the company operates, and these issues require certain personal attitudes—awareness, respect or humility in dealing with others—that need to be integrated in the whole process in a holistic way.

There is not a single, unique model of leadership development. There is a wide variety of models. But it is necessary that each school develops one. This will provide some coherence to the different programs, will help create some standards and will facilitate the task of companies when looking for specific requirements.

Reflect on the nature of the person: Beyond economics

It is worthy of mention that globalization, uncertainty and diversity put additional pressures on business schools to define a positive view of the person. With companies growing not only larger but more diverse geographically, being less rooted in a culture or a country, and experiencing the need to work with people from other cultures, professionals in international companies face a new demand for meaning. One of the critical roles of leaders is to offer meaning and context to other people. And this cannot be fully accomplished unless there is a humanistic and positive view of people in organizations, one that takes leadership and management beyond optimization and conductive behavior, towards a new territory where people's aspirations can actually find a reasonable expression in their professional jobs.

This need is also reinforced by the changing cultural roots and aspirations of the new generation of millennials joining the workforce. They are willing to make a contribution to the organizations they work for, but also have high expectations that go beyond money, compensation and job titles. They demand respect, appreciation, a sense of contribution and impact on the company and the wider society.

We propose a profile of the dimensions of human nature implicit in a humanistic view of companies and leadership (Canals, 2011b). It has the following attributes: each person is unique; she has an intrinsic dignity and has been endowed with basic human rights to be respected in the workplace and society; she has the freedom to make responsible decisions; she is responsible for the use of her rights and capabilities; she has basic material needs, but also ideals and aspirations that go beyond economic incentives or rewards; she has values that need to be respected as far as they do no cause harm to others; and she can grow her qualities and potential by serving others.

Some of these dimensions are already considered good practices around talent management or corporate social responsibility. The challenge for business schools is not only to deal with them in those areas, but to make them more horizontal across disciplines and courses, so that a more humanistic culture can emerge in companies, complementing a pure economic view of the firm. This goal has always been important, but it is becoming more relevant than ever.

Rethink program and content design

Globalization and the new business realities call for an important renovation of executive programs' content. Many schools already offer executive programs centered on global management, which is good. The challenge lies in making sure that globalization and the implications of the new realities have the right treatment in all programs.

For several years, leading business schools playing in the international arena have been emphasizing the importance of the number of foreign students and foreign faculty in a single program, the number of international alliances, the presence of the school in different countries—sometimes with a fully-fledged campus. These are highly important dimensions and strategies to tackle globalization, as the AACSB report on globalization of business education has recently pointed out (Bruner *et al.*, 2011). Nevertheless, in terms of learning, the first priority should be about how program content and design actually adjust to the new realities.

It is also important to emphasize that including more case studies on companies from other geographies, or studying national cultures deeper are important steps, but are not enough. The basic challenges in terms of program content and design are the following. The first is how real-world problems and making decisions in a specific country or region differ from problems and decisions in one's home country (Ghemawat, 2008, 2011). The second is how cross-border problems and decisions—for instance, a company based in Germany trying to optimize its global supply chain management in Asia—are taken into regular consideration in the classroom. The third is how the decision-making process in those problems needs to be framed and different individual behaviors in different cultures are taken into account. The fourth is how those issues are incorporated in a regular way in the different functional courses and programs.

In a nutshell, enriching a program with more cases from companies in other countries is always positive and provides a fresh knowledge on cross-cultural issues. But, as we have discussed, global leadership is not only about cross-cultural issues, but about heterogeneity, uncertainty, diversity and complexity. Program content and design, including case studies and other materials, should emphasize these dimensions if they want to be relevant for the business world.

Formulate a coherent strategy for globalization

The previous discussion takes us to the challenge of the globalization of business schools. Before elaborating the arguments, we should make clear two ideas. The first is that strategy is about uniqueness. Each business school needs to make a decision about its own way of dealing with globalization. In this decision, past performance, capabilities and resources, stakeholders' views and aspirations play an important role. Not every school should be global, and those that want to, do not need to follow the same pathway.

The second idea is about the strategy process by which schools define their global positioning. Some strategy scholars think in terms of strategy design as a formal process emphasizing certain rational dimensions of the environment and the resources and capabilities that a company has. Other views of strategy highlight the importance of emerging opportunistic strategies, a process of trial and error, or a pathway shaped by taking new steps as they come up. Both approaches can be useful. Perhaps a flexible combination of both approaches is required, in part as the natural outcome of the increasing uncertainty that globalization brings about and the degree of diversity that senior executives should include in their decision-making process when dealing with international operations.

A useful way to think about global strategy is to define it as the combination of goals, policies, people, resource allocation, action plans and business configuration to serve international students and companies, and achieve a certain outcome. This strategy should be coherent with the mission and vision of the business school, from which goals and policy issues should stem in a natural way. The consideration of resource allocation and operations configuration could be better understood when analyzing the global profile of a business schools, defined by two variables (see Figure 8): geographical scope and activities.

Figure 8 helps describe the global profile as the specific geographical scale that a school adopts for its functions and units. For our purpose, we define four geographies where business schools develop their activities: the

Figure 8: Global strategies for business schools: A profile

Areas and activities	Geographical scope			
	Local	Regional	Continental	Global
Faculty				
Staff				
Students				
Executive education participants				
Corporate clients and recruiters				
Program content				
Campus location				
Internships and field work				
Alumni				
Partnerships				

local, home market; the regional market—which includes several neighboring countries; the continental market—which includes many countries in a continent, even some distant ones; and the global market—with two or more continents involved.

The specific areas or activities for business schools to be considered in the different geographic contexts are: faculty and staff, students (and senior managers participating in executive programs), corporate recruiters, corporate clients, program content, campus location and program delivery, internships and field work, alumni, and partnerships.

Experience with a number of international business schools help us consider that the previous areas and activities do not have the same weight in defining a global strategy profile. Some of them are more relevant than others. Based on that experience, we propose the following propositions. The first is that faculty, students, executive education participants, program content and alumni are the core, most powerful areas shaping a global strategy. The impact that the other areas and activities (corporate partners, program delivery, staff or location) may have on the global strategy profile depend very much on the individual and holistic effect that each one of them has on the core, driving areas.

The second proposition is that two different schools could have well-defined global strategies, following different pathways, with different profiles. Nevertheless, we can say, in coherence with the first proposition, that without faculty, program content, executive education participants and students scoring high in those international dimensions, the impact of a global strategy will be smaller.

Implement a holistic system

In the 1980s and early 1990s, when globalization started to accelerate, many well-known companies in Europe, North America or Japan designed international organizations that had little coordination with their domestic business units. Firms such as Philips, Unilever, Toyota, Citibank or Ford, among others, started to implement radical reorganizations of their operations; some of them moved from a country-based organization to a global product-based organization or a global business-based organization. The problem is that organizational models do not offer universal solutions for every single company. Their success depends on many factors including a firm's culture and values, history, resources, capabilities and flexibility for change, and customers' behaviors and expectations. Solutions that can work well in one industry may not work in another. Models that could be good for a company in a certain industry may not be good for a competitor. The outcome of this process is that we have seen periodical restructurings and organizational shake-ups too often, which means that either the model or its implementation were not appropriate.

A basic root of that problem is how to face the challenge of combining local responsiveness to customers with global coordination of operations. These attributes of successful global business schools are based on previous contributions in the global management literature. Bartlett and Ghoshal (1989), for example, developed the transnational corporation model, which emphasizes three key dimensions: local responsiveness, global scale and learning.

Some companies forgot about other important dimensions: how to improve learning from international operations; how to transfer that learning to the rest of the organization; and how to serve customers that also have a global profile, and for which the right balance between local roots and global scope could also be very relevant.

This is a clear warning for business schools. The solution is not simple, but the message is clear. Business schools, when thinking and making decisions about globalization, need to consider how the process creates a holistic system that helps globalization improve the overall capacity of the school to serve its stakeholders better.

With this goal in mind, schools need to reflect on a number of basic dimensions of their performance as global institutions (Table 5). Some of them are the same as those highlighted by Bartlett and Ghoshal (1989). The first is the capacity for responsiveness to local customers. The second is the effective coordination of faculty and staff, resources and activities around the world. The third is a global learning process such that new ideas anywhere in the world can be easily translated into other parts of the school. These three dimensions coincide with Bartlett and Ghoshal's framework.

In the business school case, we can also observe that there are other dimensions or outcomes of effective institutions that need to be taken into account. The first is the management of global customers—mainly international companies with executive education needs in different parts of the world. The second is effective learning transfer not only of methodologies or international practices, but new ideas and knowledge around problems, capabilities

Table 5: Business schools: Dimensions of performance as global institutions

Local responsiveness

Global coordination

Learning process

Management of global customers

Learning transfer

Network effects

Ideas impact

and attitudes whose development is relevant in other parts of the organization. The third is the network effects that reinforce the external impact that schools have on their students, corporate clients and alumni, both in the sales and admissions processes in degree programs, sales in executive programs and alumni relations. The final dimension is the global impact of ideas, models and values that schools and their faculty develop around leadership, management, governances, and companies and their role in society. These ideas could be a solid pillar of the civic fabric in a society and can inspire and shape public policy, and the interaction between governments and the private sector.

Each one of those dimensions is important. But the critical lesson that companies with experience in international operations teach us is the need for creating virtuous circles, holistic models where those dimensions reinforce each other, making the school stronger in all of its operations, and more capable of developing their mission and delivering the value that their stakeholders expect from it.

Some implications for CEOs

As CEOs of international companies struggle with the uncertainty of a more volatile global economy, they realize that the future of their companies depends very much on the quality of leadership talent within their firms. Moreover, for companies with expanding operations in high-growth countries, "it is not product innovation or manufacturing competitiveness; leadership development is the number one challenge that companies have and will have over the next years," as the CEO of one of the largest German manufacturing firms said in a lecture at IESE in September 2010.

At a broader, societal level, the perception is also clear: the 2008 financial crisis was generated by irresponsible senior managers in some companies who were supervised by irresponsible regulators and government officials. Bad leadership and lack of ethical values are root causes of the global financial crisis. These perceptions also highlight that leadership is not about charismatic qualities—they may help or not—but about competency: the capacity to understand a problem or a challenge, identify solutions, set up coalitions and teams to work on them and implement them, while creating the right context and offering meaning to the people affected, being the citizens of a country or the employees of a company.

Leadership seems to be extremely relevant, in particular as companies and societies face vast, complex problems of unprecedented scale. The need for the right balance of knowledge, capabilities, skills and attitudes is critical.

CEOs need to reflect on some key aspects of global leadership development, with the conviction that this is an indispensable process for the long-term success of their organizations. The first reflection is a paradox: this is a time when we speak about leadership as never before. Experience also shows that in an age where knowledge, both in the West and the East, is more widespread than ever, and where companies spend a lot of time and money in leadership development initiatives (including more formal programs around coaching, capabilities' assessment and others techniques), leadership development is still in its early stages. It is true that there are good exceptions. We should be frank and recognize that some of those initiatives were nice to have, but never had or intended to have a big impact. We also should recognize that leadership does not develop spontaneously, even if some people have natural qualities to become leaders. Leadership needs to be rethought by business leaders, and new ideas and programs need to be developed.

The second reflection is the commitment to leadership development. Leadership development should be among top managers' key concerns, in the same way that setting a new strategic direction, launching new products or investing or divesting business units are. This means spending time thinking about the initiatives, helping design and implement them, funding them, and getting to know through them the current and future leaders of the firm. Formal programs need to be in place, including both internal initiatives, customized programs and a formal learning experience in knowledge and capabilities. These programs should be structured on the understanding that learning never stops and that great companies should constantly offer opportunities to continue the process.

CEOs' commitment to leadership development is also expressed in the time allocated to this challenge by CEOs themselves and their dialogue with HR managers. A CEO of one of the largest companies in Europe organizes biweekly meetings talking with future leaders, discussing their performance with their direct bosses, thinking about new assignments, assessing progress and making sure that their development is on track.

The third reflection is that leadership development requires long-term, strategic thinking. It also needs a good integration of the different initiatives, job assignments, special projects and formal programs. The CEO needs to make sure that all the elements for long-term leadership development are there and reviews its progress as she does with sales or financial performance. She also needs to make sure that in the programs for leadership development the focus is on the long term, and that future leaders are able to look inside the firm and outside the organization at the same time.

The fourth reflection is that the CEO needs to care about the development of well-rounded leaders. It is a caricature, but the prototype of leaders, defined by being bold, quick and tough, that may exist in some countries and cultures, is misleading. Good leaders need a balanced development of knowledge, capabilities, interpersonal skills and attitudes. This takes time to articulate and frame, and is costly to design and deliver. But companies need them. What would be the use of a complex aircraft if the pilot is not an expert in flying it? We need leaders—pilots—who know how to take a company to the next level and how to integrate and develop people in this process.

Finally, the fifth reflection is the regular assessment of leadership development. This is a more complex challenge than assessing financial performance or productivity of manufacturing plans, but it should be done. The assessment process is not the most important thing; the real challenge is to foster leadership development. But people need to know how effective a firm is in doing so. In the past, business analysts, media and other senior executives used to assess a CEO's success in terms of the economic performance and value creation added during the CEO's tenure. We know how incomplete this assessment is. In the future, we will assess the success of a CEO by the quality and pool of leadership talent within a company. This may be the longest-lasting legacy of a CEO. Financial profitability is about the past. Leadership development is about the future.

I have argued that companies need to become respected institutions in society (Canals, 2010). It is not enough for companies to be profitable or develop good products. They need to generate respect among a wide group of stakeholders. Leadership development is a key pillar in this effort. In this process CEOs need to lead this process and take responsibility for the final outcome.

Leadership development is such an important issue for society—not just for companies—that firms and CEOs will be judged in the future by their contribution in tackling this important challenge. Companies and CEOs who do a good job in this area will become references for the rest of society, and will also show that admired companies are not only good at delivering financial performance, but also at developing leaders who understand the challenges that they need to tackle, the decisions that they need to make, and the actions that they must undertake to put the decisions into practice.

NOTE

1 I am very grateful to Robert Bruner, Carlos Sánchez-Runde, Josep Valor and Eric Weber for their useful suggestions and comments on an early draft.

REFERENCES

Adler, N. J. (2001) "Global Leadership: Women Leader." In M. Mendenhall, T. Kuhlmann and G. Stahl *Developing Global Business Leaders* (Westport, CT: Quorum Books): 73–97.

Aristotle. (1980) *The Nicomachean Ethics* (Oxford: Oxford University Press).

Bartlett, C. and Ghoshal, S. (1989) *Managing Across Borders* (Boston, MA: Harvard Business School Publishing).

Bass, B. M. (1995) *Leadership and Performance Beyond Expectations* (New York, NY: The Free Press).

Bennis, W. (1989) *On Becoming a Leader* (Reading, MA: Addison-Wesley).

Bhagat, R. S. and Steers, R. M. (2009) *Culture, Organizations and Work* (Cambridge: Cambridge University Press).

Bruner, R. F., De Meyer, A., Ghemawat, P., Gómez, J., Lenway, S., Rao, M., Snyder, E., Tapie, P. and Teegen, K. (2011) *Globalization of Management Education: Changing International Structure, Adaptive Strategies, and the Impact on Institutions* (Tampa, FL: Association for the Advancement of Collegiate Schools of Business).

Canals, J. (2010) *Building Respected Institutions* (Cambridge: Cambridge University Press).

Canals, J. (ed.) (2011a) *The Future of Leadership Development* (Houndmills: Palgrave Macmillan).

Canals, J. (2011b) "In Search of a Greater Impact: New Corporate and Societal Challenges for Business Schools." In J. Canals (ed.) *The Future of Leadership Development* (Houndmills: Palgrave Macmillan): 3–30.

Conaty, B. and Charan, R. (2010) *The Talent Masters* (New York, NY: Crown Business).

Conger, J. and Benjamin, B. (1999) *Building Leaders* (San Francisco, CA: Jossey-Bass).

Ghemawat, P. (2008) "The Globalization of Business Education Through the Lens of Semiglobalization." *Journal of Management Development* 27.4: 391–414.

Ghemawat, P. (2011) "Responses to Forces of Change: A Focus on Curricular Content." In R. F. Bruner *et al. Globalization of Management Education: Changing International Structure, Adaptive Strategies, and the Impact on Institutions* (Tampa, FL: Association for the Advancement of Collegiate Schools of Business): 105–156.

Gundling, E., Hogan, T. and Cvitkovich, K. (2011) *What Is Global Leadership?* (Boston, MA: Nicholas Brealey).

Javidan, M., Dorfman, P., Sully de Luque, M. and House, R. J. (2006) "In the Eye of the Beholder: Cross-cultural Lessons in Leadership from Project GLOBE." *Academy of Management Perspectives* 20.1: 67–91.

Jokinen, T. (2005) "Global Leadership Competencies: A Review and Discussion." *Journal of European Industrial Training* 29.2/3: 199–216.

Kanter, R. M. (2010) "Leadership in a Globalizing World." In N. Nohria and R. Khurana (eds) *Handbook of Leadership Theory and Practice* (Boston, MA: Harvard Business School Publishing): 569–610.

Kotter, J. (1990) *A Force for Change: How Leadership Differs from Management* (New York, NY: Free Press).

Levy, O., Beechler, S., Taylor, S. and Boyacilliger, N. (2007) "What Do We Talk About When We Talk about Global Mindset? Managerial Cognition in Multinational Corporations." *Journal of International Business Studies* 38: 231–258.

McCall, M. W. and Hollenbeck, G. P. (2002) *Developing Global Executives* (Boston, MA: Harvard Business School Press).

Nohria, N. and Khurana, R. (eds) (2010a) *Handbook of Leadership Theory and Practice* (Boston, MA: Harvard Business School Publishing).

Nohria, N. and Khurana, R. (2010b) "Advancing Leadership Theory and Practice." In N. Nohria and R. Khurana (eds) *Handbook of Leadership Theory and Practice* (Boston, MA: Harvard Business School Publishing): 3–26.

Osland, J. S. (2008) "An Overview of the Global Leadership Literature." In M. Mendenhall, J. S. Osland, A. Bird, G. Oddou and M. Maznevski (eds) *Global Leadership: Research, Practice and Development* (London: Routledge): 34–63.

Osland, J. S. and Bird, A. (2006) "Global Leaders as Experts." In W. Mobley and E. Weldon (eds) *Advances in Global Leadership* (Stamford, CT: JAI Press), vol. 4: 123–142.

Osland, J. S., Taylor, S. and Mendenhall, M. E. (2009) "Global Leadership: Progress and Challenges." In R. S. Bhagat and R. M. Steers *Culture, Organizations and Work* (Cambridge: Cambridge University Press): 245–271.

Pérez-López, J. A. (1993) *Fundamentos de dirección de empresas* (Madrid: Ed. Rialp).

Podolny, J., Khurana, R. and Besharov, M. L. (2010) "Revisiting the Meaning of Leadership." In N. Nohria and R. Khurana (eds) *Handbook of Leadership Theory and Practice* (Boston, MA: Harvard Business School Publishing): 65–106.

Ready, D. A., Hill, L. A. and Conger, J. A. (2008) "Winning the Race for Talent in Emerging Markets." *Harvard Business Review* (November): 62–70.

Sánchez-Runde, C., Nardon, L. and Steers, R. M. (in press) "Looking beyond Western Leadership Models: Implications for Global Managers." *Organizational Dynamics* 40.3: 207–213.

Snook, S. A., Khurana, R. and Nohria, N. (eds) (2011) *The Handbook for Teaching Leadership: Knowing, Doing and Being* (Thousand Oaks, CA: Sage).

Tarique, I. and Schuler, R. S. (2010) "Global Talent Management: Literature Review, Integrative Framework, and Suggestions for Further Research." *Journal of World Business* 45.1: 122–133.

Tichy, N. M. and Cohen, E. (1997) *The Leadership Engine* (New York, NY: HarperCollins).

Yeung, A. K. and Ready, D. A. (1995) "Developing Leadership Capabilities of Global Corporations: A Comparative Study in Eight Nations." *Human Resource Management* 34.4: 529–547.

CHAPTER 1.3

The ABCDs of Leadership 3.0

PANKAJ GHEMAWAT, Anselmo Rubiralta Professor of Global Strategy,
IESE Business School, University of Navarra

The ambitious title reflects an ambitious proposal: consider a new way of addressing the distinctive complexities that leaders confront in a global (or international) context by thinking through the differences and distances between countries—and acting on the implications. The model I advocate, Leadership 3.0, derives from logic, empirical research, an AACSB-sponsored survey of thought leaders worldwide, participation for more than two years in the AACSB's Globalization of Management Education Taskforce (including writing a chapter in the report on some of the ideas presented here) and action research in the classroom over an even longer period.[1] Leadership 3.0 has important change implications not only for business schools but for companies and for individuals as well. To sharpen those implications, it will be contrasted at length with two more common models for global leadership development, which are referred to here as Leadership 1.0 and Leadership 2.0.

To preview the conclusions, Leadership 3.0 is tuned to an assessment of globalization, of incomplete cross-border integration or semiglobalization, that is distinct from the national (zero globalization) world of Leadership 1.0, or the fully globalized world with which Leadership 2.0 has particular affinity. Semiglobalization, involving significant home bias, fits much better with the vast array of empirical evidence on the real state of the world.[2] It is also what underpins the logic for really trying to think outside the national box. Neither the zero international integration assumed by Leadership 1.0 nor the complete international integration often envisaged by Leadership 2.0 creates a need to go beyond single-country thinking. This is obvious in the case of zero international integration and, at the other extreme, complete international integration would create a single super-country to which all our propositions derived from single-country thinking could presumably be applied. It is worth adding that the empirical finding that markets are significantly home-biased fits well with Leadership 3.0, as does individual- and company-level evidence of rootedness.

That is all about assumptions; the implications of Leadership 3.0 are even more interesting. I summarize them, given my sense that a simple mnemonic is better than none, as the ABCDs of Leadership 3.0. Leadership 3.0 changes how business schools, companies and individuals should think about four broad areas that give rise to the ABCD acronym:

- *Aspirations*: The ideal type under Leadership 3.0 is a (self-consciously) rooted cosmopolitan—instead of the national citizens of Leadership 1.0 and the global citizens or rootless global cosmopolitans idealized by Leadership 2.0.

- *Basic structure*: Leadership 3.0 is built around action that emphasizes self-discovery *as well as* the openness to "foreigners" emphasized by Leadership 2.0 (and ignored by Leadership 1.0) and implies multiple architectural possibilities (e.g., emphasis on a particular region or on emerging markets) rather than one monolithic model, whether national or global.

- *Conceptual content*: Apart from semiglobalization, the conceptual core of Leadership 3.0 consists of taking a broad but rooted view of international differences and distances instead of treating them as insurmountable (the world of Leadership 1.0) or as negligible (as in a fully globalized world).

- *Direct experience*: Leadership 3.0 implies a need to try to reach individuals through varied experiential as well as conceptual content, but it also sees the obstacles to be surmounted more seriously (or broadly) than Leadership 2.0, with implications for what is likely to constitute a useful experience.

The first section of this chapter lays out in more detail the three types of leadership models introduced above. The next section associates the three models with different assumptions about the extent of global integration and presents some of the evidence favoring Leadership 3.0 in terms of the realism of its structural substrate. The third section uses the ABCDs to contrast the implications of Leadership 3.0 with those of Leadership 1.0 and Leadership 2.0, highlighting the broad changes required. Section 4 concludes.

Three models of leadership development

Systematic consideration of leadership and leadership development started to spread in academia and business in the early twentieth century. However, the vast majority of research through the 1970s was undertaken by North American and British scholars and was focussed on leadership in a domestic context.[3] I classify this model (or set of models) under the rubric of *Leadership 1.0*.

Leadership 1.0 has been stretched beyond the traditional Anglo-North American context by more recent attempts to develop, say (Continental) European or Japanese or Chinese models of leadership that purport to offer generally useful alternatives to the traditional model. What unites these different types of leadership models, however, is their focus on a particular national context and, relatedly, a dearth of systematic attention to cross-country variation.[4] Similar nationally focussed models can be specified for other functional areas, for example, Supply 1.0, which emphasizes national rather than international models of supply chains.

But while Supply 1.0 has ceded significant share of mind to international supply chains, matters seem not to have progressed as rapidly when it comes to leadership: Leadership 1.0 is still what mostly preoccupies the leadership development initiatives of most business schools—and businesses—judging by metrics such as class hours, research areas, and so on. So Leadership 1.0 can be described as the most common response to the challenge of leadership development, even though it is, in a sense, a "no-globalization" model.

Leadership 2.0, unlike Leadership 1.0, does attempt to go beyond the purely parochial. But its content is less easy to characterize, since researchers and educators working along these lines have followed several separate paths in a sequence that was initiated by the emergence of international business as a separate field of study in the 1950s and 1960s, and was followed (with a lag) by the development of interest in the international/global dimensions of leadership.[5]

It should be acknowledged that some of the strands of research that have resulted from such efforts, particularly research on culture, come closer than others to the approach advocated in this chapter under the rubric of Leadership 3.0. But most of this research either ignores international interactions or takes a limited view of the complications that they entail. Thus, of the five strands of nonparochial research on culture discussed in Adler's classic taxonomy, three—ethnocentric research, polycentric research and comparative research—acknowledge cultural differences but fail to consider interactions across them.[6] A fourth, "synergistic" research, does focus on cross-cultural interactions and integrating processes, but misses out on noncultural differences. And a fifth, "geocentric" research, brings in the geographic dimension but, as Adler notes, "In many [such] studies, the culture of the countries involved is completely ignored."[7] A survey of nearly one hundred studies of organizational behavior and national culture that were published in the 16 leading management journals between 1996 to 2005 suggests that relatively little has changed at least as far as the exclusive concentration on culture is concerned: "Few studies considered noncultural variables."[8]

Narrowing our focus to contributions, both practice-oriented and academic, that concentrate on global leadership development—the contributions grouped here under the rubric of Leadership 2.0—suggests another commonality: an emphasis on the identification and cultivation of global leadership competencies (or traits or behaviors) that contribute to successful global leadership—as distinct from traits that are important for national leadership.[9] Most of the global leadership competencies identified in the many lists of this sort take aim at the challenge of making people more open to other cultures. The ideal type is a rootless global cosmopolitan rather than the national citizen of Leadership 1.0, although Leadership 2.0 recognizes—and even focusses on—the possibility that cultural differences may be the biggest obstacle to the achievement of that ideal.

It is worth adding that Leadership 1.0 can be dovetailed with Leadership 2.0 by dichotomizing matters into the local and the global (or the particular and the universal), and looking to Leadership 1.0 and Leadership 2.0 respectively for insights in how to deal with them. Casual empiricism suggests that Leadership 2.0 is used more frequently as the global overlay on such a hybrid arrangement rather than on its own.

Leadership 3.0 can be differentiated from Leadership 2.0 by its emphasis on recognizing where individuals or companies are coming from as well as on opening them up to foreign cultures—and its acknowledgment of and attention to noncultural differences across countries as well. The ideal type in this context is not a global cosmopolitan but a rooted cosmopolitan: someone who recognizes the importance of roots at home—and maybe a very limited number of other countries (or even homes, as in the case of "biculturals")—in determining which country-contexts will appear particularly foreign and which might appear to be fairly familiar. Note that this is rather different from the low levels of identification with individual countries of the sort generally idealized by Leadership 2.0: from the perspective of Leadership 3.0, most individuals and companies are so deeply embedded in particular home-country contexts that explicitly recognizing the reality of their roots and mapping distances, cultural and noncultural, for them is an important part of figuring out what to do—and a better focus than trying to eradicate those roots entirely.[10]

Or, to restate matters, Leadership 3.0's emphasis on replacing the dichotomy of global versus local by stretching things out in space and looking at the sensitivity of flows between countries/locations to geographic and other forms of distance (as well as to discontinuities of the sort imposed by intervening national borders)—its conception of countries as embedded in multidimensional space, at highly variable distances from others—is emblematic of the model.[11] It proposes dealing with the distinctive complexities that arise in a global (or international) context by thinking systematically through the differences and distances between countries and their implications.

Some empirical evidence

One way to compare the three leadership models described in the previous section is by noting that they are tuned to different representations of how globalized the external environment is. Leadership 1.0 is tuned to what I call World 1.0: a world of nations in which borders are so impermeable that national markets are entirely separate, that is, international integration is zero. In such a world, a national focus—in leadership development and in other respects as well—makes obvious sense.

Leadership 2.0 is ideally suited to what I call World 2.0: a world in which the cross-border integration of markets is (allegedly) so high that a fully global approach is also called for in leadership development. To quote one relatively recent review of the literature on cross-cultural management, "Physical distance or time differences are no longer barriers to foreign investment. ... It is not surprising that the metaphors of a 'flat world' (Friedman, 2005) or a 'global village' (Ger, 1999) are fitting descriptions of the contemporary business world."[12] A qualification: Leadership 2.0 approaches *have* tended to pay more attention to cultural differences—although often only as something to be minimized—than might make sense in a fully flattened World 2.0 of the sort evoked by the most popular quote, from Thomas Friedman, in Table 6 below.

As a result, Leadership 2.0 has interesting things to say about cultural differences but does miss out on the other kinds of differences—administra-
tive/political, geographic and economic— that are elaborated on below: they
also exert powerful influences on international flows and should therefore be
important elements of a global leader's worldview.

Leadership 3.0 is rooted in what I call World 3.0: a world in which international interactions are significant (unlike World 1.0) but are still significantly constrained by national borders (unlike World 2.0) and also affected by
(highly variable) inter-country differences and distances[13] along geographic
and other dimensions. Note that the addition of distance effects is what takes
this beyond saying that the world isn't completely globalized. Distance effects
amount to the imposition, with considerable econometric success, of a spa-
tial structure on the international interactions that do take place—and can
also be applied to intranational interactions if national markets are not fully
integrated internally.

Given these differences across the three leadership models, empirical evidence on international interactions should shed some light on their realism
and relative suitability. In presenting the evidence, it is important to note a
preexisting bias: World 2.0 almost always wins out in popularity contests,
at least among relatively cosmopolitan groups of business executives or students. As an example, I set up a *Harvard Business Review* (HBR) blog post
in May 2011 as a survey asking which of three quotes about globalization—
corresponding to the three worldviews described above—came closest to
mirroring readers' views. The quotes and the voting patterns among several
hundred respondents are summarized in Table 6. More than 60 percent of 700
respondents picked an apocalyptic pronouncement from a journalist, Thomas
Friedman, whose image of a flat world has become emblematic of World 2.0.

The key empirical challenge, then, is to show that World 3.0—in which
national borders do significantly constrain international interactions, and
the lion's share of the international interactions that are observed take place
between countries that are close to each other geographically and along other
dimensions—is a better representation of the real world than the more popular World 2.0, in which borders and distances do not matter (except for the
cultural differences spotlighted by Leadership 2.0).

To start with some evidence on the extent of international integration, look
at various flows that could take place either domestically or across borders
and compare the cross-border component of the total with the 85–95 percent

Table 6: Popularity of three perspectives on globalization

World 1.0 11%	A. In real estate, the mantra is "location, location, location." For global brand managers, it might be "localise, localise, localise." Orit Gadiesh, Chairman, Bain and Company[14]
World 3.0 27%	B. There is a balance on the spectrum between "local" and "global" that represents the "sweet spot" ... [and makes for] "the race to the middle." Rick Waggoner, Former CEO, General Motors [15]
World 2.0 61%	C. The world got flat ... [creating] a global, Web-enabled playing field that allows for ... collaboration on research and work in real time, without regard to geography, distance or, in the near future, even language. Thomas Friedman, journalist[16]

Source: http://blogs.hbr.org/cs/2011/05/globalization_in_the_world_we.html

levels that one would expect to see if national borders did not play a role in choking off international activity. Despite all the hype about the world being flat, globalization seems to be only 10–20 percent complete. Only 2 percent of telephone calls cross national boundaries. Only 3 percent of people live outside the country where they were born. Foreign direct investment (FDI) is about 10 percent of global fixed capital formation. And after eliminating double-counting, exports account for barely 20 percent of world GDP. Note that the average of these figures is 9 percent.[17] Additional reassurance can be obtained from the raft of studies that analyze the cross-border integration of markets of various sorts[18] or from the observation that some of the biggest puzzles in international macroeconomics relate to observed degrees of "home bias" (i.e., limits to international connectedness) that greatly exceed what simple models of international interaction would lead one to expect.[19] Significant, persistent home bias fits better, of course, with World 3.0's conceptualization of national borders as significant (choke points) than with the World 2.0 insistence that they no longer matter—or, we shall see, the Leadership 2.0 version, in which national borders matter because and only because of the cultural differences that they demarcate.

It is also interesting to note that most people consistently overestimate levels of cross-border integration—leaving less room for them to take the differences and distances between countries seriously. Thus in an earlier HBR survey, roughly one thousand respondents guessed, on average, that international phone calls were 29 percent of the total, immigrants 22 percent of the world's population, FDI 32 percent of total capital formation and exports 39 percent of GDP—an average estimate of 30 percent, or more than three times the actual average. For compactness, I refer to such exaggerations about levels of cross-border integration as *globaloney*.

Experience and seniority do not mitigate globaloney; in fact, they may make it worse. Respondents with more than 10 years' experience came up with average guesses of 33 percent, and the CEOs in the sample overestimated even more, with average guesses of 38 percent! Which isn't meant to suggest that globaloney is confined to the upper echelons of management: highly internationalized groups of MBA students at leading business schools also tend to overestimate more than the general sample—particularly when it comes to categories like telephone calls (presumably a projection bias that reflects their own calling patterns). And analysis of MBA students' responses suggests that high levels of globaloney tend to be positively correlated with a tendency to believe in World 2.0, adding to the importance of presenting some data of the sort presented above, on actual levels of cross-border integration, somewhere in the MBA curriculum.

Globaloney sheds light on what the world isn't: it isn't completely globalized. But it is useful to try to reach farther by providing more of a characterization of what the world *is*. This is where international differences and distances enter the picture. A large body of statistical work, generally referred to as gravity modeling and encompassing hundreds if not thousands of studies, establishes that differences and distances of various sorts do have large, statistically significant and generally negative effects on the intensity of international trade and (less studied) other international interactions. Consider the effects of commonalities (the opposite of differences) on trade: one study suggests that countries trade 42 percent more if they share a common language, 47 percent more if they are part of a common trading bloc, 114 percent more if they share a common currency and 188 percent more if one colonized another at some point in history.[20] Commonalities or proximity along these dimensions typically also have large positive effects on cross-border flows of capital, information and people.[21] Note that these findings are, once again, inconsistent with World 2.0.

I have synthesized the gravity-modeling literature into a framework for thinking about international differences called the CAGE framework—the letters in the acronym denote, respectively, cultural, administrative/political, geographic and (other) economic differences/distances—that is fairly widely used and is elaborated on below.[22] But the most important piece of advice to be offered here is not advocacy of a particular framework but rather exhortation to use *some* framework that captures the broad panoply of differences instead of ignoring differences—or focussing on just one or two categories, for example, cultural in the case of Leadership 2.0, or geographic and economic in the context of Supply 2.0.

This advice is tantamount to an injunction against focussing the analysis of international differences on frameworks that emphasize a very limited set of international differences. In fact, an important part of the value to be derived from applying structured frameworks such as CAGE in most practical settings is that they force one to understand *which* categories and subcategories of differences matter the most in a particular industry or for a given strategy or between a particular pair of countries. In such a context, a broad menu of possibilities—as further articulated for the CAGE framework below, especially in Table 7—is a better starting point than a narrow one.

I would further argue that the combination of deep-seated home bias and strong distance effects (over widely varying distances) is what makes room for World 3.0's rooted conception of (most) companies and individuals to be most helpful. These microfoundations allow, for instance, for the possibility that a Japanese expatriate posted to the United States may face a different (and more serious) set of issues than one posted to China—or, in recognition of the fact that distance is asymmetric in its effects, than US or Chinese executives posted to Japan. While this conception of rootedness and its implications will be elaborated further below, two fundamental objections that are likely to pop up immediately—denials that individuals or multinational companies have well-defined national roots—are worth addressing right away with data that drills down, below the level of aggregate economies, to individuals and companies.

To start with individuals, note that the data presented above about immigrants and phone calls implies a predominantly domestic cast for most people's face-to-face and telephonic interactions. They can be supplemented with many kinds of other data. Residential proximity still predicts best how often friends socialize.[23] And one study of cellphone users in a rich country found that nearly three-quarters mainly stayed within a ten-mile radius over six months and tended to return to the same few places over and over.[24] Electronic connectivity has been superimposed on this rooted reality without superseding it. Look beyond phone calls, at other types of information flows.

People still get most of their news from domestic sources—as much as 95 percent even when they go online.[25] Most sources of news focus most of their coverage domestically: only 21 percent of US TV news coverage is international, and of that, one-half deals with US foreign affairs; in Europe, about 38 percent is international, but again almost one-half relates to stories involving other countries in Europe.[26] More than 85 percent of friends on Facebook are domestic rather than international.[27] The domestic component of instant-messaging communications on Microsoft Messenger is nearly 75 percent.[28] And so on. The same points about rootedness can also be made about companies. In 2004, less than 1 percent of all US companies had foreign operations, and of those, the largest fraction operated in just one foreign country, the median number in two, and 95 percent in fewer than two dozen.[29] Among the US companies operating in just one foreign country, that country was Canada 60 percent of the time (and 10 percent of the time, the United Kingdom): think why—and think in terms of CAGE commonalities. And even the largest US firms, the ones in the S&P 500, derived 54 percent of their total sales from the United States in 2010.

The largest European multinationals are generally somewhat less subject to the gravitational pull of a single large domestic market but still tend to have clear roots in their home country or region. Thus, in 2010, BASF generated 40 percent of its sales and 49 percent of its profits from Germany; adding in the rest of Europe increased these figures to 55 percent and 68 percent respectively. And Allianz wrote 28 percent of its insurance premiums in its home country, Germany, and another 51 percent in the rest of Europe. Furthermore, there has been movement by some of the very few companies that used to have headquarters in more than one country, notably Unilever and Royal Dutch Shell, to consolidate them.

Japanese multinationals are no exception to this rule of (mostly) being focussed on the home country or region. Consider Figure 9, which scales countries in proportion to where Hitachi derived its revenues from in 2010, and note that Japan accounted for 66 percent of the total and the rest of Asia for 18 percent. Hitachi's profits were dominated to an even greater extent by the home region, with Asia accounting for a total of 91 percent. Figure 10 indicates that even a company like Toyota which (unusually) has a significant presence in more than one region and whose largest market is a foreign one (the United States), derived 58 percent of its profits over the 2005–10 period from Japan and another 13 percent from the rest of Asia. Overall, data for the

Fortune Global 500 from 2001 indicate that 88 percent derived more than one-half of their sales (an average of 80 percent) from their home regions, 7 percent were biregionals that derived at least 20 percent from their revenues from two regions (but less than 50 percent from any one region), and 2 percent were tri-regionals that derive at least 20 percent of their revenues from each of the "triad" regions of North America, Europe and Asia.[30]

Furthermore, while roughly half of the Fortune Global 500's revenues and workforces are accounted for by countries other than the ones where they are headquartered, their senior leadership typically still hails from their home countries. Of the companies on the Fortune Global 500 list in 2008, 68 (i.e., 14 percent, or just over one in seven) had a non-native CEO.[31] This average does mask significant variation by country of headquarters. Leading the list were small countries, mainly in Europe: Switzerland with 71 percent nonnative CEOs, Australia with 63 percent and the Netherlands with 36 percent. The United States, in contrast, came in at 12 percent and Japan at 3 percent. And even among US technology firms started between 1995 and 2005, which might be expected to do much better on this measure—only 25 percent had at least one senior executive born elsewhere.[32] It is worth adding that Fortune Global 500 companies headquartered in the BRIC countries reported zero nonnative CEOs.

Similarly, while large multinational firms typically do include foreign directors on their boards, the majority of their directors are almost always from the company's home country. Among the world's 100 largest transnational firms, 75 percent had at least one foreign director in 2005 (up from 36 percent in 1993), but only 10 percent had a majority of foreign directors; the average board had 25 percent foreign directors.[33] Data on S&P 500 companies from the US provide a broader picture. Among the directors of those companies, only 7 percent were foreign nationals, only 9 percent had degrees from non-US institutions, and 73 percent had no international work experience at all.[34]

To summarize the discussion so far, empirical evidence on the extent and patterns of international interactions tends to support the inference of a semi-globalized, distance-dependent World 3.0 rather than the more popular conception of a completely globalized, distance-free World 2.0. And attributes of individuals and companies suggest that the rootedness highlighted by World 3.0—and again, discounted by World 2.0—has plausible microfoundations. To these empirical conclusions, one can add a purely logical consideration: fundamental differences across countries are essential for global thinking to have

Figure 9: Distribution of Hitachi's sales, 2010

Figure 10: Distribution of Toyota's profits (2005–10)

content qualitatively different from single-country thinking. In the absence of international differences, the world could simply be thought of as one giant country! And there would be no need for separate treatment of global models as opposed to single-country models. The same would apply if countries were completely isolated from each other, because ideas from single-country models could then be applied country by country. It is the intermediate level of cross-border integration highlighted by semiglobalization and emphasized by World 3.0, and by implication, Leadership 3.0, that engenders a need for distinctively global conceptions.

Changing the ABCDs

Some readers may still not be entirely convinced of the utility of drawing such a sharp distinction between Leadership 3.0 and its predecessors. In fact, most of the utility resides in important change implications not only for business schools but for companies and for individuals as well. To sharpen those implications, it will be useful to contrast Leadership 3.0 with Leadership 1.0 and Leadership 2.0—which was part of the purpose behind also discussing those two alternate models in such detail in the last two sections. This section provides a characterization—preliminary and incomplete—of the implications, organized as ABCDs:

- A stands for Aspirations: what type of global leader are we trying to create?

- B stands for Basic Structure: what is actually done to mould global leaders?

- C stands for Conceptual Content: how to think about key barriers/bridges?

- D stands for Direct Experience: how to supplement classroom content?

Leadership 3.0 differs in these aspects from its predecessors. Consider each of the aspects in a bit more detail.

Aspirations

Aspirations were prefigured by the earlier discussion of ideal types but are worth discussing separately because of how fundamental they are: rushing off to apply any leadership model without first considering aspirations in terms of type of leader seems like a bad idea.

Leadership 1.0 idealizes the creation of national citizens who are capable of paying attention to collective national (or local) concerns as well as to individual or company interests in making decisions, but whose concerns run up against and stop short at national borders. At a time when deficits in our capacity for global governance loom as a major issue, it is obviously unappealing to make pure national/self-interest the defining characteristic of a global leadership model.

Leadership 2.0, in contrast, idealizes global citizenship or rootless global cosmopolitanism over (cultural) parochiality.[35] There is something fundamentally admirable—and essential—about its emphasis on openness, and research in this vein has provided us with a host of useful insights into how to move towards that objective. However, the research literature as well as the evidence cited earlier raises fundamental questions about the aspiration to complete rootlessness. Focussing first on individuals, the overwhelming majority of people are monocultural in the sense of being rooted in a single culture. Far fewer—probably no more than 10–20 percent—might be classified as bicultural in the sense stressed by the scholars who have pioneered this strand of research: the sense of having internalized the schemas of two cultures.[36] And there is debate within the literature as to whether it is possible to be tricultural or not, suggesting, at the very least, that being a deep insider in four or more cultures is probably out of the question. With this as backdrop, the cosmopolitan ideal triggers the basic question of whether it is even feasible to imagine individuals being at equal ease in all contexts.

What *does* seem sustainable at the individual level is not symmetric engagement but symmetric disengagement: general detachment from all contexts. But this raises a host of questions. Thus, the identity-related and other psychological stresses associated with being from nowhere in particular would seem to be substantial. Then there are questions about functionality, such as those raised by research on expatriates, which tends to conclude that individuals with high levels of identification with both home and host countries are generally more effective interculturally than expatriates with low levels of identification with one or both countries.[37] There is also a diversity-related issue: a highly rated business school or corporate employer that took in people of very different backgrounds and left them all with the same detached perspective on the world would seem, at least in some respects, to be impoverishing—yet that is what many leading institutions of this sort explicitly or implicitly seem to seek to do. And to round out this list, there is the question of broader social impact: do we really want the global leaders of tomorrow to be devoid of all sense of civic or national responsibility?

Shifting to the corporate level, declarations or insinuations of rootlessness—by companies such as Coca-Cola, ABB and Banco Santander—are, for reasons elaborated in the previous section, hard to take entirely seriously. Coca-Cola, given its history, is regarded as a US company run out of Atlanta no matter what it says. ABB, despite claiming statelessness, experienced years of postmerger turmoil while the Swedes from the former Asea side and the Swiss from the former Brown, Boveri reached a *modus vivendi*. And Banco Santander is Spanish as far as its top managers and board of directors are concerned, no matter where it gets most of its revenues from.

Leadership 3.0 recognizes such rootedness and takes a very different tack from Leadership 2.0: it stresses that most individuals and companies have well-defined home countries (although they may not coincide across employees and employers), and that those roots at home play an important role in conditioning what they do, for example, by affecting what is familiar versus unfamiliar or which countries are close versus far. Better, then, to recognize and work through the effects of rootedness than to ignore it or attempt to eradicate it: denial of the multiple categories of differences doesn't make them any easier to deal with. Of course, such a recognition does have to be overlaid on a good understanding of global issues and the capability to think through strategic and functional issues against this broader backdrop to be truly effective.

In sum, the kind of cosmopolitanism advocated by Leadership 3.0 starts with a strong grasp of one's roots and what is distinctive about them, recognizes relative similarities and differences internationally, and flags the differences as particularly worth watching out for. Note that this approach described by the philosopher Kwame Anthony Appiah, among others, as rooted cosmopolitanism that entails special relationships with those who are close to us.[38] And while these earlier accounts focussed on rootedness at the individual level, similar ideas can be applied at the corporate level. Rooted cosmopolitanism sidesteps many of the problems cited in connection with rootless global cosmopolitanism: the Leadership 3.0 approach does not aspire to anything as unmanageable as being equally at ease everywhere, nor does it seek to eradicate home country roots. Additionally, this approach seems as if it might limit psychological stress, performs well in research studies such as those of expatriates, and leaves room for diversity and for business involvement in local/national causes (in contrast with the homogenized detachment that is characteristic of Leadership 2.0).

Basic structure

What exactly do leadership development efforts do to mould global leaders? Here again, the three types of leadership models vary greatly in ways that can be illustrated by considering a Japanese executive attending a leadership development program prior to an overseas posting. Under Leadership 1.0, such an executive might be exposed to Japanese or (especially if the leadership development program is run in the US or the UK) Anglo-American leadership models, but without acknowledgment of boundary conditions beyond which they may not work. And that would be problematic because Japan, for example, ranks very high on uncertainty avoidance and even more so on masculinity—which, combined with mild collectivism, leads to intense competition between groups, with manifestations ranging from contests between teams of kindergarteners to groups of employees rallying against a company's competitors.[39] And the US and the UK are outliers in terms of individualism, not to mention other cultural variables such as low levels of uncertainty avoidance.

In contrast, a pure version of Leadership 2.0 focussed on developing global competences and opening people up to foreign cultures might attach more importance to rooting out Japanese cultural "biases" but, given the usual emphasis on eradicating roots rather than elucidating their effects, probably would not pay much attention to their likely persistence, to at least some extent, and their enduring implications.[40]

Leadership 3.0 acknowledges the value of leadership basics stressed by Leadership 1.0 and of opening up to other cultures stressed by Leadership 2.0, but tries to reach substantially farther in shaping understanding of and behavior in international interactions in three respects, ordered in terms of increasing distinctness from Leadership 2.0:

- Paying explicit attention to where one is coming from and in that sense emphasizing self-discovery—for example, the high Japanese ranks on uncertainty avoidance and masculinity noted above.

- Emphasizing destinations as well as origins. A Japanese executive preparing to work in the United States is likely to benefit from preparing for the higher level of individualism there. But one preparing for China is more likely to benefit from focussing on much lower levels of uncertainty avoidance there and its usual correlates: faster-paced change and greater levels of experimentation.

- Recognizing multiple dimensions of difference across countries, not just cultural ones. On the administrative dimension, for example, a Japanese going to the US would want to note the predominance of standalone firms, fragmented shareholders and powerful professional managers there as well as the fact that it is the only developed country with employment at will (others require cause or notice to terminate workers) And a Japanese headed to China would want to reckon with Chinese state capitalism and its effects.

The third bullet point, already referred to in context of the CAGE framework, is elaborated in the next subsection. What will be expanded on here is an implication of the first two bullet points: that the architecture of global leadership development efforts can and often should be adapted to patterns of interest in particular geographies or groups of countries—or to other variables.

Adaptation to the country of origin of participants or of a company is an obvious target, although when participants come from diverse countries, this may require access to and use of systematic data on cross-country differences and focussed project assignments layered on top of a common program structure. Adaptation to specific destinations may also be possible when they are particularly large and salient—as in the above example of executives from Japan headed to one of the world's two largest economies. But for less popular destinations (or origins), aggregation at a regional level or subregional level—for example, a focus on the issues faced by Japanese executives headed to Europe—may be the best feasible option. There is a particularly strong case for paying special attention to the home region because of the observation that 50–60 percent of the international flows of people, information, real investment and products/services still occur within continental regions.[41]

Thus, in recent interactions with business schools in emerging markets, West Africa seemed an interesting focus for a leading Nigerian business school and a focus on ASEAN for a leading Filipino business school. Similarly, it is easy to imagine a Spanish business school paying particular attention to Europe or (to a lesser extent) Latin America, and a Canadian business school to the United States.

Of course, regions are not the only basis on which one might unbundle one leadership development model into many possible submodels. Other groupings of countries, such as emerging markets, may merit more focus given long-run forecasts of GDP growth and the fact that a significant number of large Western companies have already reorganized to pay more attention to them. Or one could think of customizing by individual needs—as noted above, a major emphasis for Leadership 3.0 given its recognition of rootedness—by dealing differently, for example, with individuals who have relatively limited overseas interactions versus those about to be sent out as expatriates (especially if the expatriates are all destined for one or a few countries). In a very large organization, one might even distinguish between "traditional" expatriates and inpatriates, short-term assignees, international business travelers and self-initiated assignees.

The broader point is that there are many possible architectures for global leadership development, and those possibilities must be recognized if the power of contingency is to be exploited. Leadership 1.0 essentially ignores issues of global leadership and focusses attention of monolithic (national) leadership models. Leadership 2.0 is all about global leadership but again, given its underlying World 2.0 conception of a flat world—or at least one in which only cultural differences still matter, with the ideal company/individual being exempt from them—creates its own kind of presumption in favor of a unique and in that sense acultural model. World 3.0, with its focus on the lumps and bumps in the fabric of the world rather than the extent to which it is flat, calls attention to the distinctiveness of such possibilities, whereas World 1.0 and World 2.0 both lead, along different paths, towards more monolithic, less contingent leadership models.

Conceptual content

Data on semiglobalization and rootedness obviously represent important conceptual content for the Leadership 3.0 approach. Even more important are data on cross-country differences, a framework for thinking about those differences, and evidence on the importance of distance effects.

The case for superimposing consideration of cross-country differences and distance effects on the international interactions that do take place in a semiglobalized world—of using distance as well as rootedness as a key organizing principle—has already been made on empirical grounds. It is worth adding the logical point that distance is nothing more and nothing less than an attempt to stretch out the traditional dichotomy between local and global in multidimensional space. Examining distance effects seems preferable to dichotomizing them into extremes by assumption: effects strong enough to render international interactions prohibitively expensive (the localization of World 1.0) or zero (the complete globalization of World 2.0).

In addition to these empirical and logical points, a separate strand of support for the focus on differences and distances is provided by the results of a survey of academic thought leaders about what globalization-related content business schools should put into their MBA programs. The survey was conducted with Dean Bernard Yeung of the National University of Singapore Business School and with the support of AACSB International, particularly Juliane Iannarelli, its Director of Global Research.

The thought leaders' responses to questions such as the open-ended "What international elements of [function] do you believe are important for functional/general managers with expertise in the international dimension of business to master?" were collected and classified. The results revealed a strong shared sense that an understanding of differences across their countries and their implications should be the key component of what MBA students are taught about globalization. Specifically, it seemed possible to group most of the responses into six buckets of environmental/contextual differences: cultural, legal/regulatory, political, economic, financial and a miscellaneous category of "other."

These findings, in addition to being reassuringly clear-cut, dovetailed with the CAGE framework for thinking about the differences between countries that I had developed more than a decade earlier (see Ghemawat, 2001). The CAGE framework, which has already been mentioned, is laid out in more detail in Table 7.

The CAGE framework obviously suggests looking more broadly at international differences than Leadership 2.0's focus on cultural differences— let alone Leadership 1.0's inattention to differences. As noted above, what is more important than the precise categories or myriad subcategories presented is the idea of looking broadly at cross-country differences in ways that go beyond the handful of economic (and sometimes, geographic) variables that customarily receive attention. Bilateral (country-pair) attributes are to be looked at, not just the unilateral ones that are the focus of most country analysis because bilateral attributes are necessary to capture ideas such as "France is closer to Spain than is Japan." The notion of distance, rather than difference, is a way of getting at such "differences in differences." And finally, the CAGE framework derives much of its power from being customizable to the

Table 7: The CAGE framework for country-level analysis

	Cultural differences	Administrative differences	Geographic differences	Economic differences
Bilateral measures	– Different languages – Different ethnicities/ lack of connective ethnic or social networks – Different religions – Differences in national work systems – Different values, norms and dispositions	– Lack of colonial ties – Lack of shared regional trading bloc – Lack of common currency – Different legal system – Political hostility	– Physical distance – Lack of land border – Differences in climates (and disease environments)	– Differences in consumer incomes – Differences in availability of: .Natural resources .Financial resources .Human resources .Intermediate inputs .Infrastructure .Information or knowledge
Unilateral measures	– Traditionalism – Insularity – Spiritualism – Inscrutability	– Nonmarket/closed economy (home bias versus foreign bias) – Nonmembership in international organizations – Weak legal institutions/ corruption – Lack of government checks and balances – Societal conflict – Political/ expropriation risk	– Landlockedness – Geographic size – Geographic remoteness	– Economic size – Low per capita income – Low level of monetization – Limited infrastructure, other specialized factors

Source: Adapted from Pankaj Ghemawat (2001) "Distance Still Matters: The Hard Reality of Global Expansion," *Harvard Business Review* 79.8: 137–147

industry context: the critical challenge is often to figure out which differences matter the most in a particular industry.

The CAGE framework is widely used and is the centerpiece of attempts at IESE—and at some other schools—to insert globalization-related content into MBA and other leadership development programs.[42] It has also become the focus for an AACSB-led attempt to widen coverage of globalization-related content: in Spring 2012, the AACSB initiated an effort to distribute the course materials developed for IESE's GLOBE course to its other member schools.

Direct experience

The insertion of a short or module or course on global (or regional) themes into a leadership development program or curriculum, while probably necessary, is unlikely to be sufficient. For deep impact, globalization-related themes must be picked up on and elaborated in more functionally oriented courses. This is the implementation path followed at IESE, where we first inserted a short course on the globalization of business enterprise (GLOBE) into the required first-year MBA curriculum and are now working on achieving interlock with other first-year courses.

Such classroom content also needs to be—and in many leadership development efforts has been—supplemented with initiatives that are meant to emphasize direct personal exposure to and experience of peers from different countries ("diversity") or different countries themselves ("mobility"), that is, to be largely experiential. Examples include initiatives such as classroom diversity, international travel, international project work and language training.

The need for such initiatives is greatest under Leadership 3.0 because of its emphasis on rootedness. However, Leadership 3.0 also sees the obstacles to be surmounted more seriously (or broadly) than Leadership 2.0, with implications for what is likely to constitute a useful experience. Several points can be registered in this regard.

First, the categories mentioned above are neither mutually exclusive nor completely exhaustive, and there is substantial opportunity for synergy when two or more are used together, or when they are combined with other initiatives not mentioned above. Thus, collaborative partnerships and global footprint strategies can serve as structural enablers of many of these approaches. For example, exchange agreements often target increases on student diversity, and joint and dual degrees include opportunities for travel, language training and even exposure to course materials and educational methods other than those available at the home institution.

The biggest opportunity for synergy, however, is likely to reside in coupling such experiential initiatives with the kind of classroom content described earlier in this section. A focus on diversity and mobility as their key globalization-related value propositions to their students, to the exclusion of content, would risk turning educational or corporate leadership development programs into specialized offerings within the travel and hospitality sector.

Finally, experiential initiatives can usefully be arrayed in terms of the degree of immersion which, from a participant's perspective, might be said to range from aspersion or sprinkling (e.g., a trek) to submersion (attending a full-time MBA program in a foreign location). The resource-intensity of such initiatives appears to vary directly with the duration of immersion and there is pressure, therefore, to reduce it. But taking World 3.0 seriously also implies that experiential initiatives are subject to threshold effects, in the sense that to be worth pursuing they have to be pursued to more than a token extent. A program to send students from a Western context to an emerging market for a week, say, is unlikely to deliver benefits commensurate with its costs.

The last two points are emphasized because of a sense that poorly thought out experiential initiatives have become substitutes (rather than complements) for curricular content. Thus, the AACSB thought leaders' survey discussed in the previous subsection, while focussed on curricular content, also sought to elicit thoughts about, among other things, such complementary mechanisms for making leadership development more global. Of thirteen mechanisms for reinforcing "global" concepts and perspectives within business education, respondents cited national diversity of student body, joint ventures with foreign institutions, treks, and student exchanges (in decreasing order) most frequently as overemphasized and named cross-border collaborative projects most frequently as underemphasized!

Conclusions

This chapter has suggested a new approach to global leadership development that is rooted in the substrate of international interactions in a way that recognizes both their limited extent and their distance-dependence. In addition to its direct implications for conceptual content, this perspective aspires to create rooted cosmopolitans rather than national citizens or rootless global cosmopolitans. It emphasizes self-discovery—about where one is coming from and how that might influence where to go next—as well as opening up to "foreigners" and thereby also opens the door to multiple architectural possibilities in the design of global leadership development, rather than a monolithic model. And it sets some parameters—particularly the requirements of coupling with conceptual content and surmounting threshold effects—for experiential initiatives.

While these proposals are novel in several respects, perhaps the most obvious contrast is with the common wisdom that global leadership development is or should primarily be about experiential initiatives, defined broadly to include personal work experience. One example is Dodge's assertion—picked up by Mendenhall *et al.* among many others—that "classroom-type scenarios" can contribute about 20 percent to managerial learning about global leadership, with experience accounting for the remaining 80 percent.[43] Without attempting to specify a percentage split of this sort, I would suggest that at a minimum, global leadership development programs should leave participants equipped with some knowledge about ten managerially relevant aspects of globalization:

1. Levels of cross-border integration of markets of different types: products, capital, people and information (semiglobalization).

2. Levels of internationalization/globalization of firms (firms as the visible hand of cross-border integration).

3. Changes in cross-border integration over time (the two waves of globalization, the current crisis in historical perspective).

4. Drivers of changes in cross-border integration over time (technological changes, particularly in transport and communications, and policy changes).

5. Net impact of differences of various types on cross-border interactions (estimates from gravity models of the effects of CAGE variables).

6. Differences in national cultures and implications for business (objective indicators and Hofstede's five—subjective—dimensions of cultural values and implications—or other such cultural schemas).

7. Differences in business ownership and governance around the world and implications ("varieties of capitalism").

8. Distance and other geographic barriers and implications (regionalization—at international and intranational levels).

9. Economic differences and implications (wages and other factor costs; impact on arbitrage/vertical versus aggregation/horizontal strategies).

10. Benefits and costs of increased cross-border integration (in the presence of market failures).

This is a partial list, drawn from the AACSB report on the globalization of management education, which should be supplemented with coverage of international macroeconomics and geopolitics, attitudinal/value assessments and function-specific knowledge requirements. For example, in regard to the area of strategy, it would be useful to follow up material focussed on semi-globalization and the multiple dimensions of differences across countries with explicit consideration of strategies for addressing differences, of which I have offered a taxonomy elsewhere: *adaptation* or adjusting to differences to achieve local responsiveness, *aggregation* to overcome differences and achieve greater economies of scale than would be feasible with country-by-country adaptation, and *arbitrage* to exploit differences by taking advantage of differences in costs or willingness-to-pay across countries.[44] But the broader point is that if the managers you are developing into global leaders have knowledge gaps in these areas, experiential initiatives are likely to provide inefficient, hit-or-miss remediation in ways that limit their value.

NOTES

This chapter has benefited from comments by Steven Altman, Jordi Canals and Sebastian Reiche, although the opinions expressed herein are solely those of the author.

1 For a more detailed description of the AACSB-related work, see Pankaj Ghemawat (2011a), "Responses to Forces of Change: A Focus on Curricular Content." In R. F. Bruner, A. De Meyer, P. Ghemawat, J. Gómez, S. Lenway, M. Rao, E. Snyder, P. Tapie and K. Teegen *Globalization of Management Education: Changing International Structure, Adaptive Strategies, and the Impact on Institutions* (Tampa, FL: Association for the Advancement of Collegiate Schools of Business): Chapter 4. My action research in the classroom is described in more detail in Pankaj Ghemawat (2011b), "Bridging the 'Globalization Gap' at Business Schools: Curricular Challenges and a Response." In Jordi Canals (ed.) *The Future of Leadership Development* (Houndmills: Palgrave Macmillan): Chapter 2.3.

2 For a more extended discussion of semiglobalization and common misconceptions often articulated about the extent of globalization, see Pankaj Ghemawat (2007), *Redefining Global Strategy* (Boston, MA: Harvard Business School Press): Chapter 1.

3 B. M. Bass (1990) *Bass and Stogdill's Handbook of Leadership: Theory, Research and Managerial Applications*, third edition (New York, NY: Free Press).

4 What attention does get paid to cross-country variation tends to take the form of categorizing and cataloguing.

5 For a review, see Mark E. Mendenhall, Joyce S. Osland, Allan Bird, Gary R. Oddou and Martha L. Maznevski (2008) *Global Leadership: Research, Practice and Development* (London: Routledge).

6 Nancy J. Adler (1983) "A Typology of Management Studies involving Culture." *Journal of International Business Studies* 14 (Fall): 29–47.

7 Ibid., p. 42.

8 Anne S. Tsui, Sushil S. Nifadkar and Amy Yi Ou (2007) "Cross-National, Cross-Cultural Organizational Behavior Research: Advances, Gaps, and Recommendations." *Journal of Management* 33 (June): 426–478, at 454.

9 See, for instance, Allen J. Morrison (2000) "Developing a Global Leadership Model." *Human Resource Management* 39.2/3 (Summer/Fall): 117–131, or the discussion in Medenhall *et al.*, *Global Leadership*. Also note that, given the evidence presented in this chapter as well as its focus, I am excluding work that postulates that the main tasks that leaders carry out can be generalized across cultures, e.g., Rosabeth Moss Kanter (2010) "Leadership in a Globalizing World." in Nitin Nohria and Rakesh Khurana (eds) *Handbook of Leadership Theory and Practice* (Boston, MA: Harvard Business School Press).

10 For further discussion, see Pankaj Ghemawat (2011c) *World 3.0: Global Prosperity and How to Achieve It* (Boston, MA: Harvard Business Review Press, 2011), especially Chapter 15, and Pankaj Ghemawat (2011d) "Creating the Cosmopolitan Corporation." *Harvard Business Review* 89.5 (May): 92–99.

11 This characterization and its rejection of the global versus local dichotomy suggests that Leadership 3.0 might well be described as postmodern given a common definition (from Wikipedia) of the latter.

12 Tsui *et al.* (2007) "Cross-National, Cross-Cultural Organizational Behavior Research," p. 427.

13 A more general formulation, agnostic about the sign on distance effects, would highlight distance-dependence (rather than distance decay).

14 Orit Gadiesh (2005) "Think Globally, Market Locally." *Financer World-wide* (1 August); also available at http://www.bain.fr/bainweb/publications_detail.asp?id=21929&menu_url=publications_results.asp.

15 Based on an internal communication by Rick Waggoner, former CEO of General Motors, 22 September 2005.

16 Thomas Friedman (2005) *The World Is Flat* (New York, NY: Farrar, Straus and Giroux): 176.

17 For much more data of this sort and a listing of sources, see Ghemawat (2011c) *World 3.0*, especially Chapter 2.

18 For more academic treatments, see Pankaj Ghemawat (2003) "Semiglobalization and International Business Strategy." *Journal of International Business Studies* 34.2 (March): 138–152, and Edward E. Leamer (2007) "A Flat World, a Level Playing Field, a Small World After All, or None of the Above? A Review of Thomas L. Friedman's *The World is Flat*." *Journal of Economic Literature* 45 (March): 83–126.

19 See, e.g., Maurice Obstfeld and Kenneth Rogoff (2001) "The Six Major Puzzles in International Macroeconomics: Is There a Common Cause?" *NBER Macroeconomics Annual* 15.1: 339–390.

20 Pankaj Ghemawat and Rajiv Mallick (2003) "The Industry-Level Structure of International Trade Networks: A Gravity-Based Approach." Working Paper, Harvard Business School, Boston (February).

21 Pankaj Ghemawat and Tamara de la Mata (2011) "Gravity Modeling of Trade, Capital, Information and People Flows." Working Paper, IESE Business School (February).

22 For the original discussion of the CAGE framework, see Pankaj Ghemawat (2001) "Distance Still Matters. The Hard Reality of Global Expansion." *Harvard Business Review* 79.8 (September): 137–147.

23 Miller McPherson, Lynn Smith-Lovin and James M. Cook (2001) "Birds of a Feather: Homophily in Social Networks." *Annual Review of Sociology* 27: 415–444.

24 Marta C. Gonzalez, Cesar A. Hidalgo and Albert-Laszlo Barabasi (2008) "Understanding Individual Human Mobility Patterns." *Nature* 453 (5 June): 779–782.

25 Calculations by Ethan Zuckerman (2010), as reported in "A Cyber-house Divided." *The Economist* (4 September): 58.

26 See for the US and Europe respectively the Pew Project for Excellence in Journalism, "The State of the News Media: An Annual Report On American Journalism" (15 March 2010), http://www.stateofthemedia.org/2010/, and MediaTenor, "Different Perspectives: Locations, Protagonists, and Topic Structures in International TV News" (March–April 2006).

27 Johan Ugander, Brian Karrer, Lars Backstrom and Cameron Marlow (2011) "The Anatomy of the Facebook Social Graph," at http://arxiv.org/pdf/1111.4503v1.pdf

28 Jure Leskovec and Eric Horvitz (2008) "Planetary-Scale Views on a Large Instant-Messaging Network." In *Proceedings of the 17th International Conference on World Wide Web* (Beijing: ACM): 915–924.

29 The computations in this sentence and the next one are based on Bureau of Economic Analysis data and were kindly carried out at my request by Raymond J. Mataloni (Fall 2007).

30 Alan Rugman and Alain Verbeke (2004) "A Perspective on Regional and Global Strategies of Multinational Enterprises." *Journal of International Business Studies* 35.1: 3–18. Note that the percentages are based on the 365 Fortune Global 500 firms for which data were available, and that a fourth category, host region-focused, accounted for 3 percent of the sample.

31 Herman Vantrappen and Petter Kilefors (2009), "Grooming CEO Talent at the Truly Global Firm of the Future." *Prism* (February): 91–105.

32 Rachel Konrad (2007) "Immigrants Behind 25 Percent of Tech Startups." MSNBC (3 January).

33 Clifford L. Staples (2007) "Board Globalization in the World's Largest TNCs 1993–2005." *Corporate Governance: An International Review* 15.2: 311–321.

34 Egon Zehnder International, Global Board Index 2008, accessed at http://www.egon-zehnder.com/global/thoughtleadership/hottopic

35 For a modern statement, see Martha C. Nussbaum (2002) *For Love of Country?* (Boston, MA: Beacon Press).

36 See, for instance, Mary Yoko Brannen and David C. Thomas (2010), "Bicultural Individuals in Organizations: Implications and Opportunity." Introduction to special issue, *International Journal of Cross-Cultural Management* 10.1 (April): 5–16.

37 Yih-teen Lee (2010) "Home Versus Host—Identifying With Either, Both, or Neither? The Relationship between Dual Cultural Identities and Intercultural Effectiveness." *International Journal of Cross Cultural Management* 10.1: 55–76.

38 K. Anthony Appiah (2005) *Ethics of Identity* (Princeton, NJ: Princeton University Press): 227. Note that Appiah's usage of "rooted cosmopolitanism" was preceded by that of Mitchell Cohen and Bruce Ackerman.

39 Geert Hofstede (1980) *Culture's Consequences: International Differences in Work-Related Values* (Beverley Hills, CA: Sage), and http://geert-hofstede.com/japan.html

40 Again, some of the broader research on cross-cultural management pays much more attention to the enduring effects of cross-country cultural differences than do most of the contributions focussed explicitly on global leadership development.

41 See the data presented in Pankaj Ghemawat and Steven A. Altman (2011) *The DHL Global Connectedness Index, 2011* (downloadable at http://www.dhl.com/gci).

42 For more discussion of the course development effort at IESE, see Ghemawat (2011a), "Bridging the 'Globalization Gap' at Business Schools."

43 B. Dodge (1993) "Empowerment and the Evolution of Learning." *Education and Training* 35.5: 3–10, and Mendenhall *et al.* (2008) *Global Leadership*.

44 Ghemawat (2007) *Redefining Global Strategy*.

CHAPTER 1.4

Educating Leaders for a Global Century

NITIN NOHRIA, Dean and G.F. Baker Professor of Business Administration, Harvard Business School

W hen I graduated from IIT Bombay in 1984, like almost everyone else in my class, I applied to go to graduate school in America. Indeed, more than two-thirds of my graduating IIT class went to America, and most of us have stayed on to work. We were attracted to America because it was the land of opportunity. It was where the action was—where the best research was being done, where the most interesting innovation was occurring, where the best companies in the world were located, where if you had the raw talent and the hard work to back it up, anything was possible.

Indeed, the extraordinary global influence of America led Henry Luce, the founder of *Time* magazine and Jean-Jacques Servan Schreiber, the founder of *Time*'s French counterpart *L'Express*, to famously declare that the twentieth century was "the American century." One can quibble with such a sweeping generalization, but it was basically true—especially in the world of business. American firms represented a disproportionate share of the world's largest companies throughout the twentieth century, and the vast majority of innovations in business—from products to services to management practices and ideas—originated in America.

Evidence of this American century could also be found in our curriculum at Harvard Business School. We teach primarily by the case method, and over the course of two years our students study and discuss over 500 case studies. When I started teaching at HBS in 1988, over 90 percent of our cases were about American companies. Our international cases included some from Europe and a few from Japan. But you would have been hard pressed to find even a single case on a company from China, India, Brazil or any other emerging market in the first-year curriculum that all students must take. Today that seems outrageous and even derelict. Yet, rarely did anyone complain. Students and scholars came to Harvard Business School to study *American* business.

It's amazing how much the world has changed in the last quarter-century. Today, the HBS curriculum has become a lot more global. About a third of our cases focus on companies outside America. Our students now expect to learn much more about businesses and exciting innovative companies from all across the globe.

If the twentieth century was an American century, I believe the twenty-first century will be a global century; one in which many countries and regions will become worthy rivals in the global economy. To succeed in the global century, companies will need to hire—or develop—a different kind of manager. These managers will need to be more adaptable, more culturally aware, and more receptive to ideas and innovations that may seem foreign to them. Most of all, they will need the ability to spot and seize different kinds of opportunities—and to understand the global forces that are creating those opportunities—that previous generations of managers might have missed.

Good business opportunities are closely tied to value creation. If a company can create real economic value, it typically produces a healthy return for its investors and all other stakeholders. So, what will be the major opportunities for value creation in this new century?

Let me suggest that value creation in the context of global competition takes three forms: efficiency, local responsiveness, and innovation. This framework, developed in collaboration with my colleagues Sumantra Ghoshal and Chris Bartlett, provides, in my view, a useful way of thinking about how managers can identify value creation opportunities in the new global century. And when it comes to thinking about the new kinds of leaders we need to develop for this new era, it's useful to think of educating people to enhance their ability to recognize and understand opportunities through this framework.

Creating value through efficiency

The first opportunity for value creation in this new global century is through the constant pursuit of greater efficiency. The first example was Japan, which shocked the post-1945 American manufacturing juggernaut, exemplified by Detroit's Big Three, by introducing low-priced, fuel-efficient, high-quality automobiles in the late 1970s and early 1980s. Although it took some time for American consumers to accept that products made in Japan were of equal (if not superior) quality to those manufactured at home, at prices that originally seemed only feasible because the Japanese were "dumping" or otherwise engaging in unfair competition, by the mid-1980s the floodgates of global competition on the dimension of efficiency had fully opened. Japanese competition began to challenge American and European incumbents in all manufactured products—from cars to steel to consumer electronics. But the Japanese example inspired other countries, and by the end of the 1980s Taiwan and South Korea had emerged as other low-cost, high-efficiency manufacturers. To compete, the US embraced NAFTA and moved production to Mexico to benefit from lower labor costs there. As a result, some Latin American countries also joined this new battleground of labor cost-driven efficiency. By the end of the century, countries like India and China joined the fray. During the first decade of the twenty-first century, China emerged as the new global efficiency juggernaut. Yet, let there be no doubt: China is already being challenged by Vietnam and Cambodia, and other countries with yet lower labor costs are waiting in the wings.

If there is one truism in global competition it is this: the efficiency frontier keeps moving. Take any standard commodity product, and as a leader you have to be prepared for one reality: tomorrow it will be made more cheaply somewhere else in the world. There are simply too many reasonably educated new workers who are going to enter the global labor force in the next twenty to thirty years. And just like the high school-educated factory workers in the United States and Europe in the twentieth century, these workers can be trained to manufacture commodity products.

What is the takeaway for management educators? It is that being vigilant and responsive to this constantly moving efficiency frontier will be one of the key skills of an effective twenty-first-century global investor, leader or manager, and our institutions must prepare them for this reality. A manager who chose site locations and built factories in China a decade ago is now sizing up property and building new plants in Indonesia—and a few years from now, he or she will be going through the same process in Africa. In each of these successive stops, there will be new governments to deal with, and new populations to hire and train as workers. There will also be the task of deciding what to do with older operations that are no longer as competitive. They will need to be restructured to produce higher value-added goods competitively or else shut down. Not only will production locations keep shifting, market demand will concurrently evolve as the rise of manufacturing in a nation typically also opens up local demand for a wide variety of goods and services. Matching globally distributed supply chains with globally distributed demand is another complexity that global century leaders will need to be prepared for. Meeting these challenges will require people who will not ever settle for today's performance, because they realize the efficiency frontier is always moving.

Creating value through local responsiveness

A second way in which firms can create value in this emerging global century is by developing products and services that are responsive to the unique circumstances of local markets. In the twentieth century, economic growth was driven by consumers in the West. In the twenty-first century, growth will be driven as much if not more by consumers in emerging markets. And while much of what they will want to consume are the same goods and services that their Western counterparts consumed, they will also have unique demands, which if unlocked will spur yet greater growth.

The story of Tata Motors provides a good illustration. It may be an understatement to say that the twenty-first century didn't start well for Tata Motors. In 2001, it posted a loss of $1.25 billion, the largest loss ever recorded for a private-sector company in India. Tata executives realized that the company would need to take drastic measures and outlined three areas of focus: cost reduction and quality improvement, not surprisingly, but also new product introduction.

Tata Motors' leadership knew that truck penetration in India was expected to increase imminently owing to ongoing improvements in the nation's road system. The construction of the Golden Quadrilateral highway system and secondary road networks within various states was certain to increase the demand for larger trucks that could carry loads of 45 tons or more from hub to hub. At the same time, the construction of a new, all-weather tertiary road network connecting the highway to rural towns, combined with increasing traffic congestion in major Indian cities, was going to trigger demand for a vehicle that could service the "last mile" in the transportation supply chain by delivering small but full truckloads from various hubs to urban and rural consumption centers. Tata Motors realized that its core business could be threatened by the absence of both larger and smaller trucks in its product portfolio. Senior management reasoned that a smaller commercial vehicle would be a particularly attractive addition to the product line in light of the financial loss of 2001, since demand for smaller vehicles was historically less cyclical than that for medium or large vehicles.

During a strategic review session of Tata Motors executives, the idea of a "cheap, nasty and rugged vehicle for India" emerged. The company would design a product that would meet a need that was unique to India: a small truck that, with its compact size and shorter turning radius, could maneuver through India's narrow urban streets and cost-effectively transport small loads to villages and towns in rural areas that were typically served by overloaded auto rickshaws and hand-drawn carts. When it was launched in May 2005, the Tata Ace, at about $5500, cost 50 percent less than any other four-wheeled commercial vehicle in India and was significantly cheaper than pickup trucks with smaller payload capacities found in international markets. By offering a niche vehicle that met the unique needs of the Indian consumer at a price comparable to that of a three-wheeler, Tata Motors created an entirely new product category, and the vehicle was an instant hit. In 2005–6, Tata sold 30,000 Aces, exceeding all initial estimates; by 2009–10, annual sales exceeded the 100,000 mark.

A conceptual way of thinking about the Tata Ace and many other such products that have been embraced by local consumers in emerging markets is that they exploit an intimate understanding of what Tarun Khanna and Krishna Palepu call "institutional voids." The idea of institutional voids is that when you compare an emerging market with a developed one, the emerging market has a series of institutions missing that you typically take for granted in a developed economy. In developed markets, for example, you can take for granted the availability of credit, or transportation infrastructure or a well-functioning legal system. In an emerging market, many of those institutions are lacking, and if you can create businesses that exploit these voids in ingenious ways, you can generate lots of opportunities. This is exactly what the Tata Ace did by building a vehicle that could be responsive to the last-mile delivery problems that uniquely exist because of the institutional voids in Indian infrastructure.

China Mobile and Bharti Telecom are examples of other companies that deeply understood and responded to the institutional voids in the telecommunications sector in China and India respectively. Leapfrogging land-line operations to create an infrastructure and a market for cellphones, both these firms discovered something that no one else had expected: that the biggest market for cellular phones was not the corporate sector, or even the urban rich, but middle- and low-income rural and urban consumers.

The unifying thing to note about this second dimension of global competitiveness is that comes to those who are able to get close to the consumer and develop goods and services that are responsive to local needs and institutional realities. Leadership that focusses on local responsiveness requires, in many cases, a radical reimagination of business models. Tata Motors had to reengineer its business model dramatically, relying much more heavily on its vendors and outsourcing a much greater proportion of the production in order to deliver the customer a great product—first the Tata Ace and the Tata Nano—at a previously unimaginable price point. Companies that have exhibited outstanding local responsiveness over the last decade have done so because new leaders emerged and rose to the challenges and opportunities presented by local market conditions. Beyond efficiency-oriented leadership skills, this new generation of leaders brought an added marketing and business model savvy—like the Tata Motors executives who hatched the idea of a "cheap, nasty and rugged vehicle for India."

One of the results of opportunities that lie in being locally responsive is that they create opportunities for graduates of local institutions, including business schools. In the past, an expatriate educated at a leading business school in the US or Europe might be sent into an emerging market to scan for new opportunities. Increasingly, locals may have a better sense of the institutional voids and how to fill them. Competition in most markets will therefore not always be among global giants, but also with strong local firms. This will require companies and their leaders to learn how to compete with a more diverse set of competitors of different geographic origins, cultures, competencies and business models. Companies that want to operate in multiple global markets will have to build and manage global talent pipelines. It will require them to appreciate that products and business models may need to be adapted to be locally responsive.

In business schools, our curricula will need to evolve to educate students to better understand local contingency—to recognize when a standardized global solution will work and when practices will need to be more local. It will involve cultivating in our students and faculty a higher degree of cultural and institutional sensibility and humility.

Creating value through innovation

A third dimension of global competition that will provide opportunity for value creation is innovation. One of the key lessons of the twentieth century, when American business dominated the global scene, is that the most successful economies and companies are those that are the most dynamic and are the best at innovation. What makes this new global century so full of opportunity is that cutting-edge innovation is now occurring and will accelerate all over the world.

Innovation in this new global century will take two forms. First, we will continue to see the emergence of global innovations that will address as yet unmet needs; the next iPhone and iPad, a new drug that will cure cancer, the next social media application, and other products and services that we cannot even imagine but will captivate consumers worldwide. The second form of innovations will be what Vijay Govindrajan has called reverse innovations—products and services that will meet existing needs with resources that are an order of magnitude lower than is currently the case, thereby enabling billions of people to enter the circle of prosperity that others in developed markets have so long enjoyed.

One might be tempted to imagine that global innovations will continue to come from companies in developed markets and reverse innovations from companies in emerging markets. Yet, what is already happening is that the sources of innovation are becoming globally distributed—making this a competitive arena in which winners in either category can come from anywhere.

An interesting case is the Korean company Samsung. Today, Samsung ranks in the top 10 of companies filing global patents each year. It has become such a major force in consumer electronics that it has displaced Sony, once considered the iconic innovative company in the world. It is even challenging Nokia, another company that is often closely associated with the word innovation, for dominance in the mobile phone market. It is just as likely that the next major global innovation in consumer electronics (which now includes all mobile devices) will come from Samsung as from Nokia, Sony or even Apple. Samsung is a company whose products could once be found only on the bottom shelves at Wal-Mart and other value-oriented retailers; now, it has futuristic concept stores in New York and other cities that rival the flagship Apple, Nokia and Sony stores. Samsung is an example of a company that had not been an innovator, but has gone through the process of first becoming an efficient producer, then going out and competing on the global stage, and now challenging some of the major innovators in the world.

Another fascinating example of such a company is BYD, the Chinese automaker that—having already beaten GM, Toyota and Nissan to market with the first plug-in hybrid—is now at the front of the race to develop a full-size electric car for the mass market. BYD develops its own cutting-edge battery technology, and says that the lithium-ion ferrous phosphate battery used in its E6 electric car not only costs half what standard lithium-ion batteries do, but also lasts longer and uses non-toxic fluid. Whether BYD eventually ends up being successful in this race is an open question, but it is worth noting that BYD is from a country that is still considered a growing economy and until recently would hardly deserve mention when one thought of innovation in the automotive industry.

Just as we have to be open to global innovations emerging from surprising new players in different parts of the world, we have to be equally open to reverse innovations that deliver existing products and services at radically lower price points coming not just from new players in emerging markets but established global leaders. One of the best examples comes from GE, an American company that has long been at the forefront of introducing radically new global innovations. GE's new handheld electrocardiogram developed for growth markets sells for around $1,000 relative to its more advanced machines for developed markets that can sell for tens of thousands of dollars. But even a company like GE held out as a leading example of "reverse innovation" may find itself challenged by lower-cost products produced by teams with a particular insight about a market. For instance, in a recent business plan contest at HBS, a team that includes a doctor from India has developed a device that provides similar functionality to GE's handheld EKG—but instead of a standalone device, this one attaches to an iPhone. Its cost: $40.

Humanity, as a whole, is in desperate need for innovations that will address challenges of economic inclusion, environmental sustainability, healthcare and quality of life, and navigating the constantly expanding digital landscape. Companies that supply these innovations, wherever they are located, will be the winners in this new global century.

Being prepared for innovation in the global marketplace will be essential for leadership in the global century. Some of these new leaders will have the vision and passion of a Steve Jobs, who has come to almost personally symbolize innovation. This example of leadership is resonant with the view that being a great innovator requires the ability to believe you can produce something that no one else has made before. At the same time, we will also need a new breed of innovative leaders who have the humility to recognize that it is getting harder to develop a monopoly on creative talent—and that it will rarely reside only in one's own head, company or country. Thus learning how to work with others in an open ecology of innovation will become another opportunity for creating value through innovation. Leaders will have to embrace the emergence of new open collaborative models of innovation, exemplified by global innovation platforms like Innocentive, which upend our image of the great innovations coming from rare geniuses like Steve Jobs.

Innovation to some extent has always been about mastering paradoxes, and it will become even more so. It will involve listening intently to consumers all over the world and yet imagining things that they might not yet know they need or will fall in love with. It will involve making big investments in long-term R&D programs, yet also recognizing the maverick inside or outside your company who may actually come up with the next big thing. It will involve the creative combination of things that at first seem to have no connection with each or that even appear to be mutually opposed. One of the great Italian fashion design houses, for example, insists that every new design reflect some piece of art from their historical archives at the same time as it reflects a very contemporary piece of art. Preparing business school students to thrive on these paradoxes of innovation will be essential if we are going to develop leaders who will be successful in this emerging global century.

Implications for business education

This is the world for which we have to prepare global leaders. It doesn't tell you specifically—skill by skill, course by course—how to do that preparation, but at least it tells you the general sort of talents that twenty-first century global leaders will require.

For business educators, the key question is: how do we create these managers, who will need to be adept at recognizing and staying ahead of the efficiency curve, being responsive to unique local conditions in different markets, and working with colleagues to create various types of innovations?

At HBS, some of this work begins before students even arrive on campus. It's done by our admissions staff, which is intently focussed on identifying students whose backgrounds suggest they have the facility and ambition to thrive in a global economy. For instance, today three-quarters of our incoming students have spent an extended period living abroad. Once they arrive, we're seeking to expose them to global business problems every day. Today 40 percent of the new case studies written by faculty each year take place outside the United States. To support faculty in those efforts, HBS now maintains research centers in Tokyo, Shanghai, Hong Kong, Paris, Palo Alto, Buenos Aires and Mumbai.

This strategy of chasing knowledge around the world and bringing it back to our classrooms in the form of cases has served us well, but we recognize that it is no longer sufficient. So during the 2011–12 academic year, we introduced changes in our curriculum that represent our boldest innovations since adopting the case method in 1922. The primary thrust of these efforts is to introduce into our curriculum education a "field method" that will be a powerful complement to our historical focus on the case method.

Our introduction of a field method to complement our case method was inspired by a study on the future of business education conducted by our colleagues Srikant Datar and David Garvin. They argue that one of the most important future goals of business education should to narrow what some people call the "knowing–doing gap." Consider how the teaching at a business school compares with the professional preparation delivered at a medical school. We both teach theory, but medical school students undergo much more field training to learn how to translate that learning into real practice. Medical schools have an advantage here: every hospital has a constant influx of patients to which they can expose students. It's much more challenging to inject business students into real-world managerial situations. HBS pioneered the use of case studies to project students into the role of managers solving business problems, and this pedagogy was a dramatic improvement on the lectures that preceded it. But even when immersed in the best case studies, students aren't really managing—they're *imagining* what they would do if they were managers. The field method we are experimenting with tries to take this next step—how can we create educational experiences in which our students can learn from doing—where they actually have to put their knowing from the case method to use, and learn from reflecting on the actual results of their doing?

The main vehicle through which we are experimenting with introducing the field method into our curriculum is a new required first-year course called Field Immersion Experiences for Leadership Development (FIELD for short). This first-year course runs through the entire first year in parallel to the existing field method courses students have always been required to take. It involves students working in a wide variety of team-based field exercises and projects throughout the year.

One of the most ambitious aspects of this new FIELD program is to develop the global leadership capacity of our students by giving every student firsthand experience of working on a field project in emerging markets. In January 2012, we sent our entire first-year class of 900 MBA students abroad. Students worked in teams of six, and each group was assigned to work with a multinational or local company in one of ten different emerging markets around the globe. Before the trip, each team analyzed a new product or service that the company they were working with might introduce in the local market. This pre-work involved a series of exercises that built upon the lessons they were learning from their case method courses during the semester. During their one-week stays in their destination countries, they met with suppliers, interviewed potential customers, visited stores and worked to understand if the product or service they were investigating—an offering that had made sense on paper during late-night brainstorming sessions on our Massachusetts campus—seemed likely to really succeed in the local market.

As I write this, it is yet too early to offer any robust assessment of how our first attempt at developing greater global leadership capacities through this FIELD program has worked out. My early impression, however, is that it has accomplished at least part of its goals. One of the things we've heard consistently from students about their experiences abroad is that they were surprised by how innovative local companies were and how they were competing against multinationals. Students also reported that the way they pictured emerging markets from afar based on knowledge acquired from cases, book or other resources was very different than the reality they encountered while visiting. Students who visited Turkey, for instance, have returned to campus saying that they could now imagine living in Istanbul after graduating, something they couldn't have conceived of before encountering this large, modern city firsthand.

Real-life global field experiences have given our students an opportunity to test their ideas into practice—to bridge that "knowing–doing gap." Our ultimate goal is not only to better prepare our own students to fulfill the school's mission of "educating leaders who make a difference in the world," but to influence and improve how management is taught in business schools all over the world. This is what HBS originally did with the case study method, which is now used universally. Our hope is to do the same thing with the field method. How do you structure the experience? What kinds of interventions do you need from faculty? What specific company support do you need? Our commitment is to develop a new method for how to do this, and for this practice to become a standard that other institutions can embrace.

Understanding a concept intellectually is not the same as understanding it viscerally. To educate a new generation of global leaders, case studies, and lectures and conceptual frameworks (such as the one on the three dimensions of global competition I've offered above) are valuable, but to really prepare these people for the challenges they will face, we need to get them out into the markets.

Like the students who have gone through the first year of this new program, we don't have all the answers—and to a certain extent, we'll be improvising as we go. But what we do know is that we need to do a better job producing leaders who can move easily between markets to take advantage of emerging global opportunities in this new global century. The steps I've described here are the best ways I know to begin that task.

PART 2

Leadership Development in a Global Context: The Contribution of Business Schools

---

Combining Purpose and Performance:
A New Look at Global Business Schools

DIPAK C. JAIN, Dean, **INSEAD**, and **MATT GOLOSINSKI**, Director of Research, **INSEAD**

> Our loyalties must transcend our race, our tribe, our class, and our nation; and this means we must develop a world perspective.
>
> Martin Luther King Jr

The world before the Internet seems a remote, dim place, so profoundly has the technology upended everything about our lives. It has increased productivity, sparked innovation, and made the world more intimate. There's an expectation that, in the next five minutes, some other remarkable development will spring from the shimmering pool of digital alchemy.

By now, these are prosaic observations. But can we imagine taking this commonplace gloss and substituting as its protagonist *business schools* rather than *the Internet*? Does it seem possible that management education can unleash a similar torrent of creativity and value—or even produce a public image that defies the business-as-usual caricature often foremost in people's minds? Some schools *are* dedicating themselves to finding new ways to make an impact, including by putting people first and exploring a humanistic approach to management practise. Yet, on the whole, it is well past time for business schools to reframe their *modus operandi*, if not their *raison d'être*. In emphasizing integrity and a purpose larger than oneself, schools can aspire to *significance* as well as *success*. This transformation will need curricula that impart an understanding of global business evolution (see Table 8).

It's true that business has been called to be more and do more before: the Social Gospel movement in the US during the late nineteenth and early

Table 8: The evolution of global business

Time	Up to nineteenth century	Twentieth century	Twenty-first century
Focus	Land and labour: Colonialism	Free-market: Capitalism	Human capital: Entrepreneurialism
Key players	Countries	Corporations	Citizens

twentieth centuries offers one reference point. Protestant progressives criticised industrialization, urging a more constructive, equitable, and humane role for business, one that put the focus on community values and warned against what they saw as systemic flaws that encouraged greed and cut-throat competitiveness.

"Industry and commerce are in their nature productive and therefore good," wrote the theologian Walter Rauschenbusch in 1908. "But in our industry a strong element of rapacity vitiates the moral qualities of business life." [1]

Today, the global banking crisis and issues such as climate change and income inequality have raised similar concerns, challenging business and business schools alike. A 2010 Edelman survey revealed "a vastly different set of factors—led by trust and transparency—now influences corporate reputation and demands that companies take a multi-dimensional approach to their engagement with stakeholders". For the first time, trust and transparency are "as important to corporate reputation as the quality of products and services." [2] In another survey, Edelman found that 86 percent of more than 7000 global consumers believe that business needs to place at least equal weight on society's interests as on business's interests. Some 62 percent said they would help promote a brand's product or services if there is a good cause associated with them.

Perhaps the survey's most surprising takeaway is the global homogeneity of such responses. Even in emerging markets, more than 7 in 10 consumers report that they "would take action to support social purpose brands." Eight in 10 of these customers expect brands to donate a portion of their profits to a good social purpose. [3]

Of special interest to business schools is a recent Aspen Institute/Net Impact survey, which revealed that 88 percent of MBA students believe that business should play a role in addressing social and environmental issues.

Table 9: Evolution of management education

Time Period	Up to mid 1960s	Late 1960s to late 1990s	2000–present
Pedagogical Tools	Case studies	Research-driven analytical frameworks	Experiential global learning
Decision-making driven by	Judgment and intuition	Shareholder value and economic models of optimisation	Ethics and values
Success metrics	Performance	Profits	Purpose

Note: Earlier models are absorbed into later ones, which add new elements to existing frameworks.

About 90 percent of these people say that short-term thinking, rather than sustainable models, is a key driver of global financial instability. As a result, 78 percent of the students said that they expected and desired more emphasis on responsible business practise in their MBA curriculum.[4] In a 2011 survey of Net Impact's 20,000 members, 95 percent of respondents said that "having a career that makes a positive social or environmental impact on the world was important to them."[5]

Clearly the game has changed. Technology gives everyday consumers more strategic leverage through easier and instant communication, and greater access to information. Human capital has emerged as this century's innovation engine, and citizens have become key players in moving markets (see Table 9). As a consequence, business schools must articulate a better statement of their purpose and value in this environment.

Rakesh Khurana has said that the 1990s presented a "pervasive atmosphere of drift and uncertainty" that resulted in schools redefining themselves as "leadership" institutions. This shift, he suggests, occurred for lack of a better idea or else as a half-hearted attempt to resurrect management as a full-fledged profession with profound social responsibilities.[6]

Half measures are no longer sufficient, if they ever were. Companies are being pushed to go beyond corporate social responsibility (CSR) initiatives that seem more an afterthought than integral.[7] Likewise, schools must seek more substantial ways to make a difference. We need bold schools that operate, not in an incremental way, but as a *disruptive force* for social improvement, bringing together people, resources, and knowledge to solve problems and make life better for more of the planet. If schools are reluctant to rise to the challenge, then they risk being left behind, marginalized by an array of *purpose-driven* organizations already taking action at all levels.

Some of these entities, like Ashoka, Echoing Green, and Skoll Foundation, have fueled change through social innovation. Others, like the Bill and Melinda Gates Foundation, focus on global health and development. Still others, like Grameen Bank, extend financial instruments to the world's poorest. The United Nations, through a multitude of programs, including its Millennium Development Goals initiative, is working to eradicate poverty, improve education, and halt the spread of HIV/AIDS. Of course, some business schools have forged relationships with these and other organizations, an association that inspires fellowships, scholarships, competitions, and conferences. The conversation has started, the seeds have been planted. Now the task is to deepen the roots and push the flowers higher. This requires a better understanding of:

- sustainable business

- social entrepreneurship

- public policy fostering partnerships among business, government, and civic agents.

An era of transformation: Why and how schools are changing

Sustainability, social entrepreneurship, and public policy all imply a commitment to enduring value creation that touches many stakeholders. Short-term personal profits are anathema to the values that anchor these three domains. Furthermore, these endeavors all implicitly demand leaders capable of appreciating others' perspectives, since this work is rooted in the community.

A great global business school defines itself by transcending narrow conventional categories in favor of an expansive view of its mission, stakeholders, and partners. This institution embraces a *multiplicity of perspectives* in a genuine effort to gain a deeper, more diverse understanding of the problems confronting business and society. Then it finds solutions. Where once these remedies could be reliably 'Western' in their orientation, there is now increasing awareness of the need to adapt global frameworks to local contexts for best results.

Similarly, older notions about the very nature of business and success are evolving thanks to globalization and related demographic shifts among those seeking management education. Whether it's the "Facebook Generation" pushing the bounds of what social networks and digital media can accomplish, or Net Impact's "new generation of leaders who use [their] careers to tackle the world's toughest problems," expectations about knowledge acquisition and application keep progressing in exciting, demanding, and sometimes surprising ways.

Then, too, it is impossible to ignore the vast numbers of people living at or below subsistence level. (Google "poverty + YouTube" to test this assertion.) Some figures indicate that as many as 40 percent of the world lives on $2 a day.[8] UNICEF estimates that 22,000 children under the age of five die each day as a result of poverty.[9] While the majority of these people dwell in developing nations, poverty, homelessness, substance abuse, and a host of other 'urban' problems plague even the world's wealthier countries. For example, US Census figures indicate that a record 46.2 million Americans—15.1 percent of the population—were in poverty in 2010, up from 43.6 million in 2009. This represents the fourth consecutive annual increase in poverty.[10] As Harvard professor, policy adviser, and former Indianapolis mayor Stephen Goldsmith states:

> If ever there were a moment for creative civic engagement it is now. Financial insecurity, lack of educational opportunity, income disparities, and waning civic health challenge city leaders every day.[11]

The schools best suited to address these issues will have an ability to innovate and forge fruitful partnerships. They also will demonstrate a commitment to service and the passion to make a difference—in developed and emerging markets. These schools will succeed by focussing on core values and purpose.

Business schools, whether 'global' or not, should be engines of opportunity, creating and disseminating the knowledge that lets people make valuable contributions to their organizations and communities. What kind of knowledge? Consider some of the complexity that business leaders encounter today:

- Hyper-competition and resource scarcity

- Smarter consumers armed with better information

- Operations in multiple regulatory environments

- Reputational management, including social media.

To meet these challenges, the following are essential:

- Ability to drive broad stakeholder engagement, not just shareholders

- Great skill in cultivating employees in a climate of robust diversity

- Passion for success *and* significance, spurred by increased demand for business to "do more" to solve big problems.

The expertise required to thrive in this setting comes from a variety of "intelligences," such as those famously described by cognitive scientist Howard Gardner. In his model, Gardner identifies five "minds" needed for success tomorrow.[12] Managers and leaders need an eclectic portfolio of mental skills, ranging from rigorous structured thinking that comes from discipline-based training, to the ability to sift through a mountain of data quickly, finding valuable patterns and information, then combining disparate strands deftly. The same person also will need excellent soft skills to engage creatively and ethically with others whose backgrounds, customs, and experiences may be totally unfamiliar.

Whether we adopt Gardner's view or else think in categories such as mental intelligence (IQ), emotional intelligence (EQ), and moral intelligence (MQ), the point is much the same: Business schools have to cultivate multiple modalities of thought to support human capital development, which will be a preeminent source of twenty-first-century competitive advantage in every sector, as noted in Table 9. The holistic resources of reason, intuition, and moral conduct—when brought together around the core values of service and community—will be the framework schools use to create leaders who make a significant difference in the world (see Figure 11.) This diversity of thought signals something important about leadership and its responsibilities today: true success comes from mindfulness, from cultivating a mentality that transcends the limits of personal ego to recognize a greater purpose—*a personal responsibility*—toward which one directs one's talents and shapes one's thoughts, speech, and actions.

Since their start, most business schools have tried to bridge theory and practise through curricula that meld rigor and relevance. Today's global schools aim to put ideas into action; the best of them are not afraid to go "beyond business" to make an impact through creative partnerships at the nexus of business, government, and society.[13] When one unpacks these concepts, one discovers the seeds of an even more ambitious project: business,

Figure 11: A holistic model

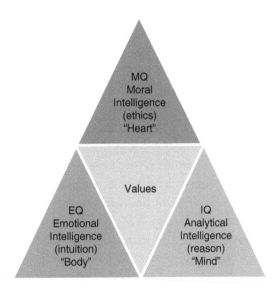

and business education, as the means to create not only material prosperity (though that too), but also greater understanding among people.

Schools once may have contented themselves with producing knowledge that optimized performance or profits alone, but now they must do that and more. Globalization is exerting pressure on schools to rethink their business models to stay relevant in a vast, hyper-competitive market. As a result, schools are forced to differentiate more as they try to deliver unique value and sharpen their brands. If the MBA formerly was a monolithic degree delivered in roughly the same way, today we see greater differences in how schools approach *what* they teach and *how* they teach it. (This is despite mission statements that can sound remarkably similar.) So, answering the question "What does a global business school look like?" requires nuance. Some factors, like international presence, a curriculum that takes a holistic market view, and diversity among students and faculty, will generate common enthusiasm among institutions. But there will be big differences in how these and other elements combine based on a school's particular strengths and resources. In other words, we cannot expect a one-size-fits-all formula. Rather, there are multiple ways of producing good results.

We *can* expect greater convergence around a related point, though: a global business school aligns purpose with performance, producing management expertise that transforms individuals, organizations, and the world. This convergence, in part, stems from environmental pressures. Management scholars and practitioners operate in a setting defined by hyper-competition with increased complexity; economic and political uncertainty; vigorous public scrutiny and skepticism; greater integration among business, government, and society; and globalization enabled by technology. Any one of these forces would be daunting. Together, they compel business schools to examine how and what they produce. The question behind all others is *whom do we serve?*

Reputation. Just as they do in the wake of every market downturn or corporate scandal, reputational challenges have emerged as a result of the recent global financial crisis. One of the visible manifestations of mainstream concern has been the Occupy Wall Street movement. Then, too, many publications have focussed on management education's reputation, including *Business Schools Under Fire* (2011), *Management Education for Integrity* (2010), and *The Journal of Corporate Citizenship* (2001–present). Perennial attention to rankings also reinforces negative impressions, since the methodology emphasizes postgraduate earnings. Rankings also tend to discourage innovation, as schools avoid doing anything that might diminish their standing in the surveys. The severity of the latest recession, coupled with greater political polarization in the US and elsewhere, adds weight to reputational issues, making them an unavoidable part of educators' strategic discussions.

Differentiation. Beyond reputation is the challenge of more competition among business schools. AACSB figures note that there are some 13,670 schools worldwide in 41 countries, with up to 2500 in India alone. Some, such as the China Europe International Business School in Shanghai, have forged partnerships with the likes of Harvard and Wharton to provide executive MBAs while aspiring to "create an Ivy League for the East."[14] Mid-tier private schools are being "sandwiched" most, while public schools and top private schools remain either good "value for money" or "value for brand."[15] This dynamic is fueled by declining demand and rising costs associated with traditional MBA programs. Controlling cost while maintaining (indeed, enhancing) value is a major challenge for nearly all schools, since tuition cannot rise indefinitely. GMAC figures indicate that tuition increases have outpaced salary increases over the last 10 years, resulting in questions about the MBA's overall return on investment. By some estimations, recouping total business school costs can take nearly a decade, or longer, for some graduates (see Table 10). Others have questioned both the financial ROI and whether the MBA can make a broader social impact.[16]

Globalization. These developments have not occurred in a vacuum, of course. They are part of the overall market forces under globalization. While goods, capital, and people have circulated across borders from antiquity, what's different today is the extraordinary rate of global change, driven as it is by technology. Globalization's *economic* impact has garnered much attention, but equally important is the social/cultural transmission brought about by increased communication. Consider the Arab Spring: recent events throughout the Middle East have been called the 'Twitter revolution' because of the role social media played in the protests. Such unexpected and mercurial change shows how quickly the landscape can shift, a fact of paramount importance to leaders in all sectors.

Globalization has integrated economics and culture in ways that affect most organizations, and these changes have impacted management education. If businesses are expected to "sense and respond" continuously to global market trends, the schools that prepare managers to thrive in this environment must be constantly aware of emerging trends and complexity too. These schools will have to adopt formal and informal mechanisms to ensure that they, as an organization, continuously learn—just as their students/graduates must.

Table 10: ROI

School	Total costs (US$)	Years to recoup
Chicago (Booth)	314,060	14.28
Columbia	319,502	12.78
Harvard	318,800	10.63
Stanford	338,612	9.67
Wharton	318,000	9.09
INSEAD	178,886	5.59

Source: Bloomberg/*BusinessWeek,* 'Ranking Return on Investment, 2011' Recoup figures based on post-MBA pay increase data. Total costs include tuition, fees, living expenses, and estimated foregone salary during MBA enrolment.

Collaboration. The specific challenges that schools face are many, including a dearth of doctoral candidates—which seriously influences the future of management scholarship. But perhaps the most significant overarching concern is balancing cost and quality. Here, schools will determine ad hoc how best to enhance their revenues (e.g., knowledge monetization) while ensuring academic excellence. There are several potential ways that schools can respond to global changes. The specifics will depend on individual institutional strengths, resources, mission, and history. As always, some of these responses will involve:

- Curriculum enhancements to stay current with market needs

- Program adjustments, including duration of offerings, to meet customer expectations

- Technological innovation to harness and integrate cutting-edge digital tools to spur innovation, collaboration, and learning

- Refining/defining sources of unique value, such as:

  o cultural diversity of students/faculty

  o opportunity to study on multiple campuses

  o greater focus on experiential learning.

We also expect schools to form inventive partnerships with peers or other institutions, such as business, government, and NGOs. Consider such collaboration as the future of competition, since fewer and fewer schools can afford to take a standalone approach to value creation. These partnerships will be most effective when they help schools stay close to the market to understand what skills are needed most in future organizations.

Going beyond: A new role for management education

Intelligence and capability are not enough. There must be the joy of doing something beautiful.

Dr Govindappa Venkataswamy[17]

Over the last 40 years management education has provided discipline-based frameworks that greatly contributed to our understanding of organizations and markets. At times, this analytical rigor has eclipsed business relevance. In the main, though, the outcome has had valuable impact. This analysis benefits from the technological power that is constantly reshaping how we live, learn, and make decisions.

Information, let alone raw data, is not the same thing as knowledge, of course. We are reminded of the great biologist E. O. Wilson who, more than a decade ago, said:

> We are drowning in information, while starving for wisdom. The world henceforth will be run by synthesizers, people able to put together the right information at the right time, think critically about it, and make important choices wisely.[18]

Today, that synthesis includes collaboration among sectors that previously operated in relative isolation from one other. Management education and business are no longer easily compartmentalized in a world whose global problems push business, government, and civic actors closer together in search of solutions. Schools have the chance to shape their curricula to better support prosperous communities and organizations, even as management educators continue preparing leaders for traditional market roles. At INSEAD, a key part of our mission for more than 50 years has been to promote collaboration. We have created a non-dogmatic learning environment that brings together people, cultures, and ideas from around the world, changing lives and helping transform organizations. Similarly, other schools have integrated interdisciplinary thinking into their curricula, such as what we have seen at Yale, Stanford, the Rotman School, and others.[19]

There also is a call for greater integration at the top level of curriculum development, as some push for a more humanistic approach to business education that puts purpose alongside performance.[20] J.-C. Spender and Jeroen Kraaijenbrink, for instance, remind us of humanism's values and history, dating back to Socrates and earlier. Humanism prizes universal tolerance, reason, equality, and individual development.

> [Humanism] puts peoples' choices, social concerns and flourishing ahead of the objectives of efficiency, economic growth, and competitive advantage that have been adopted by so many within academe, business, and elsewhere.[21]

As mentioned, many students and consumers today embrace such "purposeful" views as they seek the tools to improve the world.

These developments accompany globalization, which itself is forcing business schools to be agile in response to uncertain market realities. Reacting to the market is a fact of life for any organization. *Anticipating* market shifts before they fully occur offers even better strategic options. (Action at a still more fundamental level, where we *shape* aspects of the market rather than wait passively for change, may be best of all. This is what Peter Drucker meant when he said "the best way to predict the future is to create it.") This requires those multiple intelligences referenced above—especially the ability to analyze and synthesize data before designing creative, effective, and ethical ways to implement these fresh insights. Yet even here more is required of those seeking the visionary path. As Roger Martin, dean of the Rotman School, has said:

> Innovation is about seeing the world not as it is, but as it could be. It's about exploring really 'wicked problems' whose solutions can't be found in past experience or proven by data.[22]

If management schools want to remain relevant, if they want to orchestrate this future innovation, they will have to reinvent themselves to "go beyond" conventional expectations in at least three big ways:

- Beyond business—to embrace sustainable practise and social entrepreneurship, not just the bottom line

- Beyond the 'Western' curriculum—to explore emerging market needs

- Beyond success—to provide new models of value that reflect a greater desire to make a wise social impact.

This framework positions schools to make a difference in developed and developing markets, where management innovation is needed to address fundamental social problems, including food, energy and economic insecurity, environmental sustainability, healthcare, and more. These long-term concerns will require ongoing commitment from multiple stakeholders, including business.

In addition to revisiting mission and curriculum, schools should examine *how* they produce and disseminate knowledge. The consideration of digital technology in education is worthy of its own book. At minimum, schools must understand how to integrate the latest tools into the classroom—and even be open to new concepts of what the "classroom" entails. Distance learning, for example, is here. While, at present, it provides limited benefit when compared to the rich possibilities of a physical campus and immediate interaction with peers and professors, the technology behind distance learning should be integrated more fully into schools, complementing existing pedagogical structures. It is useful to remember that not everyone can afford traditional management education. In fact, very few among the total pool of potential students can. These tools, therefore, also open up new engagement with non-traditional market segments, such as civic innovators operating at small scale in remote locations or in informal economies. Doing so requires interaction with local government and policymakers too, but such markets are ripe for intensified public–private partnerships in critical domains, such as food scarcity. What is needed is leadership, perseverance, pragmatism, and effective governance.

Management education—and even capitalism itself—again seems at a crossroads, and all schools should be prepared to adapt or else suffer from consolidation. Interestingly, systemic changes in business teaching may begin not at the most prestigious institutions, but elsewhere, as Professor Michael Jensen has argued.

> If we're going to get new things happening, it is probably going to be not in the first phalanx of schools but in the second or the third, where they are motivated to take risks and have less to lose.[23]

Beyond business

We are moving from an older model of capitalism to a system that resembles *entrepreneurialism*.[24] This form has market and nonmarket aspects and is focussed on innovations that create community value as well as financial returns. An estimated 388 million entrepreneurs in 54 economies surveyed by the Global Entrepreneurship Monitor were starting or running ventures in 2011. This figure represents a 25 percent increase in total early stage activity (TEA) among 16 developing economies and a 22 percent TEA increase in 20 mature economies.[25] Governments, including the US and UK, have established partnerships with social entrepreneurs.[26] Facilitating this activity are regulatory reforms that streamline processes and strengthen legal institutions, according to the World Bank Group's Doing Business project.

> Overall in 2010/11, governments in 125 economies implemented 245 institutional and regulatory reforms … 13 per cent more than in the previous

year. A faster pace of regulatory reform is good news for entrepreneurs in developing economies.[27]

The entrepreneurial mindset is one with an unshakable desire to make a difference. This is perhaps even more the case with social entrepreneurs, who "identify resources where people only see problems," according to David Bornstein, author of *How to Change the World: Social Entrepreneurs and the Power of New Ideas*. He says these individuals "view the villagers as the solution, not the passive beneficiary" and harness the community's creative potential to develop solutions to poverty, illiteracy, environmental degradation, and more. Their approach is a departure from the top-down model, preferring a decentralized strategy that draws on the collective energy and insights of various "changemakers."[28]

In his 2006 Nobel Prize acceptance address, Grameen Bank founder Muhammad Yunus predicted that nearly all the world's social and economic problems would be addressed, not by government mandates, multinational corporations, or all-powerful technological innovation, but by social businesses. All three of those forces, though, have a role to play in supporting social entrepreneurship, according to Yunus.

> The challenge is to innovate business models and apply them to produce desired social results cost-effectively and efficiently. Healthcare for the poor, financial services for the poor, information technology for the poor, education and training for the poor, marketing for the poor, renewable energy—these are all exciting areas for social businesses.[29]

Some institutions, including Babson College, the University of Virginia's Darden School of Business, and the University of Michigan's Ross School, among others, have earned reputations for being strong in entrepreneurship. At INSEAD, the Social Innovation Centre has produced a range of cross-disciplinary research in areas such as corporate social responsibility and ethics, humanitarian efforts, healthcare, and social innovation itself. Likewise, INSEAD's Maag International Centre for Entrepreneurship is the school's research hub for entrepreneurship and is home to our globally recognized entrepreneurship faculty and curriculum. Management education, however, can play an even greater role in advancing social entrepreneurship. Perhaps the biggest opportunity now is finding ways to increase the speed and scale in developing frameworks for public–private engagement.

If we regard the study of social entrepreneurship as an important way to understand civic renewal, this is a project whose merits are worth integrating more fully into management education. Some of the ways schools can do this include:

- Creating a culture of inclusion that reinforces diversity, respect for others and the planet, and humanistic values

- Designing more hands-on opportunities to learn and experiment in a "safe-to-fail" environment. Doing so lets students "cut through complexity" (as Bill Gates has said)[30] and link theory with social innovation practise

- Emphasizing collaborative skills, needed for cross-cultural interaction in any modern global business, but especially needed for the multi-stakeholder engagement that defines the social innovation context, where resources may only be indirectly controlled by the entrepreneur. Developing student empathy is key for more effective conflict resolution

- Cultivating deeper relationships between the school and organizations that support social innovation at all levels (e.g., Net Impact, EABIS, Ashoka, government agencies, and various foundations)

Schools also can improve their overall curricula by creating a process that brings insights from social innovation efforts into conventional management frameworks, strengthening them. At social entrepreneurship's core is an openness to experimentation. As Bornstein writes:

> Given the way the world is changing, more people are going to have to improvise large stretches of their careers, responding to shifting needs and opportunities. Success may hinge less on what you know than on how well you learn new things, spot new patterns, take initiative, and work with others.[31]

Similarly, sustainable business practise is no longer just a "nice idea." It is a strategic/competitive imperative, so schools must integrate this element thoroughly in the curriculum and culture. In fact, the concept is now part of the World Economic Forum's annual *Global Competitiveness Report*, where it is defined along economic, social, and environmental dimensions. Sustainability is a central part of the discussion, whether in corporate board-rooms or academic conferences. Pierre Jacquet, the chief economist at the French Development Agency, made an interesting observation during the 2011 EABIS Colloquium at INSEAD. He said: "Sustainability is about trying to create values that are not so closely linked to the market. These are more transcendent values." His words resonate with those of Ban Ki-Moon. In a recent *New York Times* op-ed piece, the UN Secretary-General wrote:

> There can be no sustainable growth without development, there can be no sustainable development without protecting the planet. ... With wisdom and foresight, we can use this moment to lay the foundations for a healthy, green and inclusive economic prosperity for everyone. ... Let us make no mistake: there can be no deferring these hard choices.[32]

Business schools can strengthen their commitment to sustainable practise by including the topic in formal coursework and encouraging it through infor-mal campus and community initiatives. Some specific efforts could include:

- More field-based study that brings students face to face with the effects of environmental degradation, broadening their understanding of the stakes involved

- Action-learning modules that encourage collaboration among students and environmental and civic stakeholders to address issues related to sustainable practise

- Efforts to advance the design and development of metrics to assess sus-tainability, as greater measurement will inspire further adoption and innovation in this area

- Partnerships with companies either seeking to develop sustainability as a core value and practise, or else with firms that can provide real-world examples of how they have integrated sustainability meaningfully into their organization

- Deeper study of the history of sustainable thinking and the philosophy that informs it. For example, figures as diverse as Buddha, Aristotle,

St Francis, Goethe, Emerson, Gandhi, and Bill McKibben offer insights on the subject.

Beyond the 'Western' curriculum

If we accept the premise that business can and should advance positive change and prosperity in the world, and that globalization continues to integrate markets and cultures, then business schools must do more to prepare students for careers in the global arena. While the US model of management education remains strong internationally, "as business education becomes more global, it is becoming less American."[33] Foreign firms are showing up more often in US strategy course cases—up to one-third of the time—and new perspectives are emerging. These include a focus on higher-order purpose or vision, over short-term gain; collective wisdom rather than traditional bureaucracy; innovation and employee engagement as key adjuncts to conventional productivity.[34]

For business to make the biggest impact, it has to "think globally and act locally," to integrate at the local level, delivering value that really matters for the community, rather than merely presenting mature-market frameworks to superimpose on an emerging and/or informal market. Success in this endeavor means understanding the local context: the market needs, the social and governmental structures, the resources and impediments, and cultural values that may be diverge markedly from those in other places.

Schools can make stronger contributions by bringing new global perspectives to their students in several ways, including by:

- Greater detailed focus on emerging markets and companies through coursework, business cases, competitions, etc.

- More opportunity to study on several campuses to gain a first-hand sense of different business contexts. For example, INSEAD students study in Fontainebleau/Paris, Singapore, Abu Dhabi, and elsewhere, including in the US

- Cultivating authentic diversity in the classroom and on campus. Globalization is bringing people and cultures closer. As much as possible, the MBA experience should offer exposure to genuine diversity among students and faculty. "Genuine" is the key word, since different skin colors alone hardly constitutes diversity. Eclectic cultural, economic, and professional backgrounds better reflect the diversity that helps students gain the ability to succeed as "cosmopolitan managers"[35]

Beyond success—new conceptions of value

Nobel laureate Amartya Sen has defended market-based value creation but has called for ameliorating what he sees as systemic shortcomings that have produced economic disparity that threatens global stability. Writing even before the "Occupy Wall Street" movement, Sen noted the following"

> The economic difficulties of today do not … call for some 'new capitalism,' but they do demand an open-minded understanding of older ideas about the reach and limits of the market economy. What is needed above all is a clear-headed appreciation of how different institutions work, along with an understanding of how a variety of organisations—from the market to the institutions of state—can together contribute to producing a more decent economic world.[36]

Too often business schools incentivize and reward behavior that privileges performance over purpose and resists new interaction between business and other entities. At best, this results in success that is more narrow and limited than it might otherwise be. At worst, the mentality can contribute to reckless or unethical behavior driven by personal gain. We should instead adopt an expansive view of management education's ability to influence social change. Success is important, no doubt. But rather than think of it as an end in itself, we should consider it the foundation for *significance*.

One way to put this mindset into action is at the nexus of business, government, and society, where it can contribute to human capital development and solve problems whose complexity often baffles any one sector. This multi-stakeholder approach can fashion a new view of business and society, revising the definition of profit to focus on long-term, community-oriented outcomes as well as traditional notions. Making this arrangement work means devising mechanisms that facilitate creative engagement between the public sector and business. Getting past stereotypical thinking and outworn models is essential, as Stephen Goldsmith notes:

> With a structure designed for a simpler time, government has become ill-equipped to handle the complex task of solving our increasingly intractable

social challenges. Even more fundamentally, though, government now must deliver its assistance not through traditional rule-bound hierarchical programs but through effective civic entrepreneurs operating in dense social and community networks.[37]

What's more, globalization/global sourcing has raised questions about whether traditional managerial efficiency will itself prove sufficient "to offer a lasting competitive advantage as the diffusion of technologies and processes accelerate."[38] More likely, success will demand greater innovation, collaboration and creative ability alongside process enhancements. One example of an area where this convergence of thought leadership can make monumental differences is in humanitarian logistics—the organizing, delivery, and storing of goods to support disaster relief. At INSEAD, for instance, the Humanitarian Research Group has worked since 2001 to develop the science of humanitarian logistics and increase the capacity of humanitarian actors to respond effectively. The scholars associated with this project have worked across sectors to create partnerships among humanitarian organizations, private entities, governments, donors, and the military.[39]

Business schools have any number of opportunities to engage partners in the public sector. Global healthcare initiatives, for example, represent one high-profile, valuable contribution.

Some of the ways schools can 'go beyond' success to achieve significance include:

- Developing curricula that transcend the typical for-profit/non-profit divide, recognizing an emerging context in which a more nuanced sense of value is embraced (e.g., "people, planet, profits")

- Establishing partnerships with stakeholders in public and civic arenas to create *integrated innovation and progress centers.* These centres of excellence could develop case studies, host conferences and workshops, and actively define and solve key challenges. These centers could develop metrics to measure effectiveness of new engagement and innovation

- Adopting the framework of "Blue Ocean Strategy" (BOS) to create new market opportunities outside the conventional ones defined by head-to-head competition. BOS was created at INSEAD and is today being advanced by our Blue Ocean Strategy Institute. While BOS produces competitive advantage for organizations in the for-profit arena, its principles are well suited to cultivating fruitful engagement among business, government, and society too.

Once more we are reminded of Muhammad Yunus' conception of thinking beyond established frames of reference. In his Nobel Peace Prize speech he declared:

> I am in favor of strengthening the freedom of the market. At the same time, I am very unhappy about the conceptual restrictions imposed on the players in the market. This originates from the assumption that entrepreneurs are one-dimensional human beings, who are dedicated to one mission in their business lives: to maximize profit. This interpretation of capitalism insulates the entrepreneurs from all political, emotional, social, spiritual, environmental dimensions of their lives. This was done perhaps as a reasonable simplification, but it stripped away the very essentials of human life.

"We first," not me first

In truth, the challenges facing us go well beyond business schools, as Javier Irarrazaval Alfonzo, managing director of The Walt Disney Company (Chile), pointed out during the 2011 EABIS Colloquium. In answering a question about how we transform management education to be more enlightened, more sustainable, he said:

> It's not enough just to focus on business schools. We need lawyers and doctors and everyone else [to change] too. It's not enough that a few top business schools change. We need more holistic social change. If you don't change the minds of the kids early, it is a big challenge later for the educational world.

This is an exciting and challenging time for schools. Exciting, because of the opportunity to help create the larger engagement that Irarrazaval and others say is required for social improvement. It is also exciting because never before have we enjoyed such immediate access to so vast a repository of tools and information to inspire change, large or small. The entire world is at our fingertips, so long as we have at least a smartphone and Internet access. Digital tools are enhancing creativity and collaboration, bringing people together around the planet.

Some, like Simon Mainwaring, author of *We First: How Brands and Consumers Use Social Media to Build a Better World*, see the revolutionary potential of these tools to transform the entire market system into "capitalism for the greater good." Rather than rely on outmoded or tepid CSR efforts, Mainwaring says customers and companies have a responsibility to work together to challenge each other to "reengineer the foundational principles of capitalism to honor not only profits but also purpose, mutual self-interest, sustainability, human values, collaboration, and collective prosperity."[40] Social media, because of its immediacy and visibility, is one powerful mechanism to transform both customers and companies, he says. It can offer ways for consumers to contribute their ideas to make a brand better, or else to reward or punish firms that put profits before people.

The challenge for schools is to adapt to make maximal use of technological innovation (and to understand that we as institutions are subject to social media's global spotlight too). We need to do so in ways that complement our traditional and proven frameworks. Even more, we need schools that do not balk at engaging a range of partners to take on urgent problems facing business and society. We need schools that understand value in a new way and that have the imagination and drive to think beyond their historical strengths to meet future priorities.

Perhaps the biggest challenge for schools is to think beyond conventional notions of what education is supposed to be—intrinsically—and to what purpose it should be put. Knowledge should be a journey of self-discovery and service. That is, what you learn should elevate and illuminate your mind. Then, as you put this knowledge into action, you should strive to create both success and significance in the world. Too often, we see business in a diminished form, optimizing performance at the cost of purpose. We need both.

We need to learn the right things for the right reasons and then put them to the right use. This is the core of ethical conduct and wisdom. It is also the future of management education, if schools have the courage to make this journey.

NOTES

1 Walter Rauschenbusch (1907) *Christianity and the Social Crisis* (New York, NY: Macmillan): 268. Rauschenbusch argues that single-minded focus on profit cheats consumers of quality. He also draws unflattering links between "speculative finance" and belligerent international politics (p. 270).

2 "2010 Edelman Trust Barometer," 6, at http://www.edelman.com/trust/2010.

3 "Citizens Engage! Edelman goodpurpose Study 2010," at http://www.edelman.com/insights.

4 "MBA Perspectives 2009," at http://www.netimpact.org.

5 "Business as Unusual 2011," 1, at http://www.netimpact.org.

6 Rakesh Khurana (2007) *From Higher Aims to Hired Hands: The Social Transformation of American Business Schools and the Unfulfilled Promise of Management as a Profession* (Princeton, NJ: Princeton University Press).

7 For an excellent overview of CSR today, including how some firms are integrating these efforts into their business core to make a real impact, see N. Craig Smith, C. B. Bhattacharya, David Vogel, and David I. Levine (2010) *Global Challenges in Responsible Business* (New York, NY: Cambridge University Press).

8 Daryl Collins, Jonathan Morduch, Stuart Rutherford, and Orlanda Ruthven (2009) *Portfolios of the Poor: How the World's Poor Live on $2 a Day* (Princeton, NJ: Princeton University Press).

9 UNICEF (2010) "State of the World's Children 2010," at http://www.unicef.org/sowc.

10 www.census.gov/hhes.

11 Stephen Goldsmith (2010) *The Power of Social Innovation: How Civic Entrepreneurs Ignite Community Networks for Good* (San Francisco, CA: Jossey-Bass): xviii.

12 These are: the Disciplined Mind, the Synthesizing Mind, the Creating Mind, the Respectful Mind, and the Ethical Mind. See Howard Gardner (2008) *Five Minds for the Future* (Boston, MA: Harvard Business School Press).

13 Most management educators are aware of periodic trends that have taken some schools farther from practitioners and, instead, in a more theoretical direction—a development sometimes derided as "physics envy." The 1959 Ford and Carnegie reports on business education are often cited as a watershed in prescribing greater academic rigor—at the expense of relevance—among US management institutions.

14 "Tutors to the World," *The Economist*, 9 June 2011, at http://www.economist.com/node/18802722.

15 "Trouble in the Middle," *The Economist*, 15 October 2011, at http://www.economist.com/node/21532269.

16 Christopher F. Schuetze, "Gauging the Value of your MBA." *New York Times* (Global), 20 October 2011; and Shrikant M. Datar, David A. Garvin and Patrick G. Cullen (2010) *Rethinking the MBA: Business Education at a Crossroads* (Boston, MA: Harvard Business Press).

17 Venkataswamy was an ophthamologist who, upon mandatory retirement, founded the Aravind Eye Hospital in Madurai, India. He mortgaged his home to raise the funds to open the facility, whose purpose was to provide free or low-cost cataract surgery. He died in 2006.

18 E. O. Wilson (1999) *Consilience: The Unity of Knowledge* (New York, NY: Vintage Books): 294.

19 For a helpful gloss on these changes, see Santiago de Onzono (2011) *The Learning Curve: How Business Schools are Re-Inventing Education* (Houndmills: Palgrave Macmillan): Chapter 8.

20 See, for example, Heiko Spitzek, Michael Pirson, Wolfgang von Amann, Shiban Khan, and Ernst von Kimakowitz (eds) (2009) *Humanism in Business* (New York, NY: Cambridge University Press); Michael Pirson and Paul R. Lawrence (2010) "Humanism in Business—Towards a Paradigm Shift." *Journal of Business Ethics* 93.4: 553–565; Ernst Von Kimakowitz, Michael Pirson, Heiko Spitzeck, Claus Dierksmeier, and Wolfgang Amann (2001) *Humanistic Management in Practice* (Houndmills: Palgrave Macmillan); Claus Dierksmeier, Wolfgang Amann, Ernst Von Kimakowitz, Heiko Spitzeck, and Michael Pirson (2011) *Humanistic Ethics in the Age of Globality* (Houndmills: Palgrave Macmillan); and Wolfgang Amann, Claus Dierksmeier, Michael Pirson, Heiko Spitzeck, and Ernst Von Kimakowitz (2011) *Business Schools Under Fire: Humanistic Management Education as the Way Forward* (Houndmills: Palgrave Macmillan).

21 "Humanizing Management Education." In *Business Schools Under Fire*: 258.

22 Roger Martin (2009) *The Design of Business: Why Design Thinking is the Next Competitive Advantage* (Boston, MA: Harvard Business School Press).

23 "Insights from the W. Edward Deming Memorial Conference." In *Business Schools Under Fire*: 101.

24 See, for example, data from OECD, such as "Understanding Entrepreneurship" (2006) and "Measuring Entrepreneurship" (2009).

25 Donna J. Kelley, Slavica Singer, and Mike Herrington (2012) *Global Entrepreneurship Monitor: 2011 Global Report*, at http://www.gemconsortium.org/docs/2201/gem-2011-global-report.

26 "Let's Hear those Ideas." *The Economist*, 12 August 2010, at http://www.economist.com/node/16789766.

27 The World Bank (2012) *Doing Business 2012: Doing Business in a More Transparent World* (Washington, DC: The World Bank and International Finance Corporation).

28 See Bornstein's "In the Fight Against Poverty, It's Time for a Revolution." *The New York Times*, 12 January 2012. There he cites Michael Harrington's 1962 poverty study, which defined the poor as "internal exiles" whose pessimism prevents them from capitalizing on opportunities. Entrepreneurs are trying to devise means

to improve the poor's "capacity to aspire" in ways that transcend existing social services, which Bornstein sees as "fragmented" and ill-suited to solve the fundamental problem.

29 http://www.nobelprize.org/nobel_prizes/peace/laureates/2006/yunus-lecture-en.html.

30 In his 2007 Harvard commencement address, Gates said: "Cutting through complexity to find a solution runs through four predictable stages: determine a goal, find the highest-leverage approach, discover the ideal technology for that approach, and in the meantime, make the smartest application of the technology that you already have." See http://news.harvard.edu/gazette/story/2007/06/remarks-of-bill-gates-harvard-commencement-2007.

31 David Bornstein and Susan Davis (2010) *Social Entrepreneurship: What Everybody Needs to Know* (New York, NY: Oxford University Press): 82.

32 "The Clock is Ticking," *The New York Times*, 1 November 2011.

33 "Tutors to the World," *The Economist*, 9 June 2011.

34 See, for example, "Management: Last Bastion of American Hegemony?" CNNMoney, 27 October 2011; Peter Cappelli, Harbir Singh, Jitendra Singh, and Michael Useem (2010) *The India Way: How India's Top Business Leaders Are Revolutionizing Management* (Boston, MA: Harvard Business Press); and "India: The Future of Management Education?" *Bloomberg BusinessWeek*, 17 September 2010.

35 S. Iñiguez de Onzono (2011) points out this challenge of creating managers who are citizens of the world, able to thrive in multicultural environments. See *The Learning Curve*: 139.

36 "Adam Smith's Market Never Stood Alone." *Financial Times*, 10 March 2009.

37 *The Power of Social Innovation*: xxi. It is important to note that Goldsmith makes a point in his book to say that he is not in favor of total privatization and that he believes government does indeed have a constructive role to play.

38 "The Global Management Education Landscape" (2008): 18. Global Foundation for Management Education, at http://www.gfme.org/landscape/landscape.htm.

39 See, for example, Rolando Tomasini and Luk Van Wassenhove (2009) *Humanitarian Logistics* (London: Palgrave Macmillan), particularly Chapters 5–7, which discuss cross-sector information and knowledge management, and the importance of transparency and accountability to reduce politicization and manipulation of aid, while also improving planning.

40 Simon Mainwaring (2011) *We First* (New York: Palgrave Macmillan): 4.

What Role Management Development Has to Play in Growing International Companies

PEDRO NUENO, José F. Bertran Professor of Entrepreneurship, IESE Business School, University of Navarra, and President, CEIBS

Introduction

M anagement development must prepare managers to successfully address the issues they will find in their day-to day-work applying proven management knowledge. From quantitative management frameworks, like the balance sheet or the income statement, through the more conceptual, like the marketing plan or the corporate strategy, we have management knowledge with universal value, but it is affected by specific variables when the scope of the management process is global. Over the years, management scholars have studied the process of internationalization and its impact on management. In this chapter we will try to follow the process of specific global management knowledge creation and its application to management development programs.

The international dimension

Crossing borders with business is as old as business itself. We could put it differently: borders never stopped business when the opportunity was clear. There is evidence going back more than 2000 years. But if we look to corporations more close to how we understand them today, we see also that they travelled very early when their products appealed to distant markets, in spite of the difficulties. Otis Elevators equipped the George Washington Monument in Washington in 1888, and the Eiffel Tower in Paris in 1899. Nestlé deployed through Europe and the Americas in the early twentieth century. Singer Sewing Machines was a leader in Europe and the Americas as early as the 1860s.

We can imagine the difficulties of operating internationally a century and more ago, with the limited available logistics, underdeveloped financial systems, government controls, unavailability of qualified people, language barriers and so on.

Growing academic interest in the process of internationalization
American companies

The 1960s saw a surge of academic interest in the process of business internationalization. Raymond Vernon, at the Harvard Business School, catalyzed the study of business crossing borders through his teaching and doctoral supervision. Yahir Aharoni, working for his doctorate at Harvard under the supervision of Vernon and others, did a rigorous analysis of the process of foreign direct investment that was published by the Division of Research of the Harvard Business School as *The Foreign Investment Decision Process* in 1961.[1] John Stopford, Louis Wells, Robert Stobaugh and many other academics did their doctoral thesis under Raymond Vernon in the 1960s on the analysis of the process of internationalization. Many of them would focus later their careers on it.

At another level, Peter Drucker, with his masterpiece *The Age of Discontinuity*[2] brought experienced-based organized knowledge in the step of going global to the business community with his capacity to communicate business relevance. For Drucker, the world economy had entered a new era in which things would be different, and he labelled the irreversible process "globalization."

The Harvard Business School followed the study of the process using its famous "case method" approach with the work of Robert Stobaugh. The speed of foreign direct investment by American companies had grown so much that the unions became very alarmed. If companies invested abroad they exported jobs, and this would be bad for America. The press took up the issue in negative headings. The US Department of Commerce was concerned and agreed to do a study with the Harvard Business School. The study, published by the US Department of Commerce[3] and by Harvard University,[4] concluded that foreign direct investment created jobs in America, and should companies not follow this path they would weaken and would end up losing portions of their domestic market to imports from foreign companies.

The fast-growing process of corporate internationalization was also perceived by some leaders as a political threat. Would foreign investment be a new form of political conquering? Raymond Vernon helped also to evaluate the issue as one of the variables of the process, contributing ideas to manage this aspect.[5]

European foreign direct investment

European companies also increased their globalization speed in the 1960s and 1970s, but never with the concentration, volume and impact of the US companies. Looking for some more European developments in foreign direct investment, we can notice that even within the European Union crossing borders always implied dealing with different languages, cultures and therefore customer behaviors, as well as different regulations and cost structures. These small, specific but not easy markets allowed the growth of strong specialized mid-size companies that managed to become world champions and conquered relevant global market shares in medium or small total markets. Hermann Simon has studied this phenomenon in depth and coined the name "hidden champions" for these small and mid-size global players, many of which are European companies.[6,7]

Japanese foreign direct investment

Japanese companies also accelerated their globalization efforts and marched together to Europe and America with relevant concentration in the 1980s. The process involved many acquisitions of companies that perhaps did not have too much future but could be a good launching pad for strong Japanese players. The strength of Japanese companies was based on technology and operations (being labelled "The Toyota Manufacturing System,"[8] an effective operations model that allowed substantial quality and productivity improvements).

The sudden growth of important international investment by Japanese companies in Europe and America also created a certain alarm there, as Lawrence Franko analyzes in his book *The Threat of Japanese Multinations – How the West can Respond.*[9]

By the mid-1980s the world market was defined by Kenichi Ohmae[10] as a "triad," namely Europe, the USA and Japan, and he explored the main characteristics of global competition. Ohmae summarizes his analysis in three messages for corporations that wanted to succeed in his "triad" global market: (1) foster the capacity to work with others (competition with cooperation);

(2) seek a model that is rooted not on differential aspects of regions within the "triad," but on similarities in production and consumption; (3) be committed: develop a global culture and a global perspective in the corporation, and base it on a well-designed global infrastructure.

The new emerging world

The 1990s saw the acceleration of internationalization towards Latin America, India and China, and the twenty-first century added Africa. The "triad" grew to a group of seven key areas. The tremendous growth of the global market probably contributed to many companies modifying their managerial model into one that could fit this huge reality. We can find excellent suggestions for a better understanding of these new markets coming from outstanding practitioners like Stephen Roach of Morgan Stanley,[11] considered one of the leading experts on Asia, or relevant academics, like Martin Wolf, who includes in his analysis the key aspects of Asia, Africa and Latin America.[12] Tarun Khana and Krishna Palepu as well as John Quelch, from the Harvard Business School, present in their work practical toolkits to develop this "global model" of strategy formulation and practical execution, proposing the details to examine in every functional area and the approach to integrate them in a globally coherent way.[13]

As the global market grew, the approach to guide management clearly evolved around the idea of an in-depth, locally sensitive, analysis, and an adequate balancing of the local analysis to formulate a general model that could fit the different realities and satisfy their critical requirements. The formulation of this model, well presented by Khana and Palepu, as indicated above, was initiated by C. K. Prahalad and Ives Doz in the 1980s.[14]

Global differences and similarities

As efforts were made to develop global managerial approaches, a debate erupted about how global markets really were. *The World is Flat* by Thomas L. Friedman[15] was a bestseller and had quite an impact on introducing the idea that as global growth accelerated, the critical aspects of markets would converge, and companies would undergo soft development as global players. The assumption of the flat world was taken as a basis to define management models, including that by Victor Fung, William Fung and Jerry Wind in their book *Competing in a Flat World*,[16] an excellent example of designing successful management models that handle international differences without entering into their details.

But looking at the same reality other leading researchers directed their attention to the importance of international differences and the fact that, when well measured, in spite of fast growth, there was still a long way to go. Pankaj Ghamawat is the intellectual leader of "careful globalization" and the need to pay due regard to local differences in the formulation of global management models.[17]

Management development programs

If we look at the way management schools serve what they perceive as the management needs of the markets, we observe that leading schools tend to increase their global reach and that their offer of programs is similar regardless the continent in which they are based. Most schools offer the Master of Business Administration, the MBA, a program that requires full-time involvement for one or two years for people in their late twenties. Most also offer Executive MBA programs that are similar in content to the MBAs, aimed at people in their thirties with relevant experience of work in corporations or institutions; these Executive MBAs or graduate programs are on a part-time basis and require intensive work. Some schools also conduct a doctoral program (DBA or PhD), intended for advanced academic studies of management. These programs take four or more years of intensive research-based work.

The other category of study offered by many business schools is the programs addressed to executives or entrepreneurs with experience. There is a wide variety of programs, ranging from general management programs that require several weeks or even months of work, although the programs may be split into one-week or one-day modules spread over a long period of time, to focussed programs that address a functional area (strategy formulation, for instance) or specific problem areas (mergers and acquisitions, for example).

A third important format of management development is the company-specific programs, designed to fit the specific needs of corporations at a given moment. A company might have gone through an important acquisition process and want the resulting new management team to approach the future with adequate attention to operating opportunities (synergies, for instance) through the development of a new corporate culture. A training program addressing these issues is often considered helpful.

MBA programs were born in the first years of the twentieth century. The Harvard Business School, for example, launched its MBA in 1908. But executive education can be considered to have been born after the Second World War. Frank Folts, a professor at the HBS, received a request to organize a training program for people who had been assigned management responsibilities unexpectedly during the war, when other more experienced people had had to take direct responsibilities at the front. This training activity, which Harvard remembers as "The War Effort," was transformed after the war into the Advanced Management Program (AMP), a general management program that has been a reference for executive education worldwide since then.

Teaching methods

A professor is expected to add value to his or her students through what happens in the classroom under his or her direction. The content that will enrich the students may be made up of information such as data, frameworks, concepts, history, forecasts, hypotheses, and so on. Students can be enriched through the development of their capacities: to analyze, communicate, convince, lead, and many others. The Harvard Business School also made a breakthrough contribution to management education with the case method. Malcom McNair, a Harvard professor, as early as 1954 presented a history of the case method at the HBS.[18]

A key person in the stimulus of the production and utilization of cases, as well as in the better understanding of cases as a learning tool, was Professor Andrew R. Towl. He became Director of the Division of Case Development soon after he joined the HBS in 1944. He also collaborated in the launching of the Intercollegiate Case Clearing House, with the objective of promoting the case method as a learning tool across schools all over the world.

Another excellent book on the case method came about thirty years later, when the objectives set by Andrew Towl had been achieved and the case method had attained international leadership. In this instance, the authors interviewed more than eighty professors around the world who used the case method and developed a comprehensive and practical manual on this teaching methodology.[19]

Three leading business schools were born in Europe that followed the Harvard program portfolio as well as the class approach. These were INSEAD in France, IMEDE in Switzerland (known later as IMD), and IESE in Spain. IESE was perhaps the closest European school to Harvard, a fact acknowledged by the Dean of the Harvard Business School, George Baker, in a speech in Barcelona, on 22 June 1966. This was, on the occasion of the graduation of the first MBA class of IESE, which Baker referred to as having "a very similar approach to the Harvard model."[20] Baker said in his speech that he expected a long-standing international collaboration of IESE and HBS, given their close relationship and similar approaches, and mentioned Latin America as their first challenge. Indeed both schools have collaborated in Latin America and in Europe. In the early 2000s, Harvard and IESE extended their collaboration to Asia where they offered together with the China Europe International Business School (CEIBS) a General Management Program addressed to top Chinese CEOs. The program, almost fifty years after Dean Baker's forecast, was heavily based on the case method. And in 2008, marking the centenary of the Harvard Business School, sitting in a class as a guest, observing a case discussion at HBS with Chinese CEOs, and with an IESE professor teaching, was retired Professor Andrew Towl, the director of case development in the 1940s. In an interview published on 3 September 2011 in the business magazine *Expansion*, Dean Nithin Nohria, of the HBS, confirmed the close coincidence in approach between the Harvard Business School and IESE.

Basic framework

As indicated above, the vitality of any field of activity requires a continuous process of research that advances the frontier of basic knowledge. This is true of management, and every functional area has seen progress in better understanding of the key aspects in the field as well as in tools for better implementation of key tasks.

If we look at operations, we see how considerable knowledge has been contributed to a better handling of the basic framework of operations, the value adding chain. Probably the definition of operations as a field of knowledge goes back to the post-1945 period, following publication of Jack Wolff's book *The Production Conference*.[21] The approach to managing a "value adding chain," with key decisions such as what to produce and what to purchase, has an intellectual pillar in *Purchasing and Materials Management*.[22] The field of operations experienced an important input by Japanese knowledge development around the "Toyota Production System," as already noted.

Similar developments can be found in other functional areas. Derek Abell and John Hammond produced one of the key pillars for the marketing area, bringing frameworks for developing the marketing mix, how elements can be combined in a coherent way and finally integrated effectively in corporate strategy.[23] Scholars including Chris Argyris,[24] Abraham Zaleznik,[25] and Ralph Hower[26] contributed to establishing the field of human behavior. And we can find similar efforts in other functional areas.

At the same time, other scholars of the management field were looking for frameworks to integrate the various functional areas in one specific direction called "strategy." The key contributor in this area is most likely Michael Porter with his early work *Competitive Strategy*,[27] followed by many other bestselling publications. His model of the "five forces" has become a standard framework to set up a realistic strategic direction. Strategy implementation required a close connection with the corporate structure. This was pioneered by Alfred Chandler with his in-depth studies of leading American companies.[28]

Another integrative framework came from the perspective of creating new companies or new units within a company, or reorganizing the company, and this has been covered under the label of entrepreneurship. Entrepreneurship became a component of management education in the early 1970s when the HBS launched courses on Starting New Companies in its MBA, and MIT offered MBA students courses on How to Write a Business Plan. The Business Plan is the "entrepreneurial" format of the Strategic Plan.

Howard Stevenson, a professor at HBS, is a leader in bringing entrepreneurship to the classroom and contributing to the international spread of teaching entrepreneurship. His *Entrepreneurship, What It Is and How to Teach It* of 1983 was followed by many other publications.[29] Authors also furthered the critical development of business plans, including La Rue Hosmer of Michigan Business School.[30]

Entrepreneurship is without doubt the management area that has experienced the fastest growth in leading business schools in the last twenty and more years. IESE launched the first European MBA course on entrepreneurial management in 1974. This course required students to develop a business plan. The author participated in this effort and contributed some publications.[31]

There are other fields of "integrative" knowledge with a relevant impact on management that are also key to management development institutions. We could mention economics, which has to be seen both as a theory providing a general framework to business, but also as an environment of international scope and interrelationships that affects most aspects of business in continuously changing ways.

Ethics and corporate social responsibility are also general integrative knowledge areas that have a key impact on management as the environment (economy, technology, culture, law) changes. Management schools have always attached great importance to these subjects, and among the required reading for all doctoral students at Harvard Business School in the early 1970s were William Frankena, *Ethics*[32] and Clarence Walton, *Corporate Social Responsibilities*.[33]

Leadership can be considered another integrative framework. Energy, skills, negotiation, and other capacities must be put to work to transform strategy into action, and action into the desired results. Leadership is about this. See, for example, *The Future of Leadership Development* edited by Jordi Canals.[34]

The application to international management development programs

As we have tried to describe, the vitality of the management education sector stimulates a continuous development of knowledge either in the functional areas of management (finance, marketing, operations, human behavior, and others) or in the so-called integrative and horizontal fields (strategy, entrepreneurship, economy, ethics, and others). It is important to make sure that this knowledge is incorporated to management practice. Following Peter Drucker, management is not a science but a practice and can be compared to medical practice. There is considerable scientific development in medically related areas (biotechnology, for example), as there is in many technical areas that can be applications in medicine. But when doctors face the patient they must apply this knowledge and this is the medical practice. To apply this pool of managerial knowledge several aspects need to be taken into account.

Understanding the world

The world has growing similarities but many differences continue to exist (legal, cultural, economic). This situation occurs with a changing speed and uncertainty. The result is that risks and opportunities may appear and disappear.

In one way or another the key elements of this international changing reality must be in the background of any management development program today. This can be accomplished through a combination of lecture/discussions directly addressing the topic plus the fact that any other teaching materials (cases, notes, books) pick up relevant aspects of the theme.

Developing a global corporate culture

The author had the opportunity to meet many of the executives who were sent to China to open that market for their corporations in the 1980s and 1990s. They had a highly coincident profile: many were in their sixties (they often said that if they had not taken that job they would most probably been asked to retire), had a long international experience with their corporations, knew them well (had been in many positions in different business units), had a general management perspective, were enthusiastic about people, entrepreneurial and loved their companies. Talking to them, it was possible to see how they were adapting their company's culture to the environment, preserving the first but taking into consideration the key aspects of the second.

Corporate strategy implies ways to address customers, favours product innovation and has specific industrial and logistical requirements. Accounting and financial frameworks, even though they are standard, may have different approaches to reporting, accessing the capital markets or financing working capital and investments. Balancing these practices with a specific environment is also an art and requires a good understanding of both the managerial frameworks and competitive environments. The way these two areas are integrated in different world environments elicits a common approach through this corporate culture.

Looking after global opportunity

Fast creation of value—entrepreneurial growth—requires identification of opportunities and rapidly transforming them into business processes that satisfy them. Opportunities may be global, as in the case of a new pharmaceutical formula. But global development may offer opportunities in areas that are mature markets in Europe or in America, as is the case of the automotive industry in China. Global development may also lead to new ways of doing things, and therefore new opportunities. Probably the threshold of civilization today is reached when it is possible to have access to a mobile phone. This is creating many opportunities for companies like Vodafone in Africa to launch, among other things, medical services through the phone.

Exploiting opportunity requires what Howard Stevenson called "bottom up" strategy formulation. This means a process of listening to the organization in search of opportunity.

Designing an international management development program

The need for management development

The process of globalization combined with the fast evolution of industries and technologies makes management development increasingly necessary. The possibility to leave intensive day-to-day activity and be able to see it from a certain distance, combined with the opportunity to imagine oneself in a variety of radically different environments that exist today, is a tremendous enrichment for a manager. Companies can expect a return from developing their managers in the form of better management that will imply efficiency, innovation, and entrepreneurship.

As a professor of management, the author remembers cases of managers complaining that it was not always possible to apply the things they had learned in the classroom. Corporate systems are sometimes too rigid, which may lead to a lack of coherence between the capacities available and those developed in the organization and the possibility to exercise these capacities. This should be an area of concern for those responsible for management development, and for top management particularly.

Bringing the international reality to the classroom

If we are trying to develop managers to work in an international context (and it is difficult to imagine a management context that it is not international today), it is important to make sure that the learning process takes place with an immersion in this global environment while highlighting its most relevant aspects (economic, political, cultural, uncertainty).

Since management development programs for obvious reasons have a limited duration, it is necessary to find attractive ways to present this international scenario with its important relevant content in a summarized way. In other words, what can be the content of a full course in an MBA becomes a few sessions in a program addressed to chief executive officers.

Another practical way to bring the global environment to the classroom is the utilization of the case method, using cases that deal with problems in an international context affecting companies and executives who also act at an international level.

The teaching methodology

The teaching methodology recommended is the case method. The case itself can contain much international information. Imagine a case study on a company in America that has acquired another company in China and looks for integration, synergies, new opportunities in the US or in China with the products of each other's company, and so on. The case could also contain relevant information on the environments of the two companies (economic, legal, industrial, competitive).

If the case discussion is adequately managed by the teacher it can also facilitate learning from each other by the class participants. This leads to the selection of the class participants. Leading business schools have organized an international team managing executive education (promotion; admission; assignment to programs, groups or sections), which can create a rich diversity inside the classroom in terms of nationalities, types of companies, and industrial sectors. This variety of perspectives greatly enriches the "learning from each other" component.

Production of cases is growing continuously, and leading business schools from all over the world contribute to it. This means that today we can count on an enormous pool of cases available that facilitate the design of not only international programs (general or focussed on one area) but even company-specific programs addressing sets of issues especially relevant for a company at a given period of its evolution.

Creating a multinational setting

As indicated above, creating a multinational setting can be the task of an experienced management development team. The administrative program supervisors interact constantly with program participants. They talk with them and might receive positive comments but also some complaints. Together with faculty they can develop specific ways to create a multicultural class setting. There are many variables involved and this is not an easy task.

If a program takes place in a prestigious American business school participants, particularly those from emerging markets, will tend to act with care and respect. If it is the other way around, a program take place in a leading institution in a developing country or region, participants from that region may feel proud and be more radical about their views. The key to learning from each other is respect, and this is obviously the key value to be promoted in creating a corporate culture that takes the best of everybody: respect. Both faculty and staff can do much to promote this attitude in all aspects of the program and the relationships it requires. Respect given to faculty, to other class participants, and to program administrators will produce a positive and stimulating environment with increased learning potential.

Faculty

Last but not least, faculty will be the most important element to guarantee the quality and the value-adding of an international management development program. Most faculty members in leading management schools now have an international background: they were born in country A, educated partially in country B, took a PhD in management in country C, taught for a period in country D, and are finally developing a career as a professor in country E. The specifics of A, B, C, D, and E are different for professors who share lunch regularly in their school restaurant. This is quite normal today.

But professors must have their feet on the international ground, the same ground on which their program participants have their feet. And this means that professors must closely follow what goes on in the corporate world. This can be accomplished through a rich combination of interactions: basic research, case writing, problem-solving through consulting, and supervision from directorship in boards. For many leading business schools a faculty member should spend 25 per cent of his or her time, through her career, on research (which can include theoretical models, framework development, practical cases to bring problems to the classroom, books to diffuse management knowledge in a widely accessible language). Faculty members are supposed to spend another 25 per cent of their time in practical assignments as problem-solving consultants or as board directors.

With this type of background faculty members should be prepared to work comfortably in an international classroom. One could say that professors themselves have experienced many times in their life the wealth of perspectives, attitudes, and reactions most likely to be found in an international class. But it will be good to remember the words of the Professor Frank Folts, credited with launching management education at Harvard Business School after the Second World War with the AMP program, while at the same time helping as an advisor to several schools around the world, particularly Keio in Japan and IESE in Europe. He said: "You may not understand all cultural aspects of a culture that it is not yours; for those aspects you do not understand, respect." Respect, as already discussed, is the clear success factor in managing a classroom. Respect is coherent with a certain "push" to get people to participate in a comfortable way. The class needs a process with controlled timing that guides the discussion in the direction needed to produce learning points. Some professors summarize for the class looking for these "learning points," which are somewhere on the blackboard, mixed with other things, and they mark them by underlining them in the closing minutes.

Obviously experience is a key ingredient for faculty to develop these skills, but most of these things can also be learned, and there are International Teachers Programs, or organized class attendances, to learn how other professors manage an international classroom.

Conclusion

We have seen how management development programs started, how the international concern emerged and grew. We have looked at how management knowledge developed and evolved (theoretical concepts, frameworks, functional, integrative); and at how these elements were integrated into management development programs (contents, teaching methodologies). Finally, we have gone into some depth on designing international management development programs as the key elements of their success: experienced faculty and staff, and high-quality international cases.

We see the field of management development growing as the fields affecting management change at dramatic speed (the world economy, technology, competition). We see that management development is international because the field in which companies operate is every day becoming more international. But there is a great vitality in the creation of knowledge applicable to this field, and those responsible for management development must make sure that this knowledge gets into the programs in the right way. Management development must be coherent with corporate strategy.

NOTES

1 Yahir Aharoni (1966) *The Foreign Investment Decision Process* (Boston, MA: Graduate School of Business Administration, Harvard University).

2 Peter Drucker (1968) *The Age of Discontinuity* (New York, NY: Harper and Row).

3 US Department of Commerce, Bureau of International Commerce (1972) *The Multinational Corporation: Studies on US Foreign Investment, Volume I* (Washington DC; US Government Printing Office).

4 Robert B. Stobaugh (1976) *Nine Investments Abroad and Their Impact at Home: Case Studies on Multinational Enterprise and the US Economy* (Boston, MA: Graduate School of Business Administration, Harvard University).

5 Raymond Vernon (1972) *The Economic and Political Consequences of Multinational Enterprise: An Anthology* (Boston, MA: Graduate School of Business Administration, Harvard University).

6 Hermann Simon (1996) *Hidden Champions* (Boston, MA: Harvard Business School Press).

7 Hermann Simon (2009), *Hidden Champions of the 21st Century* (New York, NY: Springer).

8 Yasuhiro Monden (1987) *El Sistema de Producción de Toyota* (Barcelona: IESE, 1987, 1988) (original publication 1981).

9 Lawrence Franko (1983) *The Thread of Japanese Multinationals—How the West Can Respond* (New York, NY: John Wiley and Sons).

10 Kenichi Ohmae, *Triad Power: The Coming Shape of Global Competition* (New York, NY: The Free Press, 1985).

11 Stephen Roach (2009) *The Next Asia: Opportunities and Challenges for a New Globalization* (Hoboken, NJ: John Wiley & Sons).

12 Martin Wolf (2004) *Why Globalization Works: The Case for the Global Economy* (New Haven, CT: Yale University Press).

13 Tarun Khanna and Krishna G. Palepu (2010) *Winning in Emerging Markets: A Road Map for Strategy and Execution* (Boston, MA: Harvard University Press); and John Quelch (2004) *The Global Market: Developing a Strategy to Manage Across Borders* (San Francisco, CA: Jossey-Bass, John Wiley and Sons).

14 C. K. Prahalad and Yves L. Doz (1987) *The Multinational Mission: Balancing Local Demands and Global Vision* (New York, NY: The Free Press).

15 Thomas L. Friedman (2005) *The World is Flat* (New York, NY: Farrar, Straus and Giroux).

16 Victor K. Fung, William K. Fung and Yoram (Jerry) Wind (2007) *Competing in a Flat World* (Upper Saddle River, NJ: Wharton School Publishing).

17 Pankaj Ghemawat (2007) *Redefining Global Strategy: Crossing Borders in a World Where Differences Still Matter* (Boston, MA: Harvard Business School Publishing Corporation).

18 Malcolm P. McNair (1954) *The Case Method at the Harvard Business School* (New York, NY: McGraw-Hill); also C. Roland Christensen (1987) *Teaching and the Case Method* (Boston, MA: Harvard Business School).

19 James A. Erskine, Michiel R. Leenders and Louse A. Mauffette-Leenders (1981) *Teaching with Cases* (London, Canada: Research and Publications Division, School of Business Administration, University of Western Ontario).

20 Félix Huerta (ed.) (1967) *A Starting Point* (Barcelona: IESE).

21 Jack L. Wolff (1944) *The Production Conference* (Boston, MA: Houghton Mifflin Company).

22 Michiel R. Leenders, Harold E. Fearon and Wilbur B. England (1980) *Purchasing and Materials Management* (Homewood, IL: Richard D. Irwin).

23 Derek Abell and John S. Hammond (1979) *Strategic Market Planning* (Englewood Cliffs, NJ: Prentice Hall).

24 Chris Argyris (1960) *Understanding Organizational Behavior* (Homewood, IL: The Dorsey Press).

25 Abraham Zaleznick (1956) *Worker Satisfaction and Development* (Boston, MA: Graduate School of Business Administration, Harvard University).

26 John Desmond Glover and Ralph M. Hower (1957) *The Administrator* (Homewood, IL: Richard D. Irwin).

27 Michael E. Porter (1980) *Competitive Strategy* (New York, NY: The Free Press).

28 Alfred D. Chandler (1962) *Strategy and Structure* (Cambridge, MA: MIT Press).

29 John I. Kao and Howard H. Stevenson (1983) *Entrepreneurship: What It Is and How to Teach It* (Boston, MA: Harvard Business School); see also William A. Shalman and Howard H. Stevenson (1991) *The Entrepreneurial Venture* (Boston, MA: Harvard Business School); and Howard H. Stevenson (1998) *Do Lunch or Be Lunch* (Boston, MA: Harvard Business School Press).

30 La Rue Hosmer and Roger Guiles (1985) *Creating the Successful Business Plan for New Ventures* (New York, NY: McGraw-Hill).

31 Pedro Nueno (2005), *Entrepreneuring Towards 2010* (Barcelona: Ediciones Deusto); also, Pedro Nueno, *Letters to a Young Entrepreneur* (Barcelona: Ediciones Experiencia).

32 William K. Frankena (1963), *Ethics* (Englewood Cliffs, NJ: Prentice Hall).

33 Clarence C. Walton (1967) *Corporate Social Responsibilities* (Belmont, CA: Wadsworth Publishing Company).

34 Jordi Canals (ed.) (2011) *The Future of Leadership Development* (Houndmills: Palgrave Macmillan).

CHAPTER 2.3

Five Easy Questions

EDWARD A. SNYDER, Dean and William S. Beinecke Professor of Economics and Management, Yale School of Management

Introduction

The purpose of this chapter is to provoke useful thinking about the future of management education, or, more precisely, about the high-end segment of management education. Given that one cannot suggest where management education should focus without considering the nature of the leadership challenges for the balance of this challenging century, my intended audience includes both fellow deans and faculty members at the top business schools as well as aspiring leaders in all sectors.

To the extent that my provocations about changing management education are aggravating, I ask for forgiveness. The job of organizing business schools in the modern world is not easy, and one should not add unnecessarily to the burdens. But I do suggest a reallocation of efforts that is guided by a sense of the competencies that leaders will need going forward. In brief, leaders first must have a keen understanding of markets and competition. Second, leaders must understand how to lead, which means understanding their role within the organization, enhancing the performance of various types of teams, and the increasing power of networks in the modern economy. Yet the five questions I pose point to the importance of a third competence, the ability to understand and navigate complexity, within and across societies. Modern leaders in the for-profit sector, in the social and entrepreneurial sectors, and in government are connected to a broad mix of opportunities and challenges throughout a world which itself is non-convergent. Even when they are successful in particular settings, they must weaken presumptions of future success in favor of the recognition that they must continually assess situations, done best in my view with the classical frameworks, and rigorously attend to dissimilarities.

The Qs and As

As the title of this chapter indicates, the five questions are relatively easy to answer. I do not claim to provide the best or definitive answers to the questions posed, but my threshold answers yield implications for leaders and for top business schools. With these prefatory comments, let me proceed.

Question 1: Have market-oriented economies won?

Yes. The world's population is now approximately seven billion.[1] If one were to go back 25 or 30 years and presume that the ways of organizing economic activity in various countries had not changed in the intervening period, then we would have three billion fewer of the world's population connected to the world's market-oriented economy. Instead, the actual economic reforms in China and India alone have had a monumental effect in adding vibrancy to the world economy and to benefiting their societies. In addition, market-oriented economies have replaced planned economies in many other countries, including Russia, Central Europe, Eastern Europe, Indonesia, and various countries in Africa and Latin America.[2] One can debate the definition of the term *market-oriented economies* and also point to the many deficiencies in how various economies function, but taking the point of view of individual citizens and enterprises, the core features of markets, for example, the role of prices and wages in guiding economic activity along with the potential effects of the entry and exit of firms in many sectors, one must conclude that the shift of populations to the market has been huge.

Question 2: Have governments become more important in the context of market-oriented economies?

Yes. If one were to look at government's share of GDP over the last century by country, the growth of governments has been dramatic.[3] Beyond the share of resources under government control, governments now play a bigger role in regulating economic activity, including trade. Particular areas like competition policy have boomed, with virtually all major economies now having versions of the US antitrust laws.[4] Governments within market-oriented economies attempt to regulate many aspects of markets, including product safety, the provision of medical services, labor markets, and environmental protections.

Question 3: Have market-oriented economies converged in terms of practice?

No. I should admit that I was among the naïve Western economists involved in the economic transitions who thought that we would indeed experience convergence of practice.[5] My first substantial challenge to this view came when, during the mid-1990s, I recognized that India was not going to move quickly, or necessarily at all, to a model of property and decision rights that I viewed as efficient. It was not sufficient, or maybe even relevant, that India had English common law, a long history of democracy, and an educated segment who knew law, business, and governance issues as well as any segment in the world. For a set of complex reasons, decision-making and governance in India were not going to become like the UK or the US.

Now it is clear that there is no convergence in terms of how market-oriented economies work generally. China, the most striking case, is governed by a complex combination of important ministries in a federal context, with the Communist Party playing a substantial role in guiding the direction of the economy.[6] While I am not an expert on China despite my many experiences there since 1993, I readily appreciate its uniqueness.

Many factors underlie this lack of convergence, including economic factors themselves such as whether the country has a sound financial system, its fiscal profile, trade policies, and, as is now understood, the relative importance of natural resources in GDP. There are also non-economic factors, including culture. But the bottom line point is that one's understanding of China may be of little use in understanding India, and little applies from India to Russia. Thus, while prices and other market signals direct economic activity in many countries, the organization of the economy and the role of various institutions, including religious institutions, and the day-to-day allocations of time by senior executives in various types of enterprises are all hugely different. In these fundamental respects, there is no convergence of practice.

Question 4: Have the market-oriented economies around the world become globalized and more connected?

Yes. The consensus view about globalization is right in that we are more connected, and the relevant competitive pressures on particular economies are more weighted from outside and often from a broad scope of countries. In economic terms, the scale of global trade has expanded and, because of technology, the very definition of what can be traded has expanded.[7] My own view is that the process of globalization is far from over. We are not close to *factor-price equilibria* whereby factor prices around the globe, subject to quality differences and transportation cost effects, equalize. I realize that many countries are engaged in the erection of trade and non-trade barriers, which will slow this process.[8] Plus we see a shift to complex trade agreements involving smaller numbers of countries. But my bet is that the process will go forward and markets will find ways to realize most of the big gains.[9]

Question 5: What is the nature of the issues facing societies now?

If I were to pick two words to describe these issues, I would select *big* and *multi-faceted*. For sure, those adjectives apply to the following three categories of issues facing societies around the world:

1. Energy and the environment

2. Human capital—health and education

3. Income disparities and political pressures.

Each category of issues raises specific concerns and, more importantly,[10] advances entail efforts across major disciplines and functions. One may be tempted to say that government must play a big role or even the lead role. Yet the notion that the public sector can organize the multi-faceted and long-term approach to addressing these mega issues should give way to a more realistic view of what governments do. The bottom line is that we are faced with issues that are extraordinarily difficult.

Implications for leaders

These easy questions lead directly to three fundamental implications for leaders in all sectors for the balance of this century.

1. Leaders will operate in market-oriented economies, but within those economies, governments will play a bigger role.

2. Leaders will be more connected to other economies around the world, but these close connections will be combined with a confusing lack of convergence in terms of how these economies operate.

3. Leaders in all sectors will be asked to contribute to the solutions of mega issues that are multi-faceted and whose solutions involve efforts that span sectors.

Though not individually startling or controversial, in combination these implications suggest portrayals of future leaders—in many different countries and in many different sectors—that are quite different from earlier decades. Confronting multi-faceted, big challenges and operating in environments where there are many points of departure, future leaders will require skill sets that are weighted differently. Everyday behaviors of high-impact leaders will emphasize continual and disciplined assessment of situations, efforts to listen and leverage those within available networks, and receptivity to feedback and challenge.

Implications for management education

Management education and the MBA degree in particular over the last four decades is a success story. The huge growth of degrees and the entry of literally thousands of business schools around the world should be kept in mind when the recent and useful concerns about management education are raised. My previously articulated explanations for the success of management education during this period emphasize the importance of economic transitions and globalization, but also posit that business degrees and the MBA degree in particular have become the most useful means of developing two fundamental competencies:[11]

1. *Understanding how markets work and the unrelenting nature of competition.*

2. *Understanding how organizations function and the role of teams, networks, and individual leadership.*

This *two-competency model* has served graduates well because, first, whatever the setting and whatever the rules of the game so to speak, competition never is absent. Just consider IBM of the 1960s and 1970s, the Catholic Church over its long history, or the rise and fall of various political parties. Second, as former Stanford GSB Dean Robert Joss often emphasized, in modern society rarely does an individual exert great impact absent his or her ability to leverage organizations, teams, and networks.[12] We may revere Steve Jobs as an innovator, but he would have had no measurable impact absent his ability to leverage an organization, which in turn leveraged many different types of markets.

The two-competency model does not, however, incorporate the implications I have drawn above. As stated when I was announced as Dean at Yale

School of Management in January 2010,[13] the interactions within and across business and society, the connections to a world lacking in convergence, and the nature of the mega issues facing society, in combination, place a new kind of burden on future leaders, which in turn implies a *third competency*:

> 3. *Understanding the complexities within and across business and society to enable leadership in a more complex world.*

If this three-competency model is useful, then what are the implications for management education? One cannot simply say teach complexity. Yet several steps can be taken within the flow of what top business schools do, including the following:

1. Emphasize intellectual curiosity, rigor, and broadmindedness in admissions over other attributes, e.g., career progression within a particular field. The analogous point can be made regarding faculty recruitment and development.

2. Leverage assets outside the business school. The notion of an actual or *de facto* standalone business school should be resisted.

3. Create a presumption or even requirements that MBA students should take classes elsewhere (in the university or in a university) even though, as is often the case, those classes are not as 'well taught' in the sense of carefully prescribed content. (It is a good thing for MBA students to begin to listen to and leverage expertise that is not necessarily well-packaged.)

4. Create a presumption that MBA students should do exchanges in places that are different. I have nothing against students from Yale going to London, and for many it makes great sense, but my instinct is that more should go to Brazil, China, India, Indonesia, South Korea, and Turkey.

5. Foster a culture of feedback, questioning, and ongoing assessment. These are the everyday behaviors that future leaders need to help navigate complexity.

6. Connect students and faculty on an ongoing basis to peers around the world. Always look for opportunities to compare and contrast.

I hasten to offer my view that a classical and rigorous approach to developing the first two competencies is best. Our graduates are the embodiment of long-term human capital. Frameworks, disciplines, and empirical inquiry serve our students well when it comes to the core of the MBA, and by contrast we do them no favors by being less rigorous. Related to point 5 above, developing in our students an empirical orientation, grounded in disciplinary frameworks will allow them to become the types of business people who "see around corners," who pierce through complexity, and who avoid the mistakes of presuming that approaches that work in one domain are necessarily appropriate for the next.

I wish I could find a great metaphor to summarize the sense of this. I find extraordinarily appealing the notion that our future graduates will be able to put their heads down and work through difficult problems using frameworks, that they will be able to listen and leverage those immediately around them, and that they will be able to connect to those further away and assess the potential power and limitations of their approach. Pivot tables should not scare them, but they should know how to look up and pivot to see an extraordinarily complex world close to them. Opportunities abound if they develop the right values and everyday behaviors.

What should business schools do less of? My answers follow quite directly. There should be less core programming that is not rigorous within the first two competencies. International exchanges and programs in safe areas should be cut. Yet more controversial: Hire fewer traditional business school faculty members and leverage broader intellectual assets. Finally, scrap all ethics and leadership programs that do not emphasize feedback, assessment, and questioning. Top-down teaching of these critically important areas is not worth it. Finally, there is far too much emphasis on financial crises. Macroeconomics is important and has gotten more so relative to microeconomics. But policy shifts concerning particular currencies and institutions are temporal issues. The reason we have experienced financial crises is quite simple: The world is more competitive and the incumbent economies (US, Europe, and Japan) are under a lot of pressure. The nature of the flattening world is of much more import than the latest news on Greek bonds.

At the Yale School of Management, a reallocation of efforts along these lines is under way. The connections between the business school and other units at Yale are substantial and have historically been close and substantial. Yet against this assessment of the nature of the leadership challenges, including the premium on intellectual curiosity and breadth, the judgment is that the school's connections to Yale need to be strengthened and furthered. Indeed, motivated by the opportunity to leverage broader intellectual assets, one of the school's primary objectives is to become yet more integrated and involved with Yale. The school also has committed to the development of a global network of business schools, potentially positioning students and faculty to be closer to the complexities that are evidence across societies. These and other programmatic changes are explained in more detail in the Appendix.

Concluding remarks

The world of management education is not broken by any means. We are at an extraordinarily exciting period. To develop future leaders we need to focus on classical education in some core areas, and combine that approach with a set of changes that alter the developmental experiences of MBAs, with the objective that our graduates are better able to empirically assess opportunities and navigate a closer world that lacks convergence. One cannot teach complexity, but we should strive to prepare our graduates well to lead effectively in a world that features more complexity within and across societies and that is challenged by multi-faceted, mega issues.

Appendix

The Appendix describes in more detail three initiatives at the Yale School of Management to educate leaders who will understand how to navigate the complexities that exist in a closer world that lacks convergence.

The Global Network for Advanced Management

Below is a draft White Paper written for the Deans and Directors of the top business schools from around the world that are part of the new Global Network for Advanced Management, which officially launched on 26–27 April 2012 in New York City and at Yale University. The White Paper explains the motivations behind and purposes of the GNAM.

31 March 2012

THE GLOBAL NETWORK FOR ADVANCED MANAGEMENT

Motivation
In a flatter world characterized by rugged and diverse terrain, the *Global Network for Advanced Management* is an innovative approach to enable those

involved———faculty at business schools around the world, enterprises in all sectors, and students at various stages of professional development———to connect and address the leadership challenges facing business and society.

Enterprises in all sectors need leaders who understand how markets and organizations work in increasingly diverse and complex contexts. Leadership teams must understand and contribute to the big issues facing societies around the world as well as be able to work effectively in and across regions and sectors, to adapt to the different roles of governments in economies, to master increasingly complicated financial arrangements, and to draw upon ever-closer connections in the modern world. Other important considerations for leaders include an appreciation of a broad range of diversity issues, e.g., the highly variable roles of women in business, and divergent approaches to the environment and education. Leaders also must attend to fundamental questions about enterprise objectives and effective means of aligning incentives and motivating sustained effort in these extraordinarily challenging and exciting times.

The development of the *Global Network for Advanced Management* is a vital response to this diverse landscape as well as to limitations in the ways that business schools and other academic institutions are organized. As Thomas Friedman explained in compelling fashion, the world has flattened over the last three decades, as over three billion people have joined the world's market-oriented economy and businesses have become more global, in large part due to technological advances. The result, as explained recently by Joseph Stiglitz, is that the competition among countries, businesses, entrepreneurs, and employees has intensified, putting acute pressure on all countries and regions, especially the "developed economies." Over this same period of time, top business schools have developed worthwhile international partnerships for specific purposes, for example, student exchanges, joint program offerings. The partnership approach to extending the organizational reach, however, has limitations, as partnerships, typically involving schools of similar perceived quality, are drawn from a limited set of countries. In addition, given their bilateral nature, even a set of well-functioning partnerships cannot match the robust, spanning character of the global economy.

The impetus for the *Global Network for Advanced Management* is to establish a structure for far-reaching and ongoing interactions among those involved. Rather than have a US school ask, "What is the best school in China for us to partner with on a particular program?" or vice versa, the *Network* starts with altogether different questions:

- What are the new areas of economic power and growth in the global economy? What areas of economic power and growth are on the horizon?

- What leadership challenges face enterprises in the future?

- How can top talent from the broad horizons of a flatter global economy be accessed, developed, and connected?

- How can a broad set of business schools work together to address these leadership challenges and enhance leadership development around the globe?

With these questions in mind, then strategies and actions follow naturally. In contrast to the partnership model, where the focus is often on "promising tuition markets," the intention of the new approach is to build on a more meaningful definition of *global* business, to understand the importance of top talent throughout a flatter world, and to leverage the benefits of networks.

Objectives and purposes

The *Global Network for Advanced Management*[14] begins with several core objectives but not a pre-ordained agenda. In contrast to a traditional partnership agreement between schools which specifies that faculty must do certain things, the Network develops an infrastructure that creates opportunities for participating schools, enterprises, student groups, and faculty members to creatively and flexibly take advantage of the power of the network structure. Each member school has full standing in the network and can initiate programs with other participants.

One objective of the *Global Network for Advanced Management* is *the exchange among schools of cases and other curriculum content related to global business issues*. There is a clear need for such content and the network can immediately provide greater access to existing resources.

Second, the network will develop new cases and curriculum content, some involving various global enterprises, which become allied with the network.

Third, the network is committed to developing both an internet portal and website. Based on discussions involving some deans and students, the *portal will feature the capability of connecting student groups among the schools*. Thus, the finance, consulting, entrepreneurial, and marketing clubs of the various schools will be able to establish their own networks to share knowledge and build valuable relationships with fellow students around the world.

Fourth, through a series of launch meetings, the organizing deans and directors, with the benefit of dialogue with enterprise leaders with a global view, will address the central leadership question identified above, that is: What leadership challenges face enterprises in the future?

Fifth, while many schools already have student exchanges and international team experiences, network school facilitation and support will increase and enhance these learning opportunities.

Sixth, the network will allow for the development of economic indices (e.g., comparing the cost of a liter of gas at retail in network school cities/countries).

How the network can serve additional purposes for member schools

The Yale School of Management has developed the following agenda items:

1. connecting the Yale Entrepreneurial Institute (a university-wide resource involving students and faculty throughout Yale) with other groups of entrepreneurs at member schools

2. the development of Yale's Master of Advanced Management degree program, which will only be open to recent graduates of member schools and will be limited in size, that is, fewer than 20 students annually

3. the dissemination of Yale SOM's so-called Raw Cases to member schools

4. the development of new Raw Cases on global management issues with member schools

5. the development of a Fellows Program that brings faculty members from member schools to Yale for short periods of time to interact with the Yale SOM faculty

6. aligning the destinations of our "International Experience" program for first-year student teams with cities/countries where network schools are located.

These initial objectives for the Network and the further specific objectives for the Yale School of Management indicate the potential power of a new approach to organizing business schools based on a more relevant set of objectives and in a manner that reflects emerging business realities.

Expectations of member schools

Member schools will join the *Global Network for Advanced Management* for an initial period ending on June 30, 2015. The most important expectations of membership are participation and the development of an agenda to contribute to, and leverage, the network. Other specific expectations include:

1. At least two reliable points of contact, one being a Dean, Director or equivalent.

2. Regular participations in meetings and conference calls.

3. Substantial contributions of relevant information to the portal, e.g., contact information that allows for student groups to develop working relationships, contact information for relevant faculty, and notices of conferences and symposia that will be of interest to other members of the network.

4. Posting of information concerning programs with other members on the portal and where appropriate the network's website.

The Master of Advanced Management degree program

The second initiative is a document describing the Yale School of Management's new Master of Advanced Management (MAM) degree program. The MAM will provide the participating students with a deeper understanding of the complexities within and between societies, and also will enrich the learning environment at Yale SOM generally, by broadening the global diversity of the school.

MARCH 2012

MASTER OF ADVANCED MANAGEMENT (MAM)

Program overview

In the 2012–13 academic year, the Yale School of Management (Yale SOM) will launch a highly innovative one-year degree program, the Master of Advanced Management (MAM). This program will be open only to graduates of schools who are part of the *Global Network for Advanced Management*.

The program is expected to include about 20 students per year. The program also will engage a group of global enterprises.

With the support of Yale SOM faculty advisors, MAM students will develop an individualized course of study which may include courses not only at Yale SOM, but also at other graduate and professional schools at Yale. The cohort of MAM students will meet regularly with faculty, corporate and enterprise partners, MBA students, and others to explore major issues facing businesses and societies.

MAM students will have access to the full range of Yale SOM resources, including its Career Development Office. MAM students will be expected to develop relationships with Yale MBAs, Yale World Fellows, and others throughout Yale University.

Program rationale and educational objectives

The overarching purpose of the MAM program is to advance Yale SOM's mission of educating leaders for business and society. The program will bring a small group of extraordinary students from outside the US to Yale to further their educational and professional development. The MAM program also will connect top talent from a spanning network set of business schools. The program is motivated by the recognition that enterprises in all sectors need leaders who understand how markets and organizations work in increasingly diverse contexts. Senior leaders also must attend to fundamental questions about enterprise objectives and effective means of aligning incentives. This requires an appreciation of a broad range of diversity issues that are relevant to business, for example, the highly variable roles of women in business and divergent approaches to the environment and education. At the same time, leaders must understand and contribute to the big issues facing societies around the world, as well as be able to work effectively in and across all regions and sectors, to adapt to the different roles of governments in economies, to master increasingly complicated financial arrangements, and to draw upon ever-closer connections in the modern world.

Closer integration of Yale School of Management and Yale University

Thirdly, a brief description follows of curricular efforts to more closely integrate the Yale School of Management with Yale University.

Yale School of Management's close integration with Yale University plays a critical role in producing leaders who understand complexity. The school's strong ties to the University enable it to attract broadminded and intellectually curious students and faculty who think about the big picture. Furthermore, it enables Yale SOM to benefit from the University's incredible convening power to bring leaders from an expansive range of disciplines to campus.

Importantly, it also allows for a deep and wide-ranging curriculum beyond traditional MBA classes. Yale SOM students can take courses throughout the University, ranging from foreign language courses, to international relations classes, to environmental science and public health courses—all of which enrich a student's understanding of the big issues facing leaders in today's global world.

Additionally, Yale SOM is creating several courses to be taught jointly with other professional schools and departments at the University. For example, a new class on innovation in government will be cross-listed with Yale Law School and the Yale Jackson Institute for Global Affairs. This course, taught by a McKinsey partner in the firm's public sector practice, will look at actual examples of government innovation worldwide. The classroom experience will be enriched by having students from different disciplines, who approach the material from diverse perspectives.

More informally, the Yale School of Management has initiated a "Convening Yale" speaker series, to bring professors from across the University to speak at the school about a wide range of disciplines.

NOTES

1 International Data Base: World Population Summary, *U.S. Census Bureau*, available at http://www.census.gov/population/international/data/idb/worldpopinfo.php [accessed on 5 March 2012].

2 See, for example, "Central Banking Issues in Emerging Market-Oriented Economies." *A Symposium Sponsored by the Federal Reserve Bank of Kansas City*, Jackson Hole, Wyoming, 23–25 August 1990, available at http://www.kc.frb.org/publicat/sympos/1990/S90.pdf.

3 See, for example, V. Tanzi and L. Schuknecht (2000) *Public Spending in the 20th Century: A Global Perspective* (Cambridge: Cambridge University Press).

4 According to Papadopoulous (2010), "[b]y 2008, 111 countries, accounting for more than 50 percent of countries with a population exceeding 80,000 people, had competition rules in place ... 81 of these 111 countries adopted their competition law in the last twenty years." (Anestis S. Papadopoulous (2010) *The International*

Dimension of EU Competition Law and Policy (Cambridge: Cambridge University Press: 15.).

5 My first academic leadership role was as the inaugural Director of the Davidson Institute at the University of Michigan Business School. The Institute's purpose was to involve what is now the Ross School and the rest of the University in so-called transition economies.

6 Richard McGregor's 2010 book *The Party: The Secret World of China's Communist Rulers* (New York: Harper) is useful reading.

7 In the old days, things like medical services were not thought to be in the traded sector because after all most individuals have to get their medical treatment locally. But now many aspects of medical services can be provided on a global basis.

8 See, for example, Mark Landler (2009) "Trade Barriers Rise as Slump Tightens Grip." *New York Times* (22 March), available at http://www.nytimes.com/2009/03/23/world/23trade.html

9 I note that some qualify the extent of globalization by contrasting what senior executives believe about the extent of global competitive pressures and the actual extent of global trade in their sectors. See, for example, Pankaj Ghemawat (2011) *World 3.0: Global Prosperity and How to Achieve It* (Boston, MA: Harvard Business School Publishing). I believe that these qualifications are off the mark. Competitive pressures need not be manifest in high trade volumes for these pressures to be real and substantial; potential competition from global competitors may force domestic suppliers to respond by adjusting prices and quality without resulting in large trade volumes.

10 With respect to energy and the environment, I see a striking shift from the 1970s and 1980s, when we were concerned with scarcity of carbon, to now, when our fundamental problem is that we live on a carbon-rich planet, which in turn adds enormously to the challenge of reducing greenhouse gases. Technological improvements now have made huge increments of natural gas and oil resources accessible. I believe that the likelihood of scores of major sovereign governments collectively reducing use of carbon is unfortunately low. One may take some comfort in the belief that within-country coalitions will form to pressure policy changes that correlate with reductions across countries. But in any event and even in the hoped-for state of a major green technological innovation, the prices of carbon-based fuels are not fixed, and so one cannot presume that beating today's prices means that use of carbon fuels decreases dramatically. Thus, while oil is now at over $100 per barrel, in the mid-1990s, oil was priced consistently below $30 per barrel. (See, for example, "Petroleum & Other Liquids: Spot Prices." *U.S. Energy Information Administration*, available at http://www.eia.gov/dnav/pet/pet_pri_spt_s1_d.htm.) The key point is that a large share of the world's carbon reserves would come to market at much lower prices. To the extent the world does experience global environmental changes, another set of challenges will emerge, i.e., how to either mitigate these changes or organize responses to them. Issues concerning human

capital issues are high on everyone's list of big issues in the context of our modern economy where the value of human capital exceeds all other types. Among the many things that Gary S. Becker and Kevin M. Murphy have taught me about these issues, one salient point is that governments rarely make the necessary invest-ments in human capital because the political discount rate is high. The related issues concerning income disparities in the modern economy are a global phenom-enon and are certainly not specific to particular US tax policies. Over the last three decades or even longer, the returns to skill have increased, and so income distribu-tions have widened. The difficulty I see in virtually every country I visit is that market outcomes cause political challenges. Put differentially, it is more difficult to sustain political support around market outcomes given the income disparities now experi-enced. See Gary S. Becker and Kevin M. Murphy (2010) "Explaining the Worldwide Boom in Higher Education of Women." *Journal of Human Capital* 4.3: 203–241.

11 See, for example, Edward A. Snyder, Christine Poon, Joseph Thomas, and Andrew Policano (2011) "The Management Education Industry." *AACSB Annual Deans Conference Plenary Session*, Phoenix, Arizona (20 February); Edward A. Snyder (2011) "U.S. Business Schools and the MBA: A Long Perspective." *EFMD Annual Meeting of Deans and Directors*, Lyon, France (25 January); Edward A. Snyder (2009) "Globalization of Management Education." *Plenary Speaker at AACSB Annual Deans Conference*, San Francisco, CA (5 February); and Edward A. Snyder and S. Iniguez (2006) "Are Business Schools Becoming Truly Global?" *AACSB Dean's Conference*, San Diego, CA (6 February).

12 See, for example, Steven E. F. Brown (2005) "It's About People, Not Product." *Silicon Valley/San Jose Business Journal* (27 February), available at http://www. bizjournals.com/sanjose/stories/2005/02/28/smallb2.html?page=all

13 Inaugural speech at Yale University, 21 January 2010, available at http://mba.yale. edu/news_events/CMS/Articles/7075.shtml

14 The confirmed schools are Asian Institute of Management (The Philippines), EGADE Business School (Mexico), FGV São Paulo, Fudan University (China), Graduate School of International Corporate Strategy Hitotsubashi (Japan), I.Empresa (Spain), Hong Kong University of Science and Technology Business School (China), INCAE Business School (Costa Rica), INSEAD (France, Singapore), Koç University Graduate School of Business (Turkey), London School of Economics and Political Science (UK), National University of Singapore (Singapore), Universidad Católica de Chile (Chile), Renmin University of China School of Business (China), Seoul National University Graduate School of Business (South Korea), Technion-Israel Institute of Technology (Israel), UCD Michael Smurfit Graduate Business School (Ireland), University of Cape Town (South Africa), University of Ghana (Ghana), University of Indonesia (Indonesia), and Yale School of Management (USA). In addition to these academic institutions, several global enterprises, for example, Blackstone, Cargill, The Clinton Foundation, Honeywell, McKinsey, WPP, and Visa are involved in offering advice on the development of the *Global Network for Advanced Management*.

PART 3

Leadership Development, Globalization and Cross-Cultural Issues

---

Globalization and Sustainable Leadership

MARTA M. ELVIRA, Professor of Managing People in Organizations, IESE Business School, University of Navarra, and **ANABELLA DAVILA,** Professor of Business Administration, EGADE, Tecnológico de Monterrey

> The mark of good and strong leadership is to ensure a steady stream of new leaders.
> The system itself must be self-perpetuating.
> Sustainable – to use the current beloved term.
> Leaders Create Leaders.
>
> > Dr Siegfried Russwurm, Managing Board
> > Member of Siemens AG

Introduction: Leadership for the long-haul

In the wake of mass layoffs, cost reductions and other drastic actions that put people second in the struggle to overcome financial challenges, firms are discovering just how costly it is to maintain the commitment and productivity of their employees. A different approach is required to build sustainable organizations where the wellbeing of multiple stakeholders is at the center of companies' goals. Such an approach takes time, but it can be done, provided that leaders adopt a longer-term, humanistic perspective. Firms with the vision to understand this and take advantage will succeed in the market (Fernandez-Araoz, 2011). While factors such as the economic environment cannot be changed, one thing that can be influenced is who the leaders will be. In fact, while many corporations report a shortage of global leaders, studies of leadership and leadership development have paid limited attention to time factors and humanistic aspects: contributing to social sustainability encompasses both.

The ability of individuals and organizations to leave a long-lasting, positive imprint as a legacy depends partly on the stability and even health of the workforce. This aspect of leadership and sustainability reflects a broader concern in organizational research recently highlighted by Pfeffer (2010). Most research has focussed on the effects of business and organizational activity on the physical environment, yet companies and their management practises profoundly affect the human and social environment as well. For instance, the *Academy of Management Learning & Education* (2010) special issue on "Sustainability in Management Education" bypasses leadership, focussing on various sustainability models, technologies, and stakeholders (Starik, Rands, Marcus, and Clark, 2010). The article authors suggest that business sustainability has significantly expanded over recent decades despite the little attention paid to it in business school courses. In any case, such courses tend to address environmental concerns as a set of legal and ethical issues; leadership and sustainability issues seem absent. The interest in "green management" (Marcus and Fremeth, 2009) is just now reaching human resources management (e.g., Jackson *et al.*, 2012), aiming to raise awareness of how managerial actions impact the environment.

Parallel to management research, reports from international institutions, such as the International Labor Organization (ILO), highlight the negative effects for working conditions in various countries related to globalization issues. Thus, the ILO is working on the concept of *decent work* built over four pillars—basic labor rights, employment, social protection, and social dialogue—looking at the role of organizations such as governments, non-governmental organizations (NGOs), and community-based institutions to promote decent work (Thomas, 2002). Business organizations play an important role in promoting sustainable working conditions that appears missing in ILO analyses. An outstanding concern is how to promote awareness in organizations about the impact on job transformation and employee outcomes. Thus, examining how leaders and leadership development programs relate to human, organizational, and social level sustainability is a timely endeavor.

The World Commission on Environment and Development (WCED) defined sustainability as "development that meets the needs of the present without compromising the ability of the future generations to meet their own needs" (WCED, 1987: 42). According to Gladwin, Kennelly, and Krause (1995) sustainability has five main components: inclusiveness, connectivity, equity, prudence, and security.[1] For our purposes, these components all relate to organizational activities and their survival.

The aim of this chapter is to reflect on how global challenges place particular responsibility on leaders and leadership development models, keeping in mind sustainability and its main components. We take seriously the endurable aspects of people needed to be supported and developed for these responsibilities. First, we outline some challenges for leadership and leadership development derived from globalization. Second, we overview models of leadership competencies in diverse cultural contexts. Then, we comment on a few aspects of studying, developing, and practicing leadership to generate theory and research, joining recent calls for the emergence of more ethical, humanistic, inclusive, sustainable, responsible, and effective ways of leading and managing organizations within their world context, that is, the environment broadly understood (Bolden *et al.*, 2011; Voegtlin, Patzer, and Scherer, 2012). Finally, we discuss three issues of particular interest for current leadership development programs in a global context: the transferability of leadership effectiveness, as well as gender and age diversity considerations. Ultimately, this approach requires a focus around identity of individual leaders, and identity of the firm to commit to long-term development of people around community-oriented values.

Globalization's influence on leadership development

Because other chapters in this book cover theories of leadership development, we overview here only a number of conceptual and applied approaches, aiming to identify the most relevant themes for sustainability in a global context.

Background and definitions

Much has been written about globalization, especially regarding issues of trade, market liberalization, commercial and labor international agreements. While globalization advocates also caution about its potential downsides, others argue that globalization has widened the gap between rich and poor countries (Dutt and Mukhopadhyay, 2009; Joyce, 2010) and increased the income inequality within countries (OECD, 2011). Clearly there are some negative effects for countries and industries that follow the rules of globalization, but effective solutions also emerge from the global actors who are able to influence public policies and willing to collaborate with international institutions for social change (UNDP, 2006). International agencies and academic research report on different ways to overcome the challenges imposed by globalization. Similarly, leadership studies have expanded to focus on developing the capacities of individuals and organizations and their awareness of social and economic development.

Numerous definitions of leadership and views on leadership development methods exist. Over time, theories have evolved from focussing on the leader as an individual (the hero), to a builder of teams and alliances across organizations; development programs followed those trends. By contrast today the focus on sustainability is not yet influencing leadership development programs nor addressing theoretical perspectives concerning moral principles for sustainable leadership. As Campbell *et al.* (2003) note, leadership development is dominated by individualistic approaches, focussed on five broad areas: intrapersonal attributes, interpersonal qualities, cognitive abilities, communication skills, and task-specific skills.

From a humanistic, ethical perspective, we bypass definitional debates, and build on Day's (2000) distinction between leadership and leadership development. Day argues that leadership development differs from management development by involving helping people prepare for roles and situations beyond their current experience. While management development provides knowledge, skills, and abilities to enhance performance on known tasks through the application of proven solutions, leadership development is "orientated towards building capacity in anticipation of unforeseen challenges" (Day, 2000: 582). He further distinguishes between leader and leadership development: the first concerns developing individuals in leadership roles, while the latter is a relational view of leadership as a process involving everyone in the organization.

Given this variety of perspectives, and our interest in sustainable approaches to leadership, we adopt as a guideline Ciulla's ethics-based definition of leadership, which encompasses both the individual and collective levels:

> Leadership is not a person or a position. It is a complex moral relationship between people, based on trust, obligation, commitment, emotion, and a shared vision of the good.
>
> (Ciulla, 1998: 1)

This view expands beyond the boundaries of a set of traits, behaviors, or goal-oriented social relationship, to encompass the complexity of social relationships in which leaders develop. It also stresses the desire to have a positive impact on the common, shared good. It serves us as basis to define sustainable leadership as that which based on this moral relationship with organizational stakeholders, achieves the common good in the present and works for future organizational generations to meet their needs. Conceptually, it fits well the three different aspects that encompass teaching leadership development effectively, namely: knowing, doing, and being (Snook, Khurana, and Nohria, 2011).

A quick review of recent leadership manuals suggests the pervasiveness of traditional literatures around leadership development models, but again without much consideration of sustainability. For example, the *Sage Handbook of Leadership* (Bryman, Collinson, Grint, Jackson, and Uhl-Bien, 2011) departs from the history of leadership and its research methods, overviewing macro and micro perspectives and including philosophical approaches that are often ignored. Sorenson, Goethals, and Haber's (2011) chapter focusses on the enduring and elusive quest for a general theory of leadership. One might wonder whether this elusiveness arises from downplaying the social level in favor of narrowly fitted skill and competence development. The *Handbook* does include chapters on emergent perspectives such as hybrid configurations, relational approaches, complexity leadership theory, and identity work in leadership, although these perspectives are not easy to integrate.

Similarly, the more recent *Exploring Leadership* volume (Bolden *et al.*, 2011) reviews leadership frameworks at the individual, organizational, and societal levels and thus discusses more extensively the social level, yet still not focussing on sustainability dilemmas among the emergent issues in the field. Therefore, the literature on leadership development in organizations appears underdeveloped (Canals, 2011; Melé, 2009; Pirson and Lawrence, 2010). Before proceeding with a proposal for more humanistic approaches to sustainable leadership and leadership development programs, we survey some common organizational practises in which sustainable leadership might impinge.

Leadership development programs: Selected research and practise

Because leadership development is seen as a process that occurs in different settings, researchers often note that many programs are designed for the classroom or for settings with controlled contextual forces or events (Day, 2000; 2011). Meaningful work experiences occur in the field and include practises that engage individuals in real-life problems. There are practises oriented to enhance individual social awareness such as 360-degree surveys, coaching, mentoring, networking, job assignments, and action learning (Day, 2000). Reporting on global leadership development programs, Osland (2008) indicates that classroom methods such as lectures, seminars, or self-study assignments develop initial global leadership competencies, but other practises are necessary to supplement them, including global team projects or role plays that foster exchange with other subjects. She further suggests that practises with high impact in the development of global leadership competencies relate to personal work experiences such as sophisticated simulations or international assignments.

Overall, researchers in management education and the authors' experience as professors of executive programs suggest that leadership development works best when combining classroom lectures or exercises with in-company projects. For example, Adler, Brody, and Osland (2001) study the Women's Global Leadership Forum, an American company's initiative to develop global leadership skills, create an internal network and develop both global and local recommendations for enhancing support for career advancement and success. The authors report that global organizational competencies highlight a stakeholder orientation and the ability to successfully manage organizational change, uncertainty, create learning systems, and manage cross-cultural ethical issues (Adler, Brody, and Osland, 2001).

From practitioners' perspective, a number of global initiatives promote leadership development among their client firms. For example, the well-recognized Aspen Institute's mission is to foster values-based leadership. It encourages individuals to reflect on ideas that define a good society. The Aspen Institute does this primarily in four ways: seminars, young-leader fellowships around the globe, policy programs, and public conferences and events (Aspen Institute, 2011). Other organizations rank leadership development programs across the world (from business publications such as Bloomberg's *BusinessWeek* to accrediting institutions such as the European Foundation for Management Development [EFMD]) including trends and lessons from corporate universities and leadership centers.

A quick overview of these leadership development awards and practises suggests that most ranking and ranked organizations are US-based and potentially biased toward definitions of leadership based on American models, even if such companies work internationally. For example, among *BusinessWeek's* top 20 best companies for leadership in 2011, all are from the US except Nestlé and IKEA. In fact, "Nestlé: A human company" is the company's leadership development program motto, which focusses on employee well-being. As Laurent Freixe, Chief Executive for Europe, notes: "Nestlé understands the business of food and how it develops from a local knowledge." The main challenge of large organizations such as Nestlé is to align global strategies with leadership development. The company's diverse workforce (from 80 countries) requires leadership development oriented to the successful implementation of global strategies.

In order to do so, the firm seeks to create a strong culture based on values, developing talent rather than importing it, and favoring internal promotion. The Nestlé Company has developed a leadership competency framework in which its development programs operate. It is based on: inspiring people, opening up, adding value, and dealing with others. The impact of this framework promotes what the company calls a High Performance and Wellness Culture—where wellness includes a holistic view of life/work balance, attitudes of positive thinking, feedback, active listening, and of course caring about your health with good nutrition and active lifestyle. This example illustrates an effort to match strategy with sustainability for individuals via wellness concepts across a diverse global workforce.

Naturally, many other companies have created their own programs. Infosys, for instance, also implements a global leadership program with a long-term view of building a talent pipeline from within the firm through Infosys' Leadership Institute. This Institute is a small group of leadership promoters with the mandate to develop its own leadership development and influence the field itself. Considering that large organizations have certain requirements to develop a global view of leadership, these examples provide evidence that firms are not only investing important resources on company-specific development programs, but also creating development centers for that purpose.

Examining other industry-wide comparisons of leadership development programs and practises by different types of organization in multiple sectors, it appears that the effectiveness criteria evaluated rarely include long-term, sustainability concerns. Similarly, the training industry ranks the Top 20 Leadership Training Companies based on criteria that include programs' geographic reach and other quality criteria without sustainability impact (sample criteria include thought leadership, assessments or research to support programs, geographic reach and participants trained; company size and growth potential; industry recognition; innovation and impact, etc.). Also Carter, Ulrich, and Goldsmith (2011) suggest six steps for an effective leadership development program: business diagnosis, assessment, program design, implementation, on-the-job support, and evaluation. We question if other criteria such as sustainability as defined earlier in this chapter are beyond their purpose. In sum, our review of conceptual and practical approaches to leadership development suggests a relatively limited attention to its impact on the sustainability of individuals, organizations, and world societies. Keeping with this framework, we now turn to the challenges that leading sustainable organizations around the globe entail for effective leadership development for leadership development (Sánchez-Runde, Nardon, and Steers, 2011).

Assessing leadership competencies in cross-cultural models

To lead effectively across national cultures and countries, managers need to understand their own cultures and those of other countries. A number of books address the theme of developing global leaders (e.g., Brown, 2007; McCall and Hollenbeck, 2002; Steers, Sanchez-Runde, and Nardon, 2010). Among those studies, the GLOBE Project stands out in the effort to identify organizational foundations/values that unify leadership identity and unity amid diversity of global conditions (Javidan, Dorfman, Sully de Luque, and House, 2006). These authors find that to succeed, global leaders need to have a global mindset, tolerate high levels of ambiguity, and show cultural adaptability and flexibility.

Building on existing and accepted cultural models (such as those of Hofstede and Trompenaars), GLOBE studies have conceptualized and developed measures several cultural dimensions. These dimensions serve to distinguish among countries' and societies' cultures as well as to determine proper management practises: performance orientation, future orientation, human orientation, institutional collectivism, in-group collectivism, gender egalitarianism, power distance and uncertainty avoidance. The authors conclude that cultural attributes impact organizations and the ability of leaders to work effectively across different societies. Therefore, we would expect leadership development processes to be similarly influenced by culture.

By extension, GLOBE's culture attributes have been extended to leadership. Evidence suggests that leader attributes, behavior, status, and influence vary considerably as a result of culturally unique forces in the countries or regions in which the leaders function. The authors conclude by acknowledging that cross-cultural theory is inadequate to clarify and expand on the diverse cultural universals and cultural specifics elucidated in cross-cultural research, given each society and culture's preferred leadership qualities.

For our purpose what matters most is that GLOBE has empirically identified universally perceived leadership attributes that are contributors to or inhibitors of outstanding leadership. From the large number of leadership attributes the project identified a more understandable, comprehensive grouping of 21 primary and then six global leadership dimensions, which differentiate cultural profiles of desired leadership qualities: charismatic/value-based, team-oriented, participative, human-oriented, autonomous, self-protective. People within cultural groups seem to agree in their beliefs about leadership, reflected in a set of *leadership profiles* developed for each national culture and cluster of cultures (Javidan *et al.*, 2006: 73).

From these dimensions, in fact, the GLOBE study specifies a set of universal facilitators of leadership effectiveness across the various world regions despite cultural differences:

- Being trustworthy, just, and honest

- Having foresight and planning ahead

- Being positive, dynamic, encouraging, motivating, and building confidence

- Being communicative, informed, a coordinator, and team integrator

Likewise, the findings point to some universal impediments to leadership effectiveness, namely: being a loner and asocial, being non-cooperative and irritable, and being dictatorial. Regarding culturally contingent leader attributes, the list includes: being individualistic, being status conscious, and being a risk taker. These attributes are all analyzed at the individual level and matched to the regions' culture.

Companies' challenges reflect these dilemmas. Bruno di Leo, General Manager, IBM Growth Markets, notes that there is no leadership style that is unique, and succeeds globally: the different cultural environments in the world require a process of nurturing a defined set of leadership competencies, not just related to the individual but also to the company. Di Leo underlines the need for defining a company-specific portfolio of leadership competencies, and then build a leadership development process for nurturing these across the executive pool. Some of the competencies he suggests coincide with

GLOBE's universal facilitators of leadership (e.g., relation to the external local environment, client relationship capability, organizational building capability, corporate responsibility); others reflect the management of diversity as the crucial factor for executive leadership in a global setting.

Another important global trend that affects abilities valued in global leaders relates to social networks. That relationship-building is paramount to leadership seems fairly obvious, but appears especially so for future generations. Specifically, Marina Gorbis, president of the Future Institute, speaks of *social-structing*. From social networks and online markets she explains how, over the last 40 years, we have shifted from centralized to highly decentralized and distributed modes of communication, a shift with fundamental effects on all aspects of society, including education, health, and business. One of the implications is that people will increasingly be able to create value outside institutional structures, a phenomenon that has already been unfolding in Silicon Valley, Europe and other places. In her envisioning of a human-centered future, Gorbis stresses that changes in the way we organize after several decades putting in place new technologies infrastructure have allowed us to work in increasingly decentralized and distributed ways. These tools are expected to reinvent the way we organize: people are now able to create and produce value outside institutional structures. An example would be Wikipedia, where volunteers provide content outside of institution boundaries. This trend provides opportunities for social-structuring, that is, "organizing around our social connections rather than against them" (Gorbis, 2011). In this new way of organizing, networks and social skills are critical leadership assets, as are persuasion abilities across different media (from video to social media fluency).

In short, these findings suggest that while differences among countries exist, there are also similarities in effective cross-leadership, and thus the cross-cultural dimensions may serve as a foundation for more universalistic leadership development. Developing global leaders in today's context of limited supply of suitable professional candidates and designing programs that help develop a global mindset in leaders is a challenge for organizations in the new millennium. Again, as Fernandez-Araoz, Groysberg, and Nohria (2011) note, the long-term perspective helps develop from within in order to build a pool of talent available for needed roles (notwithstanding external searches), that is, leaders able to relate to the diverse stakeholders and problems found across the world. This requires not just a global-focussed approach, but also the mindset to integrate it within a comprehensive development program.

Also, work experience and international assignments are the most effective mechanisms for developing global leadership capabilities (Conner, 2000).

Bringing it all together: A humanistic approach to leadership

In this chapter we have argued for the need for organizational approaches to leadership development mindful of long-term/sustainable solutions for leaders and society, and reviewed existing frameworks and trends all revolving around relationship building and identity values. This encompassing approach, we surmise, is the basis for a humanistic understanding of leadership development.

The root of the current crisis has been widely attributed to a lack of or to mediocre leadership in many firms and political institutions, not to lack of knowledge or technical skills (e.g., Canals, 2011). When referring to business education, the phenomenon has been termed *the humanistic deficit* (Canals, 2011: 11), a description that could aptly be applied to leadership development models beyond school settings. Despite the originally well-intentioned efforts to base business education on socially responsible ideals,

> some management and financial theories and a stronger role of capital markets as drivers of modern capitalism have displaced some of those early ideals in the business world. The force of pragmatism on getting results irrespective to what happens on individuals working in the organization has become the dominant paradigm in the practice of management.
>
> (Ghoshal, 2005)

The outcome has been the growth of impersonal organizations where the human role is understated and individuals are often treated as just one more resource. The claim that people are important is stronger than ever, but in reality many decisions are taken without considering the impact on either people or companies. Consequently, individual commitment toward firms in the long term has decreased. A potential conclusion must be refocussing business education as well as leadership development in firms on serious research that places individuals at the core of organizational and social systems.

As a step forward in leadership development and in line with leadership as identity work, we propose exploring individuals' own values relative to their expected leadership role. Yet values that are also conformed to ethical parameters outside each individual is what might allow respect for others' diversity and freedom. Thus, outside stakeholders play a central role in recognizing and legitimizing leadership. From a stakeholder-management perspective, individuals, organizations, and the state all play roles in balancing interests and behaviors. Morality is connected with responsibility for the systemic consequences. A notable feature of this developmental model is that it recognizes that the fundamental needs of leader development change as individuals take on greater responsibilities for a larger number of stakeholders. Business leaders accept and assume responsibility for consequences of their actions both on the systemic level as well as the individual level (Pirson and Lawrence, 2010: 559).

First, at the individual level, the humanistic paradigm shift proposed by Pirson and Lawrence (2010) seems especially relevant to address challenges of sustainability and improvement in societal trust. Their model offers an alternative to the merely "economistic" view of human beings, emphasizing relational and community orientation. Based on the philosophical perspective of humanism (i.e., a relational human being) free agents pursue value-based social interactions. In the economistic view the role of leader requires constant negotiation to clarify goals and outcomes with followers, who are considered human resources rather than human beings, with the overall goal of efficiency maximization, rendering culture rather mechanistic (typical transactional leader).

Building on Day's (2000) distinction between leadership development focussed on the development of individuals (leaders) versus the development of social structures and processes, the humanistic approach emphasizes team and organizational development, moving from individual to collective-level identities (a shift from heroic-centric views toward considering leadership as a collaborative and relational process). This approach harkens back to Ciulla's view of leadership as a moral relationship, which forms the foundation for sustainable leadership defined in terms of achieving stakeholder, organizational, and social common good for present and future generations.

Along the same lines, transformational leadership models (see Bass and Avolio, 1994) fit better this humanistic approach to leadership. Based on moral values, transformational leaders actively balance their personal interests while engaging followers to do so the same, inspire followers, stimulate them intellectually, and engage them emotionally in the organization. They create cultures where people understand and commit to the organizational objectives, maintaining positive long-term relationships with each other, and contribute toward performance goals collectively. Moreover, humanistic leaders are compelled to contribute to society in the public arena broadly speaking (Lawrence, 2007). Businesses are engaged in resolving social issues. Thus, sustainability and corporate responsibility are endorsed factors in the humanistic view of organizations. Although this *true* humanism and its positive impact helps organizations focus on high-performance cultures and moral values (Melé, 2009), it does not appear to have reached leadership development models.

Second, at a systemic level, as mentioned at the beginning, although sustainability clearly encompasses both human and physical resources, the emphasis globally thus far has been disproportionately on the latter. Pfeffer (2010) notes that organizational research on sustainability is primarily concerned with the effects of organizations on the physical, not the social environment (Ambec and Lanoie, 2008; Marcus and Fremeth, 2009). In the rare studies that consider the social effects of organizational activities, the focus tends to be on the consequences of management practices for individuals' health and well-being and their participation in civic activities (Putnam, 2000). Despite the efforts of business to conserve natural resources and reduce operational waste (Ambec and Lanoie, 2008), it is hard to find similar efforts aimed at leadership development. The limited focus on attention, Pfeffer argues, is a result of the ideology of the primacy of markets and shareholder interests (Ghoshal, 2005; Rosanas, 2011).

Being a socially responsible business ought to encompass the effect of management practises on employee physical and psychological well-being. This is not to the detriment of organizational performance: for example, the Great Place to Work performance data suggests that human sustainability may be good for companies' profits as well. Given these calls for research and available evidence, Pfeffer attributes the limited importance given to the human dimension of sustainability to two causes: visibility of consequences in terms of results and ideology. Therefore, attention should be paid to this issue, starting with leadership development to raise awareness and capabilities toward social responsibility and people for their own sake.

Finally, leading in today's business landscape requires theories that cross organizational boundaries and are sensitive to globalization phenomena. Echoing Jensen and Sandström (2011), we propose stakeholder theory to acknowledge the responsibility that organizations have toward the larger community and with other societies. From the globalization movement perspective, individuals with global leadership competencies encounter diverse stakeholders with their diverse interests and demands. Our research shows that salient as well as silent stakeholders' call for social inclusiveness, which demands a horizontal relationship with organizations instead of a vertical relationship of subordination (Davila and Elvira, 2009; 2012). For leadership development the implication is programs with strong social and political awareness components to help leaders understand that in the global arena there are new power relations and new dimensions of responsibility (Jensen and Sandström, 2011). New global competencies emerge: the ability to establish meaningful dialogue instead of the classic negotiation skills, to initiate relationships with diverse stakeholders, and to establish accountability as good corporate citizens.

If the economic perspective of business is pushing labor institutions to remove labor market protection the stakeholder approach to business is seeking to strengthen it. For example, in Latin America, evidence from prior studies suggests at least three critical aspects of leadership in a stakeholder model: investment in employees—salary and benefits levels as well as education, training, and development; cooperative efforts in labor relations; and community-centered CSR practises (relative to distant global initiatives) (Davila and Elvira, 2012).

The stakeholder management perspective has highlighted the ethical obligation of an organization toward its stakeholders, typically stressing corporate social responsibility (CSR) (e.g., Clarkson, 1995). In addition, the sustainable development components of inclusiveness, connectivity, equity, prudence, and security require a stakeholder approach for influencing management. For example, our stakeholder approach to leadership development stresses the need to initiate relationships and build networks for dialog for social and economic inclusion beyond negotiation for business agreements. Sustainability also includes the need for action and sustainable leadership requires the organizational backing to pursue change (Morsing and Oswald, 2009). Under this view, leader effectiveness transcends financial performance by establishing consensual and legitimate solutions with organizational stakeholders (Voegtlin et al., 2012). The stakeholder perspective requires that leadership development programs focus their attention in a set of macro-level issues (contextual), meso-level matters (organizational), and micro-level interactions (personal) (Voegtlin et al., 2012).

Current challenges for sustainable leadership development

Among the many concrete areas that deserve special attention, we focus now on four that are common to the global community and that relate to social development, and which we consider are critically relevant for a long-term agenda on leadership sustainability.

Building global and local legitimacy: Globalization challenges multinational corporations (MNCs) that operate in differing business contexts (e.g., established and emergent economies) to gain legitimacy within both the local and the global institutional environments. In general, organizational legitimacy obtains when the organization copes with its social environment and its activities are desirable and appropriate within a society's system of norms, values, beliefs, and definitions (Suchman, 1995). Organizations need more than material and technical resources to operate; they also need the social acceptance and trustworthiness of the community (Scott, 2008). Although organizational legitimacy has been studied from the strategic perspective, that is, as a resource that can be managed, developed, or assessed, it is a construct usually sought by organizations because of pressure from external forces such as regulation (e.g., legislation), social norms (e.g., values and routines), or cognitive maps (e.g., cultural systems and symbols) for success (Scott, 2008). By contrast, from an institutional perspective, organizations obtain legitimacy when they adopt a wider cultural approach that makes them replicate other organizations' structures or patterns already present and accepted in the environment. That is, organizational isomorphism is produced because of the presence of coercive, mimetic, or normative institutional mechanisms (DiMaggio and Powell, 1983).

   In both perspectives of organizational legitimacy, sustainability requirements place leadership development in a central role, though from a different angle. That is, if organizational legitimacy is viewed strategically, it implies the development of managerial competencies for organizational control, design, and change. If organizational legitimacy is seen as an institutional component of a specific organizational field, managers require being responsive to cultural norms and other social demands to create organizations perceived as legitimated. Empirical research indicates that MNCs stress global CSR issues (e.g., general environment conservation) over country-specific socio-economic needs (e.g., job creation, natural habitats) (Husted and Allen, 2006). Building on the organizational legitimacy framework, leadership development programs should move further than product- or market-driven strategies and pay increasing attention to local needs and stakeholders.

Transferability of leaders' effectiveness: A paradox related to investment returns for leadership development programs in a global context concerns the sustainable transferability of talent from one company to another, and/or one specific region to the global arena. Reflecting on this paradox, we mean that companies seek to invest in developing leaders who, when they leave, probably make companies lose some of the investment, but they themselves cannot usually capitalize on the investment either.

Given research showing the drawbacks of hiring stars from one organization and the lack of applicability to other contexts, the challenge of developing globally effective leaders dovetails with the broader issue of star performers. Groysberg, Sant, and Abrahams (2008) affirm the benefits for firm performance afforded by having high-performing, or "star," workers. While wondering how portable employees are stars to other organizations, the authors find that it depends on the position, besides the person, team or organization. All these factors enter into the leadership development equation. Companies need to consider that different jobs require different human capital skills. Workers in jobs that require high-order skills are less transferable to other locations. Therefore, the decision on how to develop human capital skills, or leadership in our case, depends more on the job skills requirements. Within investment banks, for example, the retail brokers are more portable and can easily be hired from the outside because they work individually. The opposite applies to institutional salespeople, who should be developed from within and retained. Understanding such differences, and developing leadership programs accordingly, is crucial for companies attempting to attain sustainable competitive advantages.

Beyond worker position, we surmise that leaders' portability rests also on individuals' cross-cultural abilities, including those described above from GLOBE studies (e.g., some universal attributes such as honesty, trustworthiness, foresight, dynamism, and communication skills, and other culture-specific abilities).

Taking gender into account: For organizations to operate effectively amid the complexity of global transformations in economic, political, and social terms, developing leadership across all segments of society seems paramount.

As organizations such as the World Economic Forum declare, "empowering and educating girls and women and leveraging their talent and leadership fully in the global economy, politics and society are fundamental elements of the new models required to succeed in today's challenging landscape" (Hausmann, Tyson, and Zahidi, 2011: v). Human capital is the most important determinant of a country's competitiveness. Public policies targeting women's education will contribute to diversity leadership development, which in turn might provide alternative and innovative solutions to sustainable growth challenges. Companies that adopt a human development policy for their workforce assure that both male and female individuals will have the same opportunities to flourish (Hausmann *et al.*, 2011).

Along these lines, Denise Kingsmill points out that one of the greatest challenges in global management is precisely diversity: "True diversity in the context of business is about focusing on the differences in the way people think, and the differences in approach, clearly leaving to one side the issues of nationality, race or gender." In the context of the underlying causes of the current financial crisis, Baroness Kingsmill talks of the groupthink that dominated institutions and the company boards, wherein alternative approaches to problems simply were not aired or even discussed. She concludes by emphasizing that corporate leadership needs to move forward by incorporating diversity of thought, and diversity of approach.[2]

A persistent diversity challenge for organizations has been incorporating women into leadership to capitalize on the focus on diversity (Las Heras and Chinchilla, 2011; Ely, Ibarra, and Kolb, 2011), an aspect that is increasingly important given the persistent differences between men and women in reaching leadership positions and which should underpin principles for the design and delivery of women's leadership programs. Conceptualizing leadership development as identity permits grounding personal identity in the leadership role (Quinn, 2004). Ely *et al.* (2011: 488) offer three design principles for effective design of leadership programs for women: (1) include issues and methods to raise awareness of gender biases; (2) develop a learning environment that promotes mutual support for safeguarding women's identity work, and (3) motivate participants on their own leadership purpose, and connect with other participants to meaning, values and purpose (see also George and Sims, 2007). The goal is for women leaders to focus on developing and enacting identities that advance the values and purposes for which they stand. Overall, women leadership development programs would build more than traditional leadership roles because they would connect the different roles women have in our society. This shared, collective purpose resembles what we call humanistic leadership. It also considers diversity of stakeholders and prepares organizations to maximize leadership potential in its talent pool.

Developing young leaders: Universities too contribute to the development of global leadership programs at both graduate and undergraduate levels. For example, the Global Leadership Advanced Center (GLAC) of San José State University exemplifies a program attractive to students. The mission of the GLAC is the advancing, fostering, and disseminating of knowledge on global leadership and its development. GLAC offers assessment, training, coaching, mentoring, experiential learning, and global projects. In particular, this Center promotes research methods to develop global leaders, and its Global Leadership Passport Program assesses the global skills of the students and prepares them for global work. The Center takes advantage of its location in the Silicon Valley to encourage and train people to apply technology and innovation for the good of the local community (GLAC, 2011).

Managerial implications and conclusions

The content of academic and managers' work on leadership development and what we discuss in relation to sustainability, affects what is studied, published, and institutionalized in organizations (Ferraro, Pfeffer, and Sutton, 2009). To counterbalance the limited, "economistic" view of business, which also affects leadership, we can expand sustainability to represents a set of values and beliefs, or an ideology toward more humanistic, stakeholder-focused, sustainable solutions.

> There is no reason why building sustainable companies should focus just on the physical and not the social environment. It is not just the natural world that is at risk from harmful business practices. We should care as much about people as we do about polar bears (...) and also understand the causes and consequences of how we focus our research and policy attention.
> (Pfeffer, 2010: 43)

Organizations, therefore, need to pay special attention to contributing to a sustainable leadership mindset. That is, leadership development programs could be enriched to incorporate themes emerging from today's complex, uncertain, and global environments. One avenue to do so consists of framing leadership development actions under an umbrella sustainability paradigm. Thus, themes such as the financial crisis, social media communication and technology, stakeholder management and the like could be approached from this perspective.

Similarly, we argue that sustainable leadership development implies tackling the development of individuals via the development of organizations and their communities. This focus places organizations' responsibility for leadership development within a larger role of service to their industries and communities, one that enhances economic and social growth. When businesses are concerned about their responsibility for preserving a sustainable environment they should innovate in strategies that are inclusive of a broad group of stakeholders. Beyond CSR initiatives, business organizations with a leadership role have rescued communities devastated from natural disasters or funded cultural events that preserve local traditions. For managers, the challenge is how to expand the view of leadership development programs and practises at the organizational and community level.

To achieve this goal requires developing a comprehensive set of human resources management (HRM) policies, structures, and practises. From a social sustainability perspective, HRM plays a central role within and outside organizations. In redesigning traditional HRM practises, such as performance management, leaders should be evaluated in terms of, for example, their value alignment with and contribution to the social and economic development of their organization's community. Similarly, HRM practices such as training and development, or labor relations, could consider how employees might best meet the needs of diverse, critical stakeholders in society (Davila and Elvira, 2012). Enhancing individuals' ability to cultivate effective social relationships across a broad spectrum of cultures and a diverse set of stakeholders would also boost future leaders' environmental adaptation and organizational success. Compensation policies should therefore be consistent with these practises, providing incentives as well as rewards for socially sensitive leadership behaviors. In sum, sustainable leadership development requires underlying HRM practises to leverage employees' potential by facilitating transitions between individuals' current roles and future demands.

Successful global leaders effectively work with diverse and multiple stakeholders, with a human-centered perspective, and the social good in mind. Witness the examples of successful companies that operate in permanently turbulent environments, such as in Latin America. There, institutional shortcomings have forced firms to focus on human development and on building talent up in order to survive in the long run. In the absence of stable government or systems such as social security or education, firms play decisive roles. In Colombia, for instance, companies such as Indupalma and Hocol have created infrastructures to reach undeveloped regions and provide education for employees. In Mexico, companies such as CompuSoluciones contribute substantially to the training of technology experts. These companies have earned their license to operate: they developed markets where none existed before, by recognizing that their employees, along with their families, communities, and regions, are their most important stakeholders. These stakeholders, though less obvious than stockholders, are no less vital for a company to exist in the face of great difficulties. Convinced of this logic, these companies have implemented humanistic talent management policies, generating virtuous circles that radiate outward like shockwaves. The investment these companies make in human and social capital lays the groundwork for economic development across the region, fostering the creation of new businesses and industries that will eventually enrich the local economy. Furthermore, these companies gain an enviable asset—namely, well-trained, committed teams, with turnover rates well below industry averages.

Some argue that such practises work only in times of prosperity. Especially in periods of crisis, they say, the fastest way to cut costs is to let go of those employees whose jobs can be outsourced. Yet, fastest is not necessarily the most sustainable. Research shows that companies that uphold their commitments to their people come out of crises in better shape. For example, the US-based software business SAS reaffirmed its policy of investing in people in 2009 and, despite the economic crisis, ended the year with record profits and an even more committed workforce. As CEO Jim Goodnight likes to say, "My chief assets drive out the gate every day. My job is to make sure they come back." As more companies begin to "look closer to see farther," they realize that true success belongs to those capable of combining market objectives with long-term, humanistic leadership development.

NOTES

Speech delivered at the 2011 Global Executive MBA Graduation ceremony, IESE Business School http://www.iese.edu/Aplicaciones/News/view.asp?id=3107&k=siegfried_russwurm_leaders_create_leaders

1 Inclusiveness concerns a broader vision of the world, including in it both humans and nature, for ecological efficiency and social sufficiency to be achieved. Connectivity demands understanding of world's problems as interconnected and interdependent in an ecosystem. Central to equity is the fair distribution of resources and property rights, while prudence expresses the idea of an economic, social and environmental conscience where all human activities consider the impact generated in the short and long term. Finally, security refers to provide a safe, healthy and high quality of life for current and future generations (Gladwin et. al., 1995).

2 The views of Laurent Freixe, Baroness Denise Kingsmill, Bruno di Leo and Kees Storm were presented during the 2011 IESE Conference on "Globalization and Leadership Development in an Integrated World", Barcelona April 8, 2011.

REFERENCES

Adler, N. J., Brody, L. W., and Osland, J. S. (2001) "Going beyond Twentieth Century Leadership: A CEO Develops his Company's Global Competitiveness." *Cross Cultural Management* 8.3: 11–34.

Ambec, S. and Lanoie, P. (2008) "Does it Pay to be Green? A Systematic Overview." *Academy of Management Perspectives* 22.4: 45–62.

Aspen Institute (2011) About the Institute, at http://www.aspeninstitute.org/about [accessed 15 November 2011].

Bass, B. and Avolio, B. (eds) (1994) *Improving Organizational Effectiveness through Transformational Leadership* (Thousands Oaks, CA: Sage Publications).

Bolden, R., Hawkins, B., Gosling, J., and Taylor, S. (2011) *Exploring Leadership: Individual, Organizational and Societal Perspectives* (Oxford: Oxford University Press).

Brown, J. (2007) *The Global Business Leader: Practical Advice for Success in a Transcultural Marketplace* (London: Palgrave Macmillan).

Bryman, A., Collinson, D., Grint, K., Jackson, B., and Uhl-Bien, M. (2011) (eds) *The Sage Handbook of Leadership* (Thousand Oaks, CA: Sage Publications).

Campbell, M., Dardis, G., and Campbell, K. (2003) "Enhancing Incremental Influence: A Focused Approach to Leadership Development." *Journal of Leadership and Organizational Studies* 10.1: 29–44.

Canals, J. (2011) "In Search of a Greater Impact: New Corporate and Societal Challenges for Business Schools." In J. Canals (ed.) *The Future of Leadership Development—Corporate Needs and the Role of Business Schools* (London: Palgrave Macmillan).

Carter, L., Ulrich, D., and Goldsmith, M. (2011) *Best Practices in Leadership Development and Organization Change: How the Best Companies Ensure Meaningful Change and Sustainable Leadership* (San Francisco, CA: Pfeiffer).

Ciulla, J. B. (1998) *Ethics, the Heart of Leadership* (Westport, CT: Quorum Books).

Clarkson, M. B. E. (1995) "A Stakeholder Framework for Analyzing and Evaluating Corporate Social Responsibility." *Academy of Management Review* 20.1: 92–117.

Conner, J. (2000) "Developing the Global Leaders of Tomorrow." *Human Resource Management Journal* 39.2/3: 146–157.

Davila, A. and Elvira, M. M. (2009) "Theoretical Approaches to Best HRM in Latin America." In A. Davila and M. M. Elvira (eds) *Best Human Resource Management Practices in Latin America* (Oxford: Routledge): 180–188.

Davila, A. and Elvira, M. M. (2012) "Latin American HRM Model." In C. Brewster and W. Mayrhofer (eds) *Handbook of Research in Comparative Human Resource Management* (Cheltenham: Edward Elgar Publishing): 478–493.

Day, D. V. (2000) "Leadership Development: A Review in Context." *The Leadership Quarterly* 11.4: 581–613.

Day, D. V. (2011) "Leadership Development." In A. Bryman, D. Collinson, K. Grint, B. Jackson, and M. Uhl-Bien (eds) *The Sage Handbook of Leadership* (Thousand Oaks, CA: Sage Publications): 37–50.

DiMaggio, P. J. and Powell, W. W. (1983) "The Iron Cage Revisited: Institutional Isomorphism and Collective Rationality in Organizational Fields." *American Sociological Review* 48: 147–160.

Dutt, A. K. and Mukhopadhyay, K. (2009) "International Institutions, Globalization and the Inequality Among Nations." *Progress in Development Studies* 9.4: 323–337.

Ely, R., Ibarra, H., and Kolb, D. (2011) "Taking Gender into Account: Theory and Design for Women's Leadership Development Programs." *Academy of Management Learning and Education*: 474–493.

Fernandez-Araoz, C. (2011) Interview, at http://www.iese.edu/Aplicaciones/News/videos/view.asp?id=3126&lang=en

Fernandez-Araoz, C., Groysbert, B., and Nohria, N. (2011) "How to Hang on to Your High Potentials." *Harvard Business Review* 89 (October): 76–83.

Ferraro, F., Pfeffer, J., and Sutton, R. (2009) "How and Why Theories Matter: A Comment on Felin and Foss." *Organization Science* 20.3: 669–675.

George, B. and Sims, P. (2007) *True North: Discover Your Authentic Leadership* (San Francisco, CA: Jossey-Bass).

Ghoshal, S. (2005) "Bad Management Theories are Destroying Good Management Practices." *Academy of Management Learning and Education* 4: 75–91.

Gladwin, T. N., Kennelly, J. J., and Krause, T. (1995) "Shifting Paradigms for Sustainable Development: Implications for Management Theory and Research." *Academy of Management Review* 20.4: 874–907.

Global Leadership Advancement Center (GLAC) (2011) About us, at http://www.sjsu. edu/glac/ [accessed on 15 November 2011].

Gorbis, M. (2011). Interview, at http://www.iese.edu/Aplicaciones/News/videos/view. asp?id=3161&lang=en.

Groysberg, B., Sant, L., and Abrahams, R. (2008) "When 'Stars' Migrate. Do They Still Perform like Stars?" *MIT Sloan Management Review* 5 (Fall): 41–46.

Hausmann, R., Tyson, L. D., and Zahidi, S. (2011) *The Global Gender Gap Report 2011*. World Economic Forum, at http://www3.weforum.org/docs/WEF_GenderGap_Report_2011.pdf [accessed on 15 December 2011].

Husted, B. W. and Allen, D. B. (2006) "Corporate Social Responsibility in the Multinational Enterprise: Strategic and Institutional Approaches." *Journal of International Business Studies* 37.6: 838–849.

Jackson, S. E., Ones, D., and Dilcher, S. (2012) *Managing Human Resources in Environmentally Sustainable Organizations* (San Francisco, CA: Jossey-Bass/ Wiley).

Javidan, M., Dorfamn, P. W., de Luque, M. S., and House, R. J. (2006) "In the Eye of the Beholder: Cross-cultural Lessons in Leadership from Project GLOBE." *Academy of Management Perspectives* 20.1: 67–90.

Jensen, T. and Sandström, J. (2011) "Stakeholder Theory and Globalization: The Challenges of Power and Responsibility." *Organization Studies* 32.4: 473–488.

Joyce, J. P. (2010) "Globalization and Inequality Among Nations." In S. Asefa (ed.) *Globalization and International Development: Critical Issues of the 21st Century* (Kalamazoo, MI: W.E. Upjohn Institute).

Las Heras, M. and Chinchilla, N. (2011) "How to Develop and Promote Leadership from the Top." In J. Canals (ed.) *The Future of Leadership Development—Corporate Needs and the Role of Business Schools* (London: Palgrave Macmillan): 241–265.

Lawrence, P. R. (2007) "Organizational Logic—Institutionalizing Wisdom in Organizations." In E. H. Kessler and J. R. Bailey (eds) *Handbook of Organizational and Managerial Wisdom* (Thousand Oaks, CA: Sage): 43–60.

Marcus, A. A. and Fremeth, A. R. (2009) "Green Management Matters Regardless." *Academy of Management Perspectives*: 17–26.

McCall, J. J. (2002) "Leadership and Ethics: Corporate Accountability to Whom, for What and by What Means?" *Journal of Business Ethics* 38: 133–139.

McCall, Jr, M. W. and Hollenbeck, G. P. (2002) *Developing Global Executives: The Lessons of International Experience* (Boston, MA: Harvard Business School Press).

Melé, D. (2009) "Towards a More Humanistic Management." *Journal of Business Ethics* 88.3: 413–416.

Morsing, M. and Oswald, D. (2009) "Sustainable Leadership: Management Control Systems and Organizational Culture in Novo Nordisk A/S." *Corporate Governance* 9.1: 83–99.

OECD (2011) *Divided We Stand: Why Inequality Keeps Rising* (Paris: OECD).

Osland, J. S. (2008) "Interactive Teaching Methods: The Stakeholder Challenge for Global Leaders." *Academy of Management Meetings: Dialog.*

Pfeffer, J. (2010) "Building Sustainable Organizations: The Human Factor." *Academy of Management Perspectives*: 35–45.

Pirson, M. A. and Lawrence, P. R. (2010) "Humanism in Business—Towards a Paradigm Shift?" *Journal of Business Ethics* 93.4: 553–565.

Putnam, R. D. (2000) *Bowling Alone: The Collapse and Revival of American Community* (New York, NY: Simon and Schuster).

Quinn, R. E. (2004) *Building the Bridge as You Walk on It: A Guide for Leading Change* (San Francisco, CA: Jossey-Bass).

Rosanas, J. M. (2011) "A Humanistic Approach to Organizations and to Organizational Decision Making." In J. Canals, J. (ed.) *The Future of Leadership Development— Corporate Needs and the Role of Business Schools* (London: Palgrave Macmillan): 143–176.

Sánchez-Runde, C., Nardon, L., and Steers, R. M. (2011) "Looking beyond Western Leadership Models: Implications for Global Managers." *Organizational Dynamics* 40.3: 207–213.

Snook, S. A., Khurana, R., and Nohria, N. (eds) (2011) *The Handbook for Teaching Leadership: Knowing, Doing & Being* (Thousand Oaks, CA: Sage Publications).

Sorenson, G., Goethals, G., and Haber, P. (2011) "The Enduring and Elusive Quest for a General Theory of Leadership: Initial Efforts and New Horizons." In A. Bryman, D. Collinson, K. Grint, B. Jackson, and M. Uhl-Bien (eds) *The Sage Handbook of Leadership* (Thousand Oaks, CA: Sage Publications): 28–36.

Scott, W. R. (2008) *Institutions and Organizations. Ideas and Interests*, third edition (Thousand Oaks, CA: Sage Publications).

Starik, M., Rands, G., Marcus, A. A., and Clark, T. S. (2010) "From the Guest Editors: In Search of Sustainability in Management Education." *Academy of Management Learning & Education* 9.3: 377–383.

Steers, R., Sánchez-Runde, C., and Nardon, L. (2010) *Management Across Cultures* (Cambridge: Cambridge University Press).

Suchman, M. C. (1995) "Managing Legitimacy: Strategic and Institutional Approaches." *Academy of Management Review* 20.3: 571–610.

Thomas, J. (2002) *Decent Work in the Informal Sector: Latin America* (Geneva: International Labor Organization), at http://www.ilo.org/wcmsp5/groups/public/@ed_emp/documents/publication/wcms_122207.pdf [accessed on 15 December 2011].

United Nations Development Program (UNDP) (2006) *Leadership Development: Leading Transformation at the Local Level*, at http://lencd.com/data/docs/234-Concept%20Note_Leadership%20Development.pdf [accessed on 29 December 2011].

Voegtlin, C., Patzer, M., and Scherer, A. G. (2012) "Responsible Leadership in Global Business: A New Approach to Leadership and its Multi-level Outcomes." *Journal of Business Ethics* 105.1: 1–16.

World Commission on Environment and Development (WCED) (1987) *Our Common Future* (Oxford: Oxford University Press), at http://www.un-documents.net/ocf-02.htm#I [accessed on 1 November 2011].

Chapter 3.2

Global Leadership in Multicultural Teams

YIH-TEEN LEE, Associate Professor of Managing People in Organizations, IESE Business School, University of Navarra

Introduction

As business activities become increasingly globalized, there is an urgent need for global leadership to ensure effective collaboration across national boundaries. Global leadership can be defined as the process of influencing the thinking, attitudes, and behaviors of a global community to work together synergistically toward a common vision and common goal (Beechler and Javidan, 2007; Bird, Mendenhall, Stevens, and Oddou, 2010; Osland, 2008). Scholars have identified key competencies of global leadership, such as global knowledge, inquisitiveness, resilience, cognitive complexity, cosmopolitanism, mindful communication, multicultural teaming, and building community and social capital (Bird and Osland, 2004; Morrison, 2000; Osland, 2008). To make these broad concepts actionable, however, it is necessary to translate them into concrete behaviors in defined contexts. This chapter focusses specifically on global leadership in multicultural teams, and discusses its various facets and development.

The use of multicultural teams in work setting has become frequent over recent decades. It is not rare that workers nowadays need to cooperate with team members with different cultural backgrounds to achieve common objectives. The proliferation of multicultural teams is also fueled by the fact that the workplace is in transit to a knowledge society, characterized by extensive information exchange and processing. Individuals possessing the most required knowledge or competencies do not necessarily come from similar cultural backgrounds. As a result, it is crucial for organizations to make sure that their multicultural teams function well.

The objective of this chapter is to offer insight on global leadership in multicultural teams. After a brief overview on the concept of multicultural teams, I will discuss key tasks/challenges in leading multicultural teams along different stages of the team process (Tuckman, 1965), and address deep-level factors contributing to global leadership development. It is important to acknowledge at the outset that there are no hard and fast rules and recipes for leading multicultural teams, and that the issues covered in this chapter are far from comprehensive. However, with an in-depth understanding of complexity embedded in multicultural teams, global leaders may be able to make sound judgments that balance multiple and often conflicting demands when leading such teams. Furthermore, the role of global leadership may not always reside on one single person. Shared leadership refers to a team property whereby leadership is distributed among team members rather than focussed on a single formally assigned leader (Pearce, 2004). It is likely that different members would assume a shared leadership role in multicultural teams when performing team tasks. Hence, even though I use the term "global leader" in this chapter, it is supposed to refer to the global leadership function assumed by multiple members in teams instead of focussing on specific individuals as a formal leader.

Multicultural teams: Concept and challenges

Multicultural teams can be defined as "a group of people from different cultures, with a joint deliverable for the organization or another stakeholder" (Stahl, Makela, Zander, and Maznevski, 2010: 439). In such teams members are jointly responsible to accomplish certain tasks despite possible cultural differences inherent in the team composition. Multicultural teams usually have the advantages of a larger pool of skills, knowledge, and viewpoints, with multiple perspectives that foster creativity (Stahl, Maznevski, Voigt, and Jonsen, 2009; Stahl *et al.*, 2010). Moreover, multicultural teams may have a wider range of capabilities to serve a variety of client needs across space and time.

However, working with multicultural teams also implies increased complexity because of the presence of cultural diversity. Culture can be defined as the "the collective programming of the human mind that distinguishes the members of one human group from those of another" (Hofstede, 2001: 9). In other words, culture is a frame of reference that shapes the way we make sense of the world. Consequently, it affects people's underlying view of the nature of teams such that members from different cultural backgrounds hold diverse assumptions and expectations on how people should work together in teams (Gibson and Zellmer-Bruhn, 2001).

Cultural diversity in multicultural teams can easily generate management challenges. For example, cultural diversity often hinders communication effectiveness and social integration in teams (Stahl *et al.*, 2009). Members from different cultural backgrounds may not share similar understanding or expectation in terms of how work should be handled. Tensions and conflict can arise and prevent multicultural teams from reaching their full potential in delivering desirable work results. As cultural diversity can be both a blessing and a curse for multicultural teams (Bachmann, 2006), global leadership is needed to ensure smooth functioning of multicultural teams so as to reap the full benefit of diversity.

One particular leadership challenge in such a context is that of leader legitimacy. Research generally suggests that teams are likely to be effective to the extent that their cultural values match those of the work environment (Halevy and Sagiv, 2008). However, in multicultural teams where multiple cultural values and preferences are *simultaneously* present, leaders may have difficulties in identifying *one* set of values or leadership style that can satisfy members from multiple cultural backgrounds. Global leaders thus face the issue of *power paradox*, which refers to "a position where parts of the team question his/her legitimacy and authority for the same reasons that make other team members give the leader the 'licence to lead'" (Zander and Butler, 2010). Although treating members differently according to their cultural values may sound like a solution, study also indicates that such differentiated leadership within groups can diminish group effectiveness through creating divergence in leader identification and member self-efficacy, which reduces team collective efficacy (Wu, Tsui, and Kinichi 2010). To resolve the challenge of power paradox, global leaders need to skillfully deploy a dynamic combination of tailoring leadership to each team member as well as group-focussed leadership that orchestrates common team norms (Maznevski and Zander, 2001). I present a framework of global leadership in multicultural teams in Figure 12, and will discuss it point by point in the following sections.

Leading multicultural teams

Adopting the classic four-stage model of team development (i.e., forming, storming, norming, and performing: see Tuckman, 1965), I will discuss specific tasks and challenges that are particularly relevant in each stage when

Figure 12: A framework of global leadership in multicultural teams

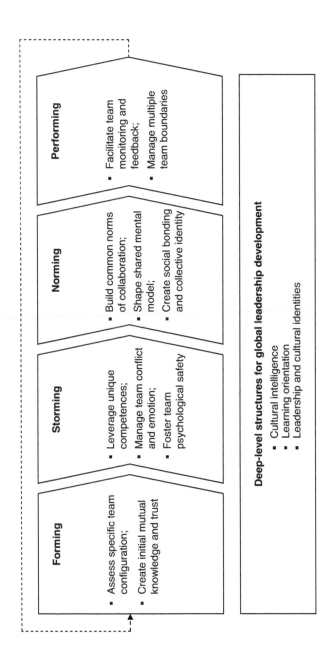

Forming
- Assess specific team configuration;
- Create initial mutual knowledge and trust

Storming
- Leverage unique competences;
- Manage team conflict and emotion;
- Foster team psychological safety

Norming
- Build common norms of collaboration;
- Shape shared mental model;
- Create social bonding and collective identity

Performing
- Facilitate team monitoring and feedback;
- Manage multiple team boundaries

Deep-level structures for global leadership development
- Cultural intelligence
- Learning orientation
- Leadership and cultural identities

leading multicultural teams. However, team processes should be understood as intertwined in a continuous and cyclical manner (Ilgen, Hollenbeck, Johnson, and Jundt, 2005). Furthermore, although certain tasks may be more pressing or salient in specific stages of team collaboration, all of them may be required at all times in leading multicultural teams.

Forming

Forming is usually the starting point of the teamwork process. In this phase, team members gather together, get to know one another and explore their similarities and differences. Global leaders need to manage such process by performing the following tasks: (1) assess specific team configuration; and (2) create initial mutual knowledge and trust.

Assess specific team configuration

Not all multicultural teams are the same (Bachmann, 2006; Maznevski, 2008). Each type of multicultural team faces distinct challenges, and different leadership modes are required to successfully lead the team (Zander and Butler, 2010). In the forming stage global leaders have to design a proper team setup that fits organizational purposes. If not given the discretion to determine team setup, they need to carefully assess team configuration and understand its implications so as to effectively lead the team.

First, the degree of diversity may differ across teams. Bicultural teams (i.e., teams involving members from two different cultures) are less diverse than team with multiple cultures. Furthermore, diversity can vary along a range of dimensions such as nationality, ethnicity, and religion. Whereas surface-level diversity (e.g., nationality and ethnicity) is more easily detectable, it is crucial for global leaders to capture deep-level diversity in teams (e.g., underlying values and assumptions) that are generally less visible but cast stronger effects on team functioning (Harrison, Price, and Bell, 1998).

Oftentimes, global leaders need to decipher issues subtler than cultural diversity, such as *power dynamics* among cultural groups. The proportion of members coming from specific cultures may determine which group has a stronger voice. The presence of a large cultural group tends to have dominant power over other cultural groups, unless other groups form some kind of coalition. Multicultural teams composed of two cultural groups of equal proportion may create a sense of equality, yet it can also engender direct power confrontation. The issue can be more delicate when it is not only the quantitative proportion of a certain cultural group that counts for power, but the subjective perception of superiority versus inferiority (often related with the level of economic development of a country or past history of confrontation), which influences the status differential in multicultural teams. Global leaders need to develop a clear sense of power dynamics in the forming stage so as to guarantee smooth collaboration.

Multicultural teams can be collocated (i.e., when members are located in the same site) or distributed (i.e., the virtual teams where members are physically working at different sites, often in different countries). Virtual multicultural teams are characterized by dispersion over many geographical sites and often time zones. Usually virtual teams face additional challenges to work together owing to enlarged geographical, cultural, and temporal distance (Cramton, 2001; Maznevski and Chudoba, 2000). Global leaders should develop a more refined understanding of the types/degrees of virtuality (Kirkman and Mathieu 2005) within teams and manage it accordingly, instead of treating virtuality as a dichotomous question (i.e., whether a team is virtual or not).

Create initial mutual knowledge and trust

During early stage of team formation, it is critical to establish mutual knowledge among team members, including basic personal information, cultural backgrounds, and specific knowledge and competencies each individual can bring to the team. Without shared experience or mutual knowledge, team members will rely on their individual past experiences to interpret persons, processes, and roles in teams, which can turn out to be very different (Cramton, 2001). They may fail to capture differences in value systems and working conditions and foster incorrect expectations of each other. Global leaders must help teams develop mutual knowledge and make sense of differences in the forming stage.

In addition to mutual knowledge, members of multicultural teams need to build up initial trust to develop into coherent teams. Whereas trust is beneficial for teams at all stages of teamwork (Jones and George, 1998), it is particularly critical in the forming stage. Without sufficient initial trust, team members may not be willing to share critical information or to accept the risk associated with relying on others (Salas, Sims, and Burke, 2005). It is more challenging to develop trust in multicultural teams where people share less common ground to build up mutual trust. Cultural differences can easily create a sense of separation (in-group versus out-group), trigger biased attribution (i.e., explaining the behaviors of members from different cultural groups in unfavorable way), and engender distrust.

Global leaders need to demonstrate trust building capabilities in two ways. First, global leaders need to gain trust from members with different cultural backgrounds. Whereas in some cultures trust for leaders is based more on leaders' formal position and interpersonal relationships (e.g., China, Japan), such trust may rely more on leaders' demonstrated competencies in other cultures (e.g., in the US: see Chua, Morris, and Ingram, 2009). Culturally adequate strategies need to be deployed to gain members' trust. Second, it is also global leaders' responsibility to cultivate trust among members of different cultural groups. Individuals from different cultures may favor a different basis of forming trust. For instance, in an individualist culture, people tend to reply more on a costs/rewards calculation and capability assessment for granting trust, whereas in collectivist cultures trust is developed more on the basis of intention and predictability (Doney, Cannon, and Mullen, 1998). Global leaders need to understand such cultural variation in fostering trust among team members from various cultures.

Storming

After their formation, teams usually enter into the storming phase in which members have to confront the differences among one another and make decisions about how to approach tasks collectively. Global leaders are expected to undertake the following interrelated tasks during the storming stage: (1) leverage unique competencies; (2) manage team conflict and emotion; and (3) foster team psychological safety.

Leverage unique competencies

To reap the benefit of diversity within multicultural teams requires a clear understanding of the unique value members from different cultures can offer to the teams. Open communication contributes to the identification of unique competencies of each team member and to the crystallization of team agreement. It helps members develop deeper mutual understanding, and is found to be significantly related to team performance (Hyatt and Ruddy, 1997). Teams with an accurate and shared knowledge of other members' expertise can better leverage unique competencies within the team. In additional to conducting basic task and social skill coverage of teams (Maznevski, 2008), global leaders may even tap into implicit benefits embedded in cultural differences in this process. In other words, global leaders need to help teams assess differences in a constructive way so that team members can develop a clear and accurate *transactive memory system* (i.e., the knowledge of team members as well as the collective knowledge of distribution of expertise, or an awareness of "who knows what" in teams: Mathieu, Maynard, Rapp, and Gilson, 2008).

One challenge global leaders have to confront is to facilitate communication in teams with the presence of cultural differences because communication norms and styles are subject to culture's influence. Whereas members from more individualistic cultures (e.g., USA, the Netherlands) are more willing to express their unique opinions, members from collectivist cultures (e.g., China, Mexico) prefer to hide their uniqueness and remain part of the group. Moreover, members from high power distance cultures (e.g., Arabic countries, the Philippines) may be quiet and express less during team discussion when high-status members are present. These cultural differences may prevent teams from identifying and leveraging unique competencies at their disposal. Global leaders have to enable teams to communicate in culturally proper way and bring out unique knowledge of members from different cultures.

Manage team conflict and emotion

Conflict is a common phenomenon in the storming process when members demonstrate their differences in direct or indirect ways. Cultural differences not only increase the likelihood of conflict but also impede a team's ability to manage affective conflict through openly discussing issues (Von Glinow, Shapiro, and Brett, 2004). Generally recognized as detrimental to team performance (Jehn, Northcraft, and Neale, 1999; Lovelace, Shapiro, and Weingart, 2001), conflict may be beneficial to teams if maintained at a healthy level and be of the right type (De Dreu, 2006; Van de Vliert and De Dreu, 1994). The capitalization of the potential benefits of team conflict depends largely on the global leaders' management of conflict.

Related to conflict is the issue of emotion. If not managed properly, conflicts in teams can fuel negative emotions, leading to breakdowns in interpersonal understanding and collaboration. Cultural diversity itself can also create anxiety and discomfort. Managing emotions in multicultural teams is more complex than that in monocultural teams because culture also affects emotional processes, including emotion appraisal, emotional experience, emotional expression, and emotion recognition (Elfenbein and Shirako, 2006).

First, people from different cultures differ in context sensitivity (Masuda and Nisbett, 2001). As a result, members of multicultural teams may work in the same objective setting yet find their emotions evoked by different stimuli within that environment. Second, people of different cultures differ in their tendency to experience particular emotional states (Aune and Aune, 1996). Consequently, members of multicultural teams are less likely to share the same emotional state following the same events, which would hinder the development of group congruence. Moreover, expression of emotion varies across culture as display rules are also conditioned by cultural norms. In some cultures individuals are not expected to express what they really feel but to display what is appropriate (e.g., displaying a smile when angry in Japan). Finally, it is more challenging to recognize emotions of people from different cultures (i.e., with lower speed and accuracy: Elfenbein and Ambady, 2002). Global leaders should be aware of these cultural differences in managing conflict and emotions in multicultural teams.

Foster team psychological safety

Closely related to the previous tasks, global leaders should create a sense of safety within the team so that members can contribute their unique values without suffering from conflict and negative emotions. Defined as a feeling that "one is not at risk of embarrassment or rejection in a particular setting or role" (Edmondson and Roloff, 2009: 186), team psychological safety help teams avoid evaluation apprehension (i.e., concern for how team members are perceived and evaluated by others), which may prevent members from communicating openly or presenting counter-arguments (Edmondson, 1999). It is more likely to preserve divergent thinking within multicultural teams when they are psychologically safe. Global leaders need to know that members from different cultures have different concerns about psychological safety in teams. For example, fear of losing face is more pertinent in collectivist societies and might hinder members from such cultures in sharing ideas or creating alternatives with others. As a result, global leaders need to pay special attention to guaranteeing a sufficient level of psychological safety in teams so that all the team members can contribute properly.

Global leaders should also ensure that uniqueness of members is not sacrificed in pursuing commonality within teams by allowing for self-verification in teams. As a process by which team members express their unique perspectives and receive acknowledgment about them from their teammates,

self-verification supports members recognizing, respecting, and sharing
their different knowledge and opinions stemming from cultural diversity
(Bachmann, 2006; Maloney and Zellmer-Bruhn, 2006). People are motivated
to stabilize their self-views. Moreover, for teams to leverage unique contributions in multicultural teams, allowing members to verify their self-views (i.e.,
express thoughts and feelings about the self) helps them feel recognized and
understood. Such feelings can in turn encourage them to offer unique ideas
that they may "otherwise have felt too inhibited to share" (Swann, Polzer,
Seyle, and Ko, 2004: 16). Global leaders should create a safe environment
in teams so that members feel enabled and motivated to contribute to their
teams.

Norming

Norming refers to the process in which team members develop shared norms
to cooperate effectively and achieve collective goals. As members with different cultural backgrounds usually hold diverse rational assumptions and
expectations on how people should work together in teams, developing shared
norms can be particularly challenging in multicultural teams. Three specific
tasks are relevant for global leadership in this stage: (1) build common norms
of collaboration, (2) shape a shared mental model, and (3) create social bonding and collective identity.

Build common norms of collaboration

As mentioned earlier, members of multicultural teams usually hold very different preconceptions about teamwork (Earley and Gibson, 2002; Gibson
and Zellmer-Bruhn, 2001). They come to teams with diverse understandings
of how to interact with each other and how to approach the team task based
on their prior cultural experiences (Janssens and Brett, 2006). Global leaders
need to address this issue and establish common norms for members to work
together. Otherwise, members would simply rely on norms shaped by their
own prior cultural understanding in collaboration and are likely to enter into
conflict over the processes to be used in performing the task.

Members of multicultural teams may have varying degree of desire or
acceptance for norms with regard to empowerment, self-management, shared
leadership, and time scheduling, just to name a few. Whereas empowerment
is usually considered valuable and can contribute to team knowledge sharing
and effectiveness (Mathieu, Gilson, *and* Ruddy, 2006), it is not held universally

desirable: in high power distance cultures, empowerment (i.e., granting individual choices) may not always produce a high level of intrinsic motivation, as it does in low power distance cultures (Iyengar and Lepper, 1999). Members from high power distance culture may even perform better under disempowered conditions (Eylon and Au, 1999). Global leaders need to understand the challenge and manage an adequate degree of empowerment when establishing team norms.

Similarly, self-managing teams, defined as "teams whose members collectively manage themselves, assign jobs, plan and schedule work, make production- or service-related decisions, and take action on problems" (Kirkman and Shapiro, 2001: 597), are found to relate to many positive team outcomes such as higher levels of productivity, safety, job satisfaction, and organizational commitment in the USA. Yet, they may not be as effective for individuals holding cultural values different from those of the USA because individuals with high power distance value may rely more on those who are in power and demonstrate resistance to self-management (Kirkman and Shapiro, 1997; 2001). This is not surprising as the concept of self-managing work teams is heavily based on the idea of empowerment discussed previously. This issue also affects the extent to which it is possible to instill shared leadership in multicultural teams. Although there is no research examining the relationship between cultural values and shared leadership to date, one may reasonably suspect that individuals from certain cultures (e.g., high power distance) will be more reluctant to undertake the role of shared leadership and expect the team leader to give clear directions in teamwork. In building norms, global leaders need to pay special attention to the predominant cultural values inherent in the teams they lead.

Individuals from different cultures also hold diverse conceptualization about time (Hofstede, 2001; Kluckhohn and Strodtbeck, 1961). Team temporal diversity regarding time urgency, pacing style, and time perspective can create temporal ambiguity, conflict of temporal interests, and different time pressure experienced by team members (Mohammed and Nadkarni, 2011). Global leaders should help members identify temporal diversity in teams and establish clear norms regarding the meaning of deadlines and criteria for priority setting so as to effectively synchronize team member behaviors. In sum, without building clear norms for collaboration, team members are likely to experience confusion and incapability to allocate tasks fairly within teams. Global leadership hence involves confronting the power paradox mentioned previously in a culture-sensitive way, and establishing norms of collaboration acceptable to everyone. In such a process, power and status difference among cultural groups may play a role in determining who adapts to whose norms. Global leaders need to be aware of possible status inequality in teams so as to maintain an adequate balance of such subtle power dynamics.

Shape a shared mental model

Members of multicultural teams also need to develop a shared knowledge structure that provides them with a common frame of reference to perceive, interpret, and react to their particular work environment. A shared mental model refers to a common knowledge structure or information held by team members (Klimoski and Mohammed, 1994). Shared mental models in teams not only facilitate coordination and communication among members, but also prevent misunderstanding and increase mutual trust within teams (Bachmann, 2006).

Shared mental models are complementary to common norms for team collaboration. Norms tend to be spelled out explicitly, whereas shared mental model tend to be more implicit. Because explicit norms cannot possibly cover all aspects of collaboration, shared mental models contribute to implicit coordination in teams that require synchronization of members' actions based on unspoken assumptions about what other team members are likely to do beyond explicitly stated norms. Global leaders have to devote time to shaping a shared mental model while leaving room for individual unique contributions as mentioned in the "storming" section.

Create social bonding and collective identity

It is not sufficient for team members to cognitively understand each other; they also need to develop an emotional connection to work together effectively. Global leadership should create social bonding beyond the initial trust developed in the forming stage. Especially, it is important for multicultural teams to develop a sense of *collective* identity and belonging in this stage, in contrast to developing trust that is dyadic among specific individuals within the team.

Creating social bonding in multicultural teams is challenging because cultural differences render similarity-based liking and attraction more difficult. Moreover, people from different cultures develop different relational templates regarding what is a proper way of maintaining a social relationship

(Lee, Reiche, and Song, 2010). For example, the work of Hinds, Liu, and Lyon (2011) suggests that the meaning of social network varies across culture in several ways. First, the expected network density and strength of ties may differ across cultures (e.g., high density in Israel, low density in the USA). Second, there are cultural differences in norms about how to build and maintain social ties—members from different cultures may not feel equally comfortable with the same way of building social bonds. Finally, culture also shapes people's expectations about the nature of relationships within work teams. Whereas in individualist cultures people tend to develop instrumental ties at the workplace, people in collectivist cultures usually expect true friendship (to some degree) to enable them to work together. Individuals exercising global leadership in creating social bonding in multicultural teams need to understand the cultural variation of such social dynamics so as to function properly.

Although a collective identity is generally beneficial to team performance (Brewer, 1996), global leaders need to be able to maintain the distinct aspects of different cultural groups in the process of collaboration. Over-emphasizing collective identity may force team members cede local identity, which leads them to discount the culturally based views and ideas from certain cultural groups (Janssen and Brett, 2006). The key task for global leaders in this regard is to balance the dual demands in fostering *sharedness* in teams (e.g., common norms, shared mental model, and collective identity), while at the same time maintaining room for the *uniqueness* of each cultural group.

Performing

Performing is the stage during which team members undertake activities that are directly involved in implementing action plans and achieving their goals at both collective and individual levels (Marks, Mathieu, and Zaccaro, 2001). Global leaders need to perform two critical tasks in this stage: (1) facilitate team monitoring and feedback; and (2) manage multiple team boundaries.

Facilitate team monitoring and feedback

Given the inherent diversity within multicultural teams, it is critical to develop monitoring and feedback mechanisms to coordinate members' effort in the action phase. Effective monitoring and feedback behaviors help teams make regular reality checks and necessary adjustments, which in turn affects the allocation of resources and consequent performance (DeShon, Kozlowski,

Schmidt, Milner, and Wiechmann, 2004). Global leaders are faced with the need to facilitate monitoring and feedback so as to ensure that team action plans are executed properly following previously agreed norms, and that each team member's unique contribution is leveraged in optimal ways.

Adequate intensity and style of monitoring and feedback, however, depend on team setting and cultural values. For example, members of virtual teams may have more difficulties in establishing clear mutual expectations and to identify with their teams. Consequently, there is a high risk that members will engage in effort-withholding behaviors (e.g., free riding) and damage trust and overall performance in teams (Shapiro, Furst, Spreitzer, and Von Glinow, 2002). Global leaders will need to enhance the intensity of monitoring and offer proper feedback to keep teams on the right track. In terms of style, people from individualist cultures tend to favor personal performance feedback, while those from collectivist cultures would prefer collective feedback. Moreover, research suggests a stronger desire for failure feedback in Japan in contrast to a desire for success feedback in the US (Bailey, Chen, and Dou, 1997). When feedback is provided in culturally congruently way, such feedback is considered as of higher quality and to be more effective (Van de Vliert, Shi, Sanders, Wang, and Huang, 2004). Global leaders need to take into account such cultural variations in facilitating effective feedback in multicultural teams.

Manage multiple team boundaries

As most team tasks require extensive interaction between members and various parties outside the team (Maznevski, 2008), global leaders need to manage team boundaries both internally and externally in order to achieve optimal performance. Internally, global leaders need to manage faultlines, or "hypothetical dividing lines that may split a group into subgroups based on one or more attributes" (Lau and Murnighan, 1998: 328). Faultlines create a sense of separation in teams (we versus they), encourage subgroup favoritism, and limit information sharing across subgroups, hence significantly affecting team learning, psychological safety, satisfaction, and expected performance (Lau and Murnighan, 1998; 2005). In fact, the challenges for leading multicultural teams rarely come from cultural diversity per se. Rather, it is how the team is partitioned into cultural subgroups and the salience of cultural faultlines that determine team cohesion and effectiveness.

Multicultural teams tend to develop strong faultlines among cultural groups (especially in global virtual teams when team members are distributed in different locations), preventing the development of social ties and effective collaboration. The issue of faultlines can be further accentuated when power is distributed unequally within teams (i.e., when a specific cultural group enjoys higher status and more power: Janssens and Brett, 2006). Global leaders need to help team members cross these internal faultlines so as to secure resources and commitment from all cultural parties in the performing phase. In order to reach this objective, global leaders need to strategically adopt different leadership modes (i.e., single, paired, rotated, and shared) when leading multicultural teams based on criteria such as the strength of fautlines and status difference within teams (Zander and Butler, 2010).

Global leaders also need to manage external boundaries to obtain critical resources (Morgeson, DeRue, and Karam, 2010). Teams require many different types of resources from outside, such as information, technology, financial and administrative support, etc. For multicultural teams, the relationship with outside stakeholders can be highly complex. As different team members may interact with different external stakeholders at different time and places, not only do global leaders need to be the bridge between teams and external world, they also have to encourage all team members to share the responsibility of maintaining external connection.

To summarize, key competencies for global leadership that stem from leading multicultural teams include: (1) a heightened level of cognitive complexity and cultural knowledge to capture subtle differences of cultural sense-making regarding teamwork (in communication, setting norms, etc.); (2) the capability to cultivate people relationships across cultures (i.e., fostering trust and mutual understanding while managing conflict and team emotions); (3) the aptitude to identify unique knowledge and skills in teams and to leverage diversity; and (4) the savvy to manage internal and external boundaries and to create a coherent team. They help individuals perform critical global leadership tasks properly in various stages of the team process as described earlier.

Developing global leadership in multicultural teams

Because global leadership typically involves a complex mix of cognitive, behavioral, and social skills, its development is never an easy and straightforward task. Oddou and Mendenhall (2008) have detailed a series of approaches for global leadership development, including conceptual learning (i.e., radically redraw provincial mental maps into global ones with *contrast*, *confrontation*, and *replacement*: Black and Gregersen, 2000), international business travel and seminars, international project teams and taskforce, global assessment centers, planned field experience, and short- and long-term international assignments, using various methods ranging from lectures, self-study, case analysis, role play, and simulation, to in-depth information exchange. Such development often goes beyond the acquisition of surface-level technical skills and requires individuals to go through a profound transformation in their deeper cognitive structures involving identity, meta-cognitive processes, and emotional regulation (Lord and Hall, 2005; Mendenhall, 2006). Unlike surface-level knowledge and skills, these deeper structures tend to more difficult (yet still possible) to change. However, developing these deeper structures can create much more profound impacts in fostering global leadership than learning laundry-list-like knowledge about cultural differences.

The next section will focus on three deeper structures critical for developing global leadership, namely cultural intelligence, learning goal orientation, and leadership and cultural identities. These qualities, once developed, enable individuals to make adequate decisions and act properly, facilitating their capability of taking initiatives and getting things done (i.e., with an action orientation), instead of being paralyzed by the novelty and uncertainty embedded in working in multicultural teams.

Cultural intelligence

As discussed in the previous section, exercising global leadership in multicultural teams requires extensive cultural knowledge for subtle judgments and decision-making. Cultural intelligence (CQ), defined as the capability to function effectively in situations characterized by cultural diversity (Ang and Van Dyne, 2008; Earley and Ang, 2003), is valuable in helping individuals deal with the complexity of leading multicultural teams (Lee *et al.*, 2010). Cultural intelligence includes features such as possessing cultural knowledge about values and norms (cognitive CQ), being consciously aware of and thinking strategically about culture (metacognitive CQ), directing attention and energy toward cross-cultural learning and interaction (motivational CQ), and generating appropriate behavior when interacting with people who are culturally different (behavioral CQ: see Earley and Ang, 2003). Individuals with high cultural intelligence will be able to capture and make sense of cultural differences in teams, and adopt the appropriate behavioral strategy to influence members from various cultural backgrounds.

Cultural intelligence also facilitates cultural learning in the process of global leadership development. Ng, Van Dyne, and Ang (2009) argue that cultural intelligence is an essential learning capability that leaders can use to translate their international experiences into effective learning in culturally diverse contexts for becoming global leaders. Therefore, cultural intelligence represents another deep-level structure to work on for developing global leadership.

Learning orientation

Assuming the responsibility of global leadership and handling the cultural diversity within multicultural teams can be very stressful. Individuals need to be able to tolerate setbacks and frustrations and constantly adjust themselves to the unfamiliar international environment. A learning orientation can be highly valuable to help individuals develop into global leaders when facing setbacks in the learning process. Learning goal orientation refers to an interpretative framework that shapes individual affective, cognitive, and behavioral responses to challenging tasks, events, and situations. It channels individual attention toward developing ability and competence for accomplishing future tasks, instead of toward performing well (and looking well) at the current ones. Specifically, learning-oriented individuals view abilities as malleable, hence prefer to set goals in terms of competence development (or mastery) instead of ability demonstration (Dweck, 1986). Consequently, learning-oriented individuals focus more on self-development and are less afraid of failure.

Scholars have demonstrated that a learning orientation is important not only for leadership development in general (Day, Harrison, and Halpin, 2009), but also for various types of cross-cultural adjustment (Gong and Fan, 2006; Wang and Takeuchi, 2007). In fact, learning-oriented individuals are more likely to emerge as leaders in multicultural teams because they feel less threatened by unfamiliar cultural diversity and take initiatives to serve the team (Paunova and Lee, 2011). Hence, cultivating a learning orientation serves as another critical path that can facilitate the progress of individuals to become global leaders.

Leadership and cultural identities

The third personal transformation is to develop a clear global leader identity, specifically about one's current and future roles in leading teams in a global context. A leader identity refers to "the sub-component of one's identity that relates to being a leader or how one thinks of oneself as a leader" (Day and Harrison, 2007: 365). Identity is important because it regulates people's understanding and motivation regarding who they are and their major goals and objectives. As a result, developing global leadership requires individuals to consciously construct a new leadership identity that incorporates the global component—in construing oneself as a global leader, such individual can better mobilize cognitive and emotional resources in handling heightened complexities related to the global context.

In multicultural teams, global leaders also need to pay attention to their cultural identity and its effects on working with their team members. The social identity theory of leadership regards leadership as a group process generated by social categorization and prototype-based influence (Hogg, 2001; Hogg and van Knippenberg, 2003). Following this vein, global leaders need to manage the dynamics between their own cultural identity and that of team members so that they can maintain a certain level of prototypicality for leveraging their leadership influence. Moreover, in a two-culture team context individuals with a bicultural identity (Lee, Masuda, and Cardona, 2010) and marginalized identity (Fitzsimmons, Lee, and Brannen, 2011; Lee *et al.*, 2010) are more likely to develop into global leaders than those holding on to a one-sided cultural identity. Developing a global identity (a sense of belonging to the global community: see Shokef and Erez, 2006) may also enable individuals to emerge as leaders in multicultural teams (Lee *et al.*, 2010). Such an identity structure may provide an important structure around which relevant knowledge is organized and serve as a source of motivational and directional forces for individuals to undertake risks pertaining to global leadership tasks. Developing dual or even multiple identities toward their team, organization, and external environment can also facilitate global leaders' role as boundary spanner in multicultural teams (Richter, West, van Dick, and Dawson, 2006). It is thus indispensable to incorporate identity work when planning for global leadership development.

Managerial implications

Given the strategic importance of global collaboration and the complexity involved in multicultural teams, CEOs and HR managers should proactively and systematically ensure that proper global leadership is in place in their multicultural teams rather than leaving it to chance. There are two important aspects that CEOs and HR managers need to pay special attention to in this regard, which will be examined next.

Global leadership identification

CEOs and HR managers should set up clear selection criteria that allow them to identify individuals with global leadership competencies to lead multicultural teams. Such criteria include general competencies such as global knowledge, inquisitiveness, resilience, cosmopolitanism, and ability to build community and social capital (Osland, 2008), as well as deeper cognitive structures such as cultural intelligence, learning goal orientation, and proper leadership and cultural identities, as discussed in the previous section. It is critical for organizations to establish a clear global leadership model beyond technical competencies to identify and select proper individuals to assume global leadership responsibilities in multicultural teams. Putting the right persons in the right places for global leadership is the first step toward smooth multicultural collaboration within teams.

Global leadership development

CEOs and HR managers also need to create proper systems and an appropriate culture to facilitate global leadership development in organizations. People with global leadership qualities still need support to develop their capabilities to their full potential. Companies may organize training activities focussing on specific skills and competencies mentioned above to facilitate global leadership development. Moreover, in addition to training, it is equally important to build up a culture and mentoring system in favor of such development such that, via the joint effects of a consistent system (including mentoring, special assignment, projects and formal courses, etc.), organizations can ensure a fit between job demands in global leadership and the capabilities of individuals concerned (Kristof-Brown and Guay, 2010; Lee and Ramaswami, forthcoming). In sum, CEOs and HR managers should enlarge the scope of their competence map by consciously and systematically incorporating global leadership in the map so as to better align their talent management with corporate strategy.

Conclusions

As global leadership encompasses a wide range of skills and capabilities, this chapter addresses global leadership in a specific context—that of leading multicultural teams. Using a process model of forming, storming, norming, and performing, I raised key tasks of leading multicultural teams and discussed the special challenges that global leaders need to address at each stage. However, it is important to reiterate that most activities mentioned in this chapter are continuous and relevant to all stages of the team process. Moreover, this chapter by no means attempts to offer a ready-to-apply recipe for managers to lead multicultural teams. Instead, I intend to show the complexity involved in performing these tasks. Global leaders face the challenge of complexity, duality, balancing conflicting demands and global–local tension, and making decisions with increasing reference points. As a result, they need to develop a deeper knowledge of culture's consequences in teams and a more comprehensive assessment of team dynamics so as to make sound judgments in leading multicultural teams. I hope this chapter will serve as a roadmap for those who aspire to become global leaders in multicultural teams as they embark on this exciting journey.

REFERENCES

Ang, S. and Van Dyne, L. (2008) "Conceptualization of Cultural Intelligence: Definition, Distinctiveness and Nomological Network." In S. Ang and L. Van Dyne (eds) *Handbook on Cultural Intelligence: Theory, Measurement and Applications* (Armonk, NY: M. E. Sharpe): 3–15.

Aune, K. S. and Aune, R. K. (1996) "Cultural Differences in the Self-Reported Experience and Expression of Emotions in Relationships." *Journal of Cross-Cultural Psychology* 27.1: 67–81.

Bachmann, A. (2006) "Melting Pot or Tossed Salad? Implications for Designing Effective Multicultural Workgroups." *Management International Review* 46.6: 721–748.

Bailey, J. R., Chen, C. C., and Dou, S.-G. (1997) "Conceptions of Self and Performance-Related Feedback in the U.S., Japan and China." *Journal of International Business Studies* 28.3: 605–625.

Beechler, S. and Javidan, M. (2007) "Leading with a Global Mindset." In M. R. Javidan, R. R. Steers and M. Hitt (eds) *Advances in International Management: The Global Mindset* (Oxford: Elsevier/JAI Press).

Bird, A. and Osland, J. (2004) "Global Competencies: An Introduction." In H. Lane, M. Maznevski, M. E. Mendenhall, and J. McNett, (eds) *The Blackwell Handbook of Global Management: A Guide to Managing Complexity* (Oxford: Blackwell).

Bird, A., Mendenhall, M., Stevens, M. J. and Oddou, G. (2010) "Defining the Content Domain of Intercultural Competence for Global Leaders." *Journal of Managerial Psychology* 25.8: 810–828.

Black, J. S. and Gregersen, H. B. (2000) "High Impact Training: Forging Leaders for the Global Frontier." *Human Resource Management* 39.2/3: 173–184.

Brewer, M. B. (1996) "When Contact is not Enough: Social Identity and Intergroup Cooperation." *International Journal of Intercultural Relations* 20.3/4: 291–303.

Chua, R. Y. J., Morris, M. W., and Ingram, P. (2009) "Guanxi versus Networking: Distinctive Configurations of Affect- and Cognition-Based Trust in the Networks of Chinese and American Managers." *Journal of International Business Studies* 40.3: 490–508.

Cramton, C. D. (2001) "The Mutual Knowledge Problem and its Consequences for Dispersed Collaboration." *Organization Science* 12.3: 346–371.

Day, D. V. (2000) "Leadership Development: A Review in Context." *The Leadership Quarterly* 11.4: 581–613.

Day, D. V. and Harrison, M. M. (2007) "A Multilevel, Identity-based Approach to Leadership Development." *Human Resource Management Review* 17.4: 360–373.

Day, D., Harrison, M., and Halpin, A. (2009) *An Integrative Approach to Leader Development: Connecting Adult Development, Identity, and Expertise* (New York, NY: Routledge).

De Dreu, C. K. W. (2006) "When Too Little or Too Much Hurts: Evidence for a Curvilinear Relationship between Task Conflict and Innovation in Teams." *Journal of Management* 32: 83–107.

DeShon, R. P., Kozlowski, S. W. J., Schmidt, A. M., Milner, K. R., and Wiechmann, D. (2004) "A Multiple-goal, Multilevel Model of Feedback Effects on the Regulation of Individual and Team Performance." *Journal of Applied Psychology* 89: 1035–1056.

Doney, P. M., Cannon, J. P., and Mullen, M. R. (1998) "Understanding the Influence of National Culture on the Development of Trust." *Academy of Management Review* 23.3: 601–620.

Dweck, C. S. (1986) "Motivational Processes Affecting Learning." *American Psychologist* 41: 1040–1048.

Earley, P. C. and Ang, S. (2003) *Cultural Intelligence: Individual Interactions Across Cultures* (Palo Alto, CA: Stanford University Press).

Earley, P. C. and Gibson, C. B. (2002) *Multinational Work Teams: A New Perspective* (Mahwah, NJ: Lawrence Erlbaum).

Edmondson, A. (1999) "Psychological Safety and Learning Behavior in Work Teams." *Administrative Science Quarterly,* 44: 350–383.

Edmondson, A. and Roloff, K. (2008) "Overcoming Barriers to Collaboration: Psychological Safety and Learning in Diverse Teams." In E. Sales, G. G. Goodwin, and C. S. Burke (eds) *Team Effectiveness in Complex Organizations: Cross-disciplinary Perspectives and Approaches* (Mahwah, NJ: Lawrence Erlbaum Associates): 183–208.

Elfenbein, H. A. and Ambady, N. (2002) "On the Universality and Cultural Specificity of Emotion Recognition: A Meta-Analysis." *Psychological Bulletin* 128: 203–235.

Elfenbein, H. A. and Shirako, A. (2006) "An Emotion Process Model for Multicultural Teams." In B. Mannix, M. Neale, and Y. R. Chen (eds) *Research on Managing Groups and Teams: National Culture and Groups* (Amsterdam: Elsevier): 263–297.

Eylon, D. and Au, K. Y. (1999) "Exploring Empowerment Cross-cultural Differences along the Power Distance Dimension." *International Journal of Intercultural Relations* 23: 373–385.

Fitzsimmons, S. R., Lee, Y.-t., and Brannen, M. Y. (2011) "Demystifying the Myth about Marginals: Implications for Global Leadership." Pre-publication conference (November 2011), IMD, Lausanne, Switzerland.

Gibson, C. B. and Zellmer-Bruhn, M. E. (2001) "Metaphors and Meaning: An Intercultural Analysis of the Concept of Teamwork." *Administrative Science Quarterly* 46.2: 274–303.

Gong, Y. and Fan, J. (2006) "Longitudinal Examination of the Role of Goal Orientation in Cross-Cultural Adjustment." *Journal of Applied Psychology* 91: 176–184.

Halevy, N. and Sagiv, L. (2008) "Teams Within and Across Cultures." In M. Peterson, P. Smith, and D. Thomas (eds) *Handbook of Cross-Cultural Management Research* (Thousand Oaks, CA: Sage): 253–268.

Harrison, D. A., Price, K. H., and Bell, M. P. (1998) "Beyond Relational Demography: Time and the Effects of Surface- and Deep-Level Diversity on Work Group Cohesion." *The Academy of Management Journal* 41.1: 96–107.

Hinds, P., Liu, L., and Lyon, J. (2011) "Putting the Global in Global Work: An Intercultural Lens on the Practice of Cross-national Collaboration." *Academy of Management Annals* 51.1: 135–188.

Hofstede, G. (2001) *Culture's Consequences: Comparing Values, Behaviors, Institutions, and Organizations across Nations*, 2nd edn (Thousand Oaks, CA: Sage).

Hogg, M. A. (2001) "A Social Identity Theory of Leadership." *Personality & Social Psychology Review* 5.3: 184–200.

Hogg, M. A. and van Knippenberg, D. (2003) "Social Identity and Leadership Processes in Groups." In M. P. Zanna (ed.) *Advances in Experimental Social Psychology* 35: 1–52 (San Diego, CA: Academic Press).

Hyatt, D. E. and Ruddy, T. M. (1997) "An Examination of the Relationship between Work Group Characteristics and Performance: Once More into the Breach." *Personnel Psychology 50:* 553–585.

Ilgen, D. R., Hollenbeck, J. R., Johnson, M., and Jundt, D. (2005) "Teams in Organizations: From Input-Process-Output Models to IMOI Models." *Annual Review of Psychology* 56.1: 517–543.

Iyengar, S. S. and Lepper, M. R. (1999) "Rethinking the Value of Choice: A Cultural Perspective on Intrinsic Motivation." *Journal of Personality and Social Psychology* 76: 349–366.

Janssens, M. and Brett, J. M. (2006) "Cultural Intelligence in Global Teams." *Group & Organization Management* 31.1: 124–153.

Jehn, K. A., Northcraft, G. B., and Neale, M. A. (1999) "Why Differences Make a Difference: A Field Study of Diversity, Conflict, and Performance in Workgroups." *Administrative Science Quarterly 44:* 741–763.

Jones, G. R. and George, J. M. (1998) "The Experience and Evolution of Trust: Implications for Cooperation and Teamwork." *Academy of Management Review 23:* 531–546.

Kirkman, B. L. and Mathieu, J. E. (2005) "The Dimensions and Antecedents of Team Virtuality." *Journal of Management* 31.5: 700–718.

Kirkman, B. L. and Shapiro, D. L. (1997) "The Impact of Cultural Values on Employee Resistance to Teams: Toward a Model of Globalized Self-managing Work Team Effectiveness." *Academy of Management Review* 22.3: 730–757.

Kirkman, B. L. and Shapiro, D. L. (2001) "The Impact of Cultural Values on Job Satisfaction and Organizational Commitment in Self-managing Work Teams: The Mediating Role of Employee Resistance." *Academy of Management Journal* 44.3: 557–569.

Klimoski, R. and Mohammed, S. (1994) "Team Mental Model: Construct or Metaphor?" *Journal of Management* 20.2: 403–437.

Kluckhohn, F. R. and Strodtbeck, F. L. (1961) *Variations in Value Orientations* (Evanston, IL: Row, Peterson and Company).

Kristof-Brown, A. L. and Guay, R. P. (2010) "Person–Environment Fit." In S. Zedeck (ed.) *APA Handbook of Industrial and Organizational Psychology* (Washington, DC: American Psychological Association).

Lau, D. C. and Murnighan, J. K. (1998) "Demographic Diversity and Faultlines: The Compositional Dynamics of Organizational Groups." *Academy of Management Review* 23.2: 325–340.

Lau, D. C. and Murnighan, J. K. (2005) "Interactions within Groups and Subgroups: The Effects of Demographic Faultlines." *Academy of Management Journal* 48.4: 645–659.

Lee, Y.-t. and Ramaswami, A. (forthcoming) "Fitting Person–Environment Fit Theories into a Cultural Context." In A. Kristof-Brown and J. Billsberry (eds) *New Directions in Organizational Fit* (Oxford: Wiley-Blackwell).

Lee, Y.-t., Masuda, A. D., and Cardona, P. (2010) "Multiple Cultural Identities in CQ and Global Leadership." Paper presented in the Annual Conference of Society for Industrial and Organizational Psychology (SIOP), Atlanta, 2010.

Lee, Y.-t., Reiche, B. S., and Song, D. (2010) "How Do Newcomers Fit In? The Dynamics between Person–Environment Fit and Social Capital across Cultures." *International Journal of Cross Cultural Management* 10.2: 153–174.

Lord, R. G. and Hall, R. J. (2005) "Identity, Deep Structure and the Development of Leadership Skill." *Leadership Quarterly* 16.4: 591–615.

Lovelace, K., Shapiro, D., and Weingart, L. R. (2001) "Maximizing Cross-functional New Product Teams' Innovativeness and Constraint Adherence: A Conflict Communications Perspective." *Academy of Management Journal* 44.4: 779–783.

Marks, M. A., Mathieu, J. E., and Zaccaro, S. J. (2001) "A Temporally Based Framework and Taxonomy of Team Processes." *Academy of Management Review* 26.3: 356–376.

Masuda, T. and Nisbett, R. A. (2001) "Attending Holistically versus Analytically: Comparing the Context Sensitivity of Japanese and Americans." *Journal of Personality and Social Psychology* 81, 5: 922–934.

Mathieu, J. E., Gilson, L. L., and Ruddy, T. M. (2006) "Empowerment and Team Effectiveness: An Empirical Test of an Integrated Model." *Journal of Applied Psychology* 91: 97–108.

Mathieu, J., Maynard, M. T., Rapp, T., and Gilson, L. (2008) "Team Effectiveness 1997–2007: A Review of Recent Advancements and a Glimpse into the Future." *Journal of Management* 34.3: 410–476.

Maznevski, M. L. (2008) "Leading Global Teams." In M. E. Mendenhall J. Osland, A. Bird, G. Oddou, and M. Maznevski (eds) *Global Leadership: Research, Practice and Development* (London: Routledge).

Maznevski, M. L. and Chudoba, K. M. (2000) "Bridging Space Over Time: Global Virtual Team Dynamics and Effectiveness." *Organization Science* 11.5: 473–492.

Maznevski, M. L. and Zander, L. (2001) "Leading Global Teams: Overcoming the Challenge of Power Paradoxes." In M. Mendenhall, T. Kuehlmann, and G. Stahl (eds) *Developing Global Business Leaders: Policies, Processes, and Innovations.* (Westport, CT: Quorum Books).

Mendenhall, M. E. (2006) "The Elusive, yet Critical Challenge of Developing Global Leaders." *European Management Journal* 24.6: 422–429.

Mohammed, S. and Nadkarni, S. (2011) "Temporal Diversity and Team Performance: The Moderating Role of Team Temporal Leadership." *Academy of Management Journal* 54.3: 489–508.

Morgeson, F. P., DeRue, D. S., and Karam, E. P. (2010) "Leadership in Teams: A Functional Approach to Understanding Leadership Structures and Processes." *Journal of Management* 36: 5–39.

Morrison, A. J. (2000) "Developing a Global Leadership Model." *Human Resource Management* 39.2/3: 117–131.

Ng, K. Y., Van Dyne, L., and Ang, S. (2009) "Developing Global Leaders: The Role of International Experience and Cultural Intelligence." In W. H. Mobley, Y. Wang, and M. Li (eds) *Advances in Global Leadership, Volume 5* (Bingley: Emerald Publishing): 225–250.

Oddou, G. R. and Mendenhall, M. (2008) "Global Leadership Development." M. E. Mendenhall, J. Osland, A. Bird, G. Oddou, and M. Maznevski (eds) *Global Leadership: Research, Practice and Development* (London: Routledge).

Osland, J. (2008) "Overview of the Global Leadership Literature." In M. E. Mendenhall, J. Osland, A. Bird, G. Oddou, and M. Maznevski (eds) *Global Leadership: Research, Practice and Development* (London: Routledge).

Paunova, M. and Lee, Y.-t. (2011) "Learning Goal Orientation and Leadership Emergence in Multicultural Teams: A Moderated Process Model." Paper presented at Academy of Management Meeting, San Antonio, 2011.

Pearce, C. L. (2004) "The Future of Leadership: Combining Vertical and Shared Leadership to Transform Knowledge Work." *Academy of Management Executive* 18.1: 47–57.

Richter, A. W., West, M. A., van Dick, R., and Dawson, J. F. (2006) "Boundary Spanners' Identification, Intergroup Contact, and Effective Intergroup Relations." *Academy of Management Journal* 49.6: 1252–1269.

Salas, E., Sims, D. E., and Burke, C. S. (2005) "Is There a Big Five in Teamwork?" *Small Group Research* 36: 555–599.

Shapiro, D. L., Furst, S. A., Spreitzer, G. M., and Glinow, M. A. V. (2002) "Transnational Teams in the Electronic Age: Are Team Identity and High Performance at Risk?" *Journal of Organizational Behavior* 23.4: 455–467.

Shokef, E. and Erez, M. (2006) "Shared Meaning Systems in Multicultural Teams." In B. Mannix, M. Neale, and Y. R. Chen (eds) *National Culture and Groups: Research on Managing Groups and Teams* (San Diego, CA: Elsevier/JAI Press): vol. 9: 325–352.

Stahl, G. K., Makela, K., Zander, L., and Maznevski, M. L. (2010) "A Look at the Bright Side of Multicultural Team Diversity." *Scandinavian Journal of Management* 26.4: 439–447.

Stahl, G. K., Maznevski, M. L., Voigt, A., and Jonsen, K. (2009) "Unraveling the Effects of Cultural Diversity in Teams: A Meta-analysis of Research on Multicultural Work Groups." *Journal of International Business Studies* 41.4: 690–709.

Swann, J. W. B., Polzer, J. T., Seyle, D. C., and Ko, S. J. (2004) "Finding Value in Diversity: Verification of Personal and Social Self-Views in Diverse Groups." *Academy of Management Review* 29.1: 9–27.

Tuckman, B. W. (1965) "Developmental Sequence in Small Groups." *Psychological Bulletin* 63.6: 384–399.

Van de Vliert, E. and De Dreu, C. K. W. (1994) "Optimizing Performance by Stimulating Conflict." *International Journal of Conflict Management* 5: 211–222.

Van de Vliert, E., Shi, K., Sanders, K., Wang, Y., and Huang, X. (2004) "Chinese and Dutch Interpretations of Supervisory Feedback." *Journal of Cross-Cultural Psychology* 35: 417–435.

Von Glinow, M. A., Shapiro, D. L., and Brett, J. M. (2004) "Can We Talk, and Should We? Managing Emotional Conflict in Multicultural Teams." *Academy of Management Review* 29.4: 578–592.

Wang, M. and Takeuchi, R. (2007) "The Role of Goal Orientation during Expatriation: A Cross-sectional and Longitudinal Investigation." *Journal of Applied Psychology* 92: 1437–1445.

Wu, J. B., Tsui, A. S., and Kinicki, A. J. (2010) "Consequences of Differentiated Leadership in Groups." *Academy of Management Journal* 53.1: 90–106.

The New Asia: Corporate Challenges and Leadership Development

RANDALL MORCK, Jarislowsky Distinguished Chair in Finance and Distinguished University Professor, University of Alberta, and **BERNARD YEUNG,** Stephen Riady Distinguished Professor and Dean, National University of Singapore Business School

Introduction

The financial crisis that erupted in 2008 exerts a lingering negative effect on the world economy, especially in the Western world. The US is recovering, but more slowly than most would like. Europe confronts a difficult sovereign debt crisis that threatens its monetary union. In the aftermath of the crisis, banks in both the US and EU are tightening credit, often citing capital structure ratio rules as the reason. In both the US and the EU, governments try to muster political will to impose fiscal disciplines, while also trying to deal with persistent high unemployment. Uncertainties about fiscal and monetary policies, and the recovery in general, make corporations hesitate to invest; and real investment remains very low.

In contrast, an economic renaissance continues in parts of Asia. Japan's rapid industrialization in the late nineteenth and early twentieth centuries gave the world a glimpse of Asians' ability to industrialize. Japan's rapid post-war reconstruction from the 1950s through the 1970s, and the Asian "four dragons" rapid growth from the 1970s through the 1990s provide further evidence that Asian economies can industrialize very quickly. Following the economic reforms China started in 1978, its economy has boomed and is now a significant contributor to global economic growth. In recent years, India also has registered strong growth. Many previously stagnant Asian economies are modernizing and industrializing fast. This Asian economic renaissance is a dramatic episode in global development history.

Growth opportunities are clearly abundant. The income gap between many Asian nations and most Western countries remains large, and huge profits remain to be made by closing it. Those profits are the cause of continuing excitement in Asian business circles. The International Monetary Fund (IMF) estimates per capita GDP, a widely used measure of living standards, for the United States at US$48,147, but at only US$5184 and US$1527 for China and India, respectively. These income gaps, together with other Asian economies' demonstrated ability to close income gaps, highlight exciting further growth opportunities. For example, if 20 percent of the Indian and Chinese combined population were to enjoy an increase in per capita income of US$10,000 in the next five years, which is quite reachable, the new-found income amounts to US$4.8 trillion. That income could buy vast quantities of consumer goods, housing, travel, and other things that Asian and Western companies produce.

But, the fact that this income gap lingers should also make us very cautious; finding a path to sustained rapid growth in much of Asia is nontrivial. Many parts of Asia are still affected by daunting illiteracy, and public health, infrastructure, and corruption problems. Too many Asian governments accept poor market institutions, dense bureaucracy, and ineptly written and inconsistently enforced laws and regulations as the way things are. In contrast to 1880s Japan and 1970s South Korea, neither India nor China has invested adequately in universal high-quality education and public health. India especially remains a primary reservoir for preventable diseases, such as polio; and one of us (Morck) recalls vividly a National Bureau of Economic Research conference where two distinguished Indian economists argued about whether, after adjusting for repeated revisions to the official definition of illiteracy, India's illiteracy rate was actually higher now than at independence. The question was left unresolved. China too underinvests in education, especially of migrants' children, and its environmental standards rival the worst pea soup fogs of Dickens's London—hardly an environment conducive to improved public health. These deficiencies constrain the pace of development and perhaps explain why China has failed yet to match South Korea's growth trajectory. An ill and ill-educated population is apt to compete poorly with the West, even a West stricken by the aftershocks of a financial crisis.

Persistent economic difficulties in the West are, moreover, not something Asians should hope for. Asia's growth, and the world's too, needs affluent consumers to buy the goods and services workers generate. The income gaps in China and Japan allow for a huge potential increase in consumption in Asia. But making good on this potential poses a huge challenge. When even a quarter of the populations of China, India, and Indonesia (about 0.7 billion consumers) start to consume like regular middle-income citizens of the West, the incremental demands on food, energy, and similar natural resources will be substantial, and the world will need either vast additional natural resources or vastly more efficient ways of using its current reserves. While the world, for example in the form of the World Bank, asks Asia to rebalance its growth drive from investment to consumption, the world clearly needs to deal the implications on resources constraints.

The world has faced such fears many times before, and has always overcome them. There will be ways to support the world's population at high levels of affluence. Seemingly looming resource constraints on growth have, in the past, been overcome by policies that make consumers and businesses highly sensitive to the real opportunity costs of resource misallocation. If the rising costs of resources are truly apparent, people change their behavior. People find cheaper substitutes that do the job just as well—as when rising copper prices led home builders to substitute PVC plumbing in the 1970s. People also become creative. Facing constraints, people with economic freedom develop product and process innovations that use less of more costly inputs to meet demand. Indeed, this is what productivity growth means: doing more with less.

The job is shared: businesses and consumers; and governments, non-profit organizations, researchers and academics can all play a role. Governments can reduce distortions by ensuring that regulations, subsidies, tax breaks, and the like do not prolong the overuse of scarce resources, and can remove impediments to flexibility and innovation, fostering better resource allocations and innovations. Academics do their part by educating a creative and innovative population, by providing aggregate learning via systematic positive taking stock of government and business experiences, and by advancing basic knowledge so as to give applied researchers in the business sector new tools for findings ways of creating more valuable outputs from less valuable inputs. The Japanese and the Four Dragons have shown remarkable adeptness at this, and China and India both look promising too.

To accommodate sustainable growth in the East, we need global coordination. The West's advanced technology, knowledge, and experience can certainly benefit the East; not utilizing them would be wasteful. Yet, the East inevitably has to rely on itself to develop indigenous solutions to meet its growth needs. Economic solutions are context-dependent, although utilization of resources and technology can be global. People with intimate knowledge of the people and environment, and actually experiencing the binding constraints, have an advantage in knowing the challenges and gaining more directly from overcoming them. If the East's economy were to rise rapidly, creating millions of new consumers, demand for the West's goods and services would rise, creating jobs and prosperity there too.

Business plays a role

Ever since their invention four centuries ago in the Netherlands, business corporations have contributed mightily to the West's economic and social pre-eminence. In recent years, both foreign and indigenous firms have been critical agents for economic transition in Asia and elsewhere. Asia's income gap gives corporations huge opportunities, but the way to benefit from these opportunities is largely uncharted.

We see several basic challenges, all pointing to the context-dependence nature of business. Clearly, multinational firms from the West have impressive technology and effective management systems-based centuries of accumulated wisdom—often gleaned from costly mistakes. They could serve as role models for Asia. Moreover, a huge literature shows how multinationals can—and often, though not always, do—generate positive spillovers in their host economies by stimulating competition and local learning. However, many North American and European business models and innovations were developed in a different context, and depend on very advanced market environments. Much attention to context is needed in the adaptation of their technology and management in Asia. Here are the challenges.[1]

The first challenge is that Asians' physical and social needs, and even their tastes, differ from those of Europeans and North Americans. Asians' tastes in food, drink, housing, cultural amenities, and any number of other things can differ from those of the median consumer in the West. As Asian consumers grow richer, their tastes may converge with those of consumers in the West—either because Asians' tastes become more Western or because Western consumers grow even more interested in sashimi and manga than they already are. Until that convergence, if it ever happens, businesses will have to adapt and adjust Western accumulated wisdom to Asian realities. This may well be a blessing. Japan, South Korea, and Taiwan have all shown how Asians can develop, produce, and market globally competitive innovations. Many of these well-known product and process innovations are based on technologies and concepts originated in the West, modified to meet Asian needs, and then marketed globally when Westerners' tastes for miniaturized electronics and high-definition flat screen televisions turned out to be similar to Asians' tastes after all. Experienced business executives can recall abundant animating examples from many parts of Asia. Japan, South Korea, China, and India have all adapted and modified some Western basic ideas and technologies to meet their consumers' needs, and the results are wondrous; more of these will happen as Asian consumers' purchasing power rises. And these successes will likely generate export opportunities into Western markets, especially if Western consumers' appreciation of things Asian continues to grow.

The second challenge is that institutional and cultural differences distinguish Asia from the West. To elaborate on these differences would take more space than we have at our disposal here. In essence, the legal, regulatory, religious, and cultural norms that govern our lives affect how we exchange ideas, how we interact more generally, and who we trust how much. The economic history of the Western World is a millennia-long saga of how, largely by trial and error, institutions—decrees, laws, regulations, religious proscriptions, and cultural norms— slowly evolved (Rosenberg and Birdzell 1986; Smith 2004). Western countries whose institutions promoted productivity growth prospered, and other Western nations fell behind until their citizens' wrath forced emulation of their more successful neighbors. Where institutions protected inefficient governance models and weakened market forces, personal relationship remained critical to sharing and cooperating, and large-scale business remained stillborn. Compared to the West, business dealings in Asia remain more relationship-based. This is a barrier to growth because the development and implementation of innovations seems to require rare combinations of talent, which can seldom be found in relatively small sets of blood relatives and close friends. Western institutions have evolved to allow people to trust strangers by forcing strangers to be trustworthy, at least for the most part. China's efforts to penalize makers of fake medicines, tainted mill products, and so on are important steps towards an economy with higher levels of trust. Bernie Madoff and other Western fraudsters show that the West has not fully licked this problem either. More importantly, perfect trust in strangers is not required to sustain an affluent society—all that is required is that people be trustworthy enough.

Here we encounter some critical issues. First, while some Asian corporations show vibrancy and creativity, many are still in a developmental stage in trying to systemize and professionalize their organizational structures. Work relationships remain intertwined with personal relationships. Second, within Asia, as among the Western countries, ample variation in market, political, and social institutional and cultural environments persists. Institutional evolution is ongoing, and just as genetic variation favors adaptation, institutional variation lets humanity run experiments to see what works best. Third, we should not over-play differences between East and West. Basic human nature is almost surely the same everywhere. Nonetheless, seemingly minor cultural differences can trip up seemingly bountiful business opportunities.

The third challenge is that the rest of Asia can follow Japan, the Four Dragons, and now possibly India and China in bypassing some developmental steps as it adopts new technology. For example, without telephone cables, many areas can start off wireless. Asia can apply modern technologies to build smart cities that utilize extensively sustainable energy, like solar and wind energy. Asia can use business analytics intelligently to cater to consumer needs more efficiently and effectively. Smart adaptations of basic technologies to local conditions can create opportunities to leap-frog over stages in which Western countries lingered for decades. Jumping over unnecessary intermediate stages can help Asia avoid waste as it attains rapid growth towards sustainable affluence. However, words are cheap. Leap-frogging ahead can be relatively simple, as in skipping over telephone networks based on landlines, but is often less straightforward. Leap-frogging opportunities can require as much creativity as any other form of innovation. And creativity seems to require the cultivation of a certain mindset.

Change in mindsets

Industrialization started in the West. In the past, business ideas originated disproportionately in the West and manufacturing took place there too. During the era of Western colonization, raw materials flowed from colonized regions to manufacturing in the West. That flow was inevitable because the West also contained the lion's share of affluent consumers and skilled workers. Locating production facilities near workers and consumers was logical.

The wave of globalization in the closing decades of the twentieth century, fueled by advances in transportation and communication technologies, generated a shift in this logic. Locating production facilities farther afield became feasible. And as Asian labour became increasingly skilled, the logic shifted further toward increased economic activity in Asia. Global corporations took to locating production in low-wage Asian economies and even collaborated with Asian companies, while relying heavily on technologies, management skills, and financial resources from developed countries.

As Asia grows, benefitting from its increasingly large-scale industrialization, another shift is taking place. Asian consumers' purchasing power is rising, and as affluent consumers become ever more evenly distributed across East and the West, straightforward business logic will increasingly favor the locating of economic activity in fast-growing Asian countries. As affluent Asians look for more varied ways to save, investing in those businesses by buying their shares and bonds will also move the financing of economic development to Asia. This spread of economic activity into Asia means that important business and technological ideas are likely to originate in both the West and the East in the future. Moreover, as manufacturing takes root throughout Asia, the head offices of major global corporations are also increasingly likely to be found in Asia. We see this geographic shift in economic activity evoking, or perhaps being evoked by, a shift in mindset.

One change in mindset will be a recognition everywhere of the significant new economic role of Asia. Business presence in the East will no longer be just for manufacturing, nor for being regional merchants. As Asian consumers grow affluent, Asian retailing is likely to provide important profits centers for Asian and Western corporations. Innovations, either imported or indigenous, aimed at attracting Asian customers will become ever more profitable, as will product and process innovations that solve resource and environmental constraints to let Asian consumers grow still more affluent. Successful corporations will become solution-providers for Asian customers, sources of Asia's ascent towards the First World, and transmitters of globally scalable innovations that originated in Asia.

We feel that this change will be accompanied by a less "top-down" and more "bottom-up" flow of information within successful businesses. In this new era, corporations will have to capture and assimilate information from multiple Asian and Western markets to make intelligent predictions about future consumer demand. They will need to become aware of possible technological and process innovations that could cater to consumers' existing and future needs effectively and efficiently. To do so, corporations will need vastly more sensitive antennae than many now possess.

Academics have long debated this issue. Friedrich von Hayek (1941) writes that management needs to be prescient about the future. Joseph A.

Schumpeter (1912; English translation 1934) writes that growth is driven by creative innovators. Ronald Coase (1937) writes about successful firms being run by experts who can assimilate information, discern market needs, and coordinate and execute teamwork effectively. David Teece, Gary Pisano and Amy Shuen (1977) combine all these to argue that successful businesses need "corporate dynamic capabilities." All these fundamental ideas on the theory of the firm were built when the world was not as globalized as now, but remain highly relevant.

The reason we see a more "bottom-up" mode of business organization spreading is that large-scale and complex problems of assimilating information, identifying opportunities, and coordinating teamwork to capture them tend to overwhelm concentrated decision-making. Von Hayek (1945) developed these ideas in correctly predicting precisely how and why market economies would ultimately prevail over central planning. The same reasoning applies to management: corporations need a robust "bottom-up" information flow to get top-level decision-making right. Somehow, big businesses will need to develop the mindset and mechanisms to let top management assimilate insights and ideas from employees, customers, and suppliers spread across vastly disparate geographic areas and cultural milieus, and to condense viable strategies and operation plans to work as a team from those insights and ideas.

In a sense, this will require something akin to democratic decision-making, a concept quite contradictory to the very concept of a business corporation. Ronald Coase (1937) quite rightly points out that a corporation's key advantage is that it puts people who are particularly good at assimilating information and assigning work to other people in a coordinated manner in charge of other people, who submit themselves to orders from the decision-maker. Hence, centralized decision-making is the whole point: it lets talented executives specialize in making speedy and effective decisions to benefit all concerned. Realistically, corporations need decision-makers, and employees have to accept centralized decisions.

It seems unlikely that letting General Motors' employees, or even SUV buyers, vote on major corporate decisions would have saved the firm from bankruptcy. But a robust "bottom-up" information flow does not require voting (although it is true that employees and consumers who disagree can "vote with their feet" by taking their skills or purchases elsewhere). Rather, we see something like the following developing: first, for top decision-makers to have access to information from all levels they have to adopt employee empowerment. A tolerance for negative feedback will have to develop. If sales personnel, who see customers doubting a product, or workers, who see flaws in production or design, are to pass that very valuable information up the chain of command, top decision-makers must learn to accept challenges to their past decisions. Flat organizational arrangements and open access systems that grant employees equal "air space" can help in this, as can clear policies of "not shooting the messenger." Perhaps just as important, top decision-makers will have to practice merit-based promotion and pay systems. Cronyism and favoritism become very dangerous if they impede the upward flow of unbiased information.

All this is far easier said than done. We suspect that a conscious shift in mindset is necessary. We worry that too many dominant corporations in Asia are family-controlled, with family members given privileged status as top decision-makers and favoured "sons" and "grandsons" treated as superior beings. Princelings can easily be as big a hindrance to progress in business as in politics. As Fukuyama (2011) shows in a huge variety of settings, our biologically based tendency to favor our genetic kin has repeatedly undermined our broader well-being. Substituting political loyalty for competence works no better than does substituting genes for talent: state-owned enterprises present the same barriers to attaining a genuinely flat organization with meaningfully open access. Some dominant corporations in Asia are foreign-owned multinationals. Regional offices are often granted limited autonomy and valued only as subordinates of headquarters.

Develop talent

Flat organizations, open access to decision-makers, and merit-based rewards are all just management formats. They are merely potential means to an end. An effective "bottom-up" information flow relies on people: a workforce filled with people able to "connect the dots" to flag problems and conceive of profitable innovations on a corporation-wide basis. People in positions to discern future consumer needs must somehow communicate that information to people with knowledge of the disparate talents of people scattered throughout the corporation so that people with a talent for organizing and directing effective teams can respond appropriately. This is not even easy to say!

Giving fuller flight to our fancy, in such a corporation, employees need to be full of curiosity, confident that asking questions will not be punished, be able to see market conditions, cognizant of capabilities inside and outside of their corporations, and willing to take a chance in offering ideas. They should also have an enterprise perspective: they should apprehend results from the perspective of the corporation as a whole, rather than one department or plant.

Calling for a wholesale change in human nature is obviously absurd. Fortunately, curiosity seems to be a fundamental human asset. Obedience is valued in old-fashioned corporations. However, that can be inconsistent with curiosity. Suppressing questioning creates blind followers.

But blind curiosity, without awareness, wastes energies. Insightful curiosity requires that people at all levels be able aware of internal and external market opportunities and experiences. That calls for creating employees exposures. Exposures enrich one's information bank and intelligent ideas are based on rich information.

Agile corporations encourage risk-taking. Old-fashioned hierarchical corporations with centralized decision-making tend to suppress risk-taking. There is value in punishing poor decisions based on self-interest and unsound logic. Yet, punishment for good risk-taking generates employees who just work according to the corporate "menu," and there will be no attempts to spot opportunities and innovations. Good risk-taking is based on a good due process of capital budgeting focussing on the overall corporate bottomline. Employees should be encouraged, even if bad luck brings in downside results.

We do not presume to predict how corporations will do all this, but we feel sure that some will manage it. The ones that do will survive and prosper; the others will either fall away or emulate their more "fit" rivals. As Asia joins the First World, economic selection is likely to grow more severe. Corporations will have to adapt more rapidly than in the past if they are to survive. Adaptable corporations have bottom-up organization, cultivate curiosity, and encourage experimentation and risk-taking. Old-fashioned hierarchical corporations, with centralized decision-making, which effectively makes them miniature centrally planned economies within larger market economies, tend to suppress questions, experimentation, and risk-taking. Not all experiments succeed, and not all risks end well. National economies need all sorts of experiments to be run and all sorts of risks to be taken so that their businesses can find the best way forward.

At both corporation and social level, experimentation and risk-taking should be encouraged, even if many efforts end in failure. Western countries cushion the costs of failure to small entrepreneurs with bankruptcy protection that encourages people to try again and social safety nets that make failure less unbearable. Developed countries' progressive corporate income tax systems also cushion the costs of failure to large corporations by imposing high taxes on successful innovators while letting unsuccessful risk-takers deduct their losses. In a very real sense, the government collects part of the upside gains from success with high taxes and pays part of the downside cost of failure by granting tax deductions.

Conclusion

The slow recovery of the US and the eurozone economies, as Asia continues its rapid growth is leading to a new distribution of consumer power. Increasingly affluent Asian consumers and rising Asian corporations stand poised to change the global economy in important ways.

First, hundreds of millions of increasingly affluent Asian consumers will undoubtedly increase global demand for natural resources. The world economy would best respond to this with heightened sensitivity to the opportunity costs of resource misallocation so that people and firms that develop product and process innovations to satisfy more consumer needs with fewer resources profit from this. Doing more with less is, in a nutshell, what productivity growth is about. Increasingly productive business organizations are the obvious solution.

Second, these sorts of innovation will arise on a global scale. The model of innovations originating in the West, and only filtering over to Asia to take advantage of cheap labor, will fall away. Driven by more evenly distributed consumer power, innovations will increasingly arise both in Asia and the West. Some of this innovation will surely entail developing entirely new technologies. But adapting existing technologies to more efficiently meet massive new Asian consumer demand could be just as important. Leap-frogging over relatively inefficient legacy technologies that persist in the West because they are too expensive to replace can let Asian consumers attain comparable levels of affluence to those enjoyed in the West, yet exert less pressure on global resource reserves.

Third, the top executives and employees of the corporations that make these things happen will, we think, adopt a new mindset. As these changes alter the balance of the global economy, the forces of economic selection will grow more severe. The corporations that adapt to these changes will, we think, be those that better make use of the information that surrounds them. Their top decision-makers will need access to information about unprecedentedly diverse consumers in unprecedentedly rapidly changing environments. To remain players in this unfolding world, we think corporations will need to encourage a robust "bottom-up" flow of information. This would let corporate leaders react to changes and opportunities, and redeploy and coordinate the corporations' physical resources and talented employees rapidly.

Fourth, this change in mindset will require that corporations also use fair merit-based reward systems. Nepotism and cronyism need not doom a firm in a stable, protected environment. It does not require a genius to continue doing things the way they have always been done. But in a rapidly changing world, exposed to the full force of economic selection, having genuinely talented people in charge becomes essential to survival. Cronyism and nepotism become unbearable costs.

Fifth, people make or break any system. The corporations that survive and prosper in the unfolding new world will encourage their employees' curiosity and welcome their questions. Universities and schools need to step forward to prepare employees for these new responsibilities.

Finally, leadership counts. In this new world economic order, corporations have many heavy burdens. Corporations have to develop leaders who can and want to embrace the above points, and hone their own skills in leading their companies accordingly in the current transformational period. We reemphasize that the critical issue is not developing leadership skills, but developing understanding and embracement of the concepts.

NOTES

1 The first two points below are developed in Pankaj Ghemawat's book, *Redefining Global Strategy* (2007).

REFERENCES

Coase, Ronald (1937) "The Nature of the Firm." *Economica* 4: 386–405.

Fukuyama, Francis (2011) *The Origin of Political Order* (London: Profile Books).

Ghemawat, Pankaj (2007) *Redefining Global Strategy: Crossing Borders in a World Where Differences Still Matter* (Cambridge, MA: Harvard Business Press).

Hayek, Friedrich von (1941) *The Pure Theory of Capital* (Chicago, IL: University of Chicago Press).

Hayek, Friedrich von (1945) "The Use of Knowledge in Society." *American Economic Review* 35 (September): 519–530.

Rosenberg, Nathan and Birdzell, Luther Earle (1986) *How the West Grew Rich: The Economic Transformation of the Industrial World* (New York, NY: Basic Books).

Schumpeter, Joseph, A. (1912/1934) *The Theory of Economic Development* (Cambridge, MA: Harvard University Press).

Smith, Mark (2004) *A History of the Global Stock Market: From Ancient Rome to Silicon Valley* (Chicago, IL: University of Chicago Press).

Teece, David, Pisano, Gary and Shuen, Amy (1997) "Dynamic Capabilities and Strategic Management." *Strategic Management Journal* 18.7: 509–531.

Accounting for Culture in the Development of Global Leaders

CARLOS SÁNCHEZ-RUNDE, Professor of Managing People in Organizations, IESE Business School, **LUCIARA NARDON**, Assistant Professor of International Business, Sprott School of Business, Carleton University, and **RICHARD M. STEERS**, Professor of Organization and Management, Lundquist College of Business, University of Oregon

U nderstanding why organizations fail or succeed typically requires, among other things, an assessment of leadership behaviors and contexts. Some experts, mostly those with a stronger psychological inclination, emphasize the figure of those in charge, their personality traits and habits, their charisma and style, their personal or task orientations, and so on. It is then the *behavior* displayed by specific individuals, particularly those at the top, which accounts for the performance of the firm. Other pundits, however, favor a sociological bias and explain performance less in terms of the behavior of the leader, and more as a function of the organizational leadership *context*, including here processes and systems, policies and practises orienting the final behavior of people in the organization. Of course, nobody will seriously disregard that both context and behaviors matter, but the fact is that scholars have traditionally felt more comfortable choosing one alternative viewpoint than trying to integrate both of them. As a result, traditional approaches to leadership in organizations suffer from partiality and excessive simplification. Consider the following scenario.

Imagine you knew very little about organizations and leadership and wanted to access the fundamental, state-of-the-art knowledge of the field. You could first check at your public or university library for books on the subject, only to find literally hundreds of titles available. What would first look like great news (there is a lot of intellectual effort around the topic) would finally disappoint and worry you because, as you began perusing the first volumes you would realize that they all talk about basically the same phenomenon, but they propose extremely different approaches, analyses, and advice for practise. On top of that, those approaches are often incompatible and contradictory, or extremely vague and ambiguous.[1] The myriad contributions to the leadership literature is actually bad news, for it confirms an apparently paradoxical reality: the less we know about a phenomenon, the more books can be written about it. Fine, you could say, rather than blindly looking on your own for books on the topic, you could consult with a few learned business school professors, some recognized academic experts in organizational leadership, and ask them how to approach the basic concepts. They will easily point you at a dozen—or more—radically different, competing theories on leadership that will keep you wondering how to make sense of it all. Armed with some patience, you could still navigate through this immense literature looking for some commonalities and agreements. Something will soon stand out but, let us warn you, you are not going to like it. You would immediately notice that most of the work of experts in the field (academic scholars, sophisticated practitioners, consultants) was done in the United States, by Americans, with the American reality in mind. While this has begun to change lately, the truth is that the overall situation is still lacking in terms of cultural and geographic balance.[2]

We then face a double challenge. First, in order to talk meaningfully about leadership and provide some practical advice, we need to work through the ambiguity and partiality of the leadership concepts that dominate the managerial landscape. Second, we need to recognize that, culturally, that landscape is much more diverse than most leadership studies to date have assumed. Both challenges are not fully independent from each other. It is our intuition that some of the excessive simplifications and ambiguities around the leadership phenomenon have a lot to do with past attempts at the mere exportation of American models and practises across borders. Some of those attempts have actually proved quite successful. Others have not. In any case, we also need to understand why those successes and failures actually happen. Accordingly, in this chapter we first review the ambiguities and partialities around the leadership phenomenon. Second, we briefly address the main challenges to bringing back the cultural context into the discussion of global leadership. Third, we discuss the three main efforts to date at integrating culture and leadership. Next, we illustrate the findings of the cross-cultural leadership research with the particularities of Chinese leadership as a way to contrast it with dominant Western views. Finally, we offer some conclusions and implications for global leadership practise.

The ambiguities of global leadership

The ambiguities of leadership go beyond emphasizing either leadership behaviors or contexts rather than accounting for both emphases. Previous work on management dualities shows that effective organizations tend to excel at reconciling apparently opposing tendencies while behaving in consistent ways (Sanchez-Runde and Pettigrew, 2003). Life might seem simpler when choosing one extreme of a duality continuum than when accommodating both sides, but only at the expense of longer-term, sustainable efficiencies. It is usually misguided to follow an *either/or* approach that frames organizational problems in terms of whether, for instance, firms need to centralize or decentralize, rely on hierarchies or networks, focus on the short or the long term, customize or mass-produce, specialize or generalize, compete on costs or differentiation, go global or stay local, explore new possibilities or stabilize current achievements, and so on. Instead, successful organizations tend to endorse *both/and* perspectives that aim at simultaneously achieving the benefits of centralizing and decentralizing, competing on costs and differentiation, keeping global and local perspectives, and so on. In fact, Evans and Doz (1992) point out that all crucial organizational challenges can and should be put in terms of underlying dualities that need conciliation rather than resolution, thus paving the way for comprehensive and sophisticated frameworks in tune with the complexities of organizational life.

Some efforts, though not many, have centered on the way to balance competing or apparently contradictory ideas and activities. These tensions have been framed as paradoxes (Handy, 1994), dilemmas (Hampden-Turner, 1990), dialectics (Mittroff and Linstone, 1993), competing goals and values (Cyert and March, 1992), and dualities (Pettigrew and Fenton, 2000). However, while we have gained important insights from this literature, the cultural variable has basically been absent, and the most that has been done in this regard has had an international and comparative approach, but one that was clearly not cross-cultural in nature. With this caveat in mind, let us review briefly how the dualistic viewpoint enlightens leadership phenomena in organizations.

Researchers in the INNFORM Program[3] in the United States, Europe, and Japan identified a basic set of leadership dualities in innovative organizations in those countries. These dualities underline four sets of issues (Sanchez-Runde, Massini, and Quintanilla, 2003): first, whether leadership needs to be concentrated in a few leading figures or should rather be distributed along all organizational levels; second, the extent to which leadership and management should be conceptualized as substantially different phenomena; third, whether organizational activities should be encouraged or directly mandated; and finally, the balancing of long-term trust building in the face of growingly temporary commitments. With the benefit of time, we now realize that while we certainly have much to win by reconciling the opposing tendencies behind those dualities, cultural considerations need to be brought into the picture from the very beginning if we are to truly realize their potential. Let us examine a couple of examples on some of the cultural issues underlying those dualities.

Take, for instance, the duality of whether organizations should think in terms of leading or managing. The standard, Western approach follows the classic distinction that talks of managers as those who "do things right," versus leaders as those who "do the right things." What the research generally reports here is that successful organizations combine both approaches rather than merely choosing one over the other. Those in positions of high responsibility in the firm will then be expected to behave as both good *leaders* and *managers*, thus "doing the right things right." This piece of advice, however, is not culture-free. In some societies, worldviews take a rather fatalist approach, and reality is seen as unfolding under the rule of preordained destiny. Individuals are not so much expected to act but to integrate themselves and follow the flow of events. Hinduism, Buddhism, and Daoism, with their different versions of karma, illumination, and "wu wei" (literally, "no action" in the Chinese language) commonly hold a bias for compliance rather than action, which is not easily compatible with typical decision-making approaches favored in the West. The notion of organizational life as something "manageable" already incorporates a cultural bias that not all cultures share. Employee leadership and motivation theories in the Indian tradition, for instance, sound rather difficult to understand for those who have not been exposed to these traditions (Kanungo and Mendonca, 1994; Schumaker, 1997). Similarly, the concept of efficiency and leader performance in traditional Chinese thought is also at odds with standard Western approaches (Jullien, 1996).

A second example of how difficult can be to extend dualistic theory across culture is illustrated along the need to reconcile the temporality of many current employment arrangements with the need of a long-term orientation to employee–organization linkages. This is the fundamental issue around the concept of organizational commitment as experienced by global companies today. The literature on organizational commitment has been quite standard in the field of organizational behavior since the fundamental work of Porter and his colleagues (Mowday, Steers, and Porter, 1982). However, when transplanted to cultures beyond the direct Western influence, things change drastically. Japanese employees are well known for their strong commitment to their organizations. Organizations become a sort of second family, and employees become deeply attached to their firms. Firms in turn reciprocate with lifelong employment contracts. Surprisingly, when researchers measure commitment in Japan and the United States, American employees tend to show stronger scores. What happens here is that commitment is so crucial to Japanese employees and they feel so serious about it, that they see the slightest want in that domain as a serious misbehavior, thus adhering to a much stricter standard. When self-assessing their commitment, Japanese employees rate themselves with lower scores simply because the standard of their commitment duties are significantly higher than American ones. A simple look at the comparative scores, therefore, would teach us the wrong lesson. The average Japanese employees, despite their lower scores, do display higher commitment than the average American employees (Lincoln and Kalleberg, 1990).

Our conceptual frameworks to deal with the ambiguities of leadership need to account for cultural differences. What is clearly established in Western environments may or may not work across boundaries. This is a crucial challenge for global companies, and it poses basic dilemmas on whether firms need to adopt a universal approach across locations or company policies and processes need to be adapted to local conditions. Before we advance in our understanding of leadership across cultures, we need to clarify the role of culture in our organization models.

Bringing culture back into the organizational picture

Since experts began to realize that organizational processes, practises, and performance cannot be fully explained without making reference to places, geographies, and cultures, some progress has been made in the field. There are signs, however, that this progress is not as straightforward as initially imagined, and the answer to this problem may have a lot to do with the way "culture" has been introduced in our research.

The first studies took an international, comparative approach. This meant that some in-depth analyses initially developed in the US would be replicated in a few other countries (mostly European) in order to establish comparisons with the American results. A first sense of differences thus emerged, but many questions were still unanswered. One main difficulty relates to the fact that everything in that research was developed in the US (literature reviews, models, and choice of variables for analysis) and later exported to third countries. As a result, anything that could prove indigenous to a certain third country was likely to remain unaccounted. If the studies included some in-depth, qualitative design, some of those issues could at least be identified. If the research followed, as most did, a questionnaire-based, quantitative approach, the issues were not even likely to appear in the radar screen. It took some time for scholars in the third countries to raise the alarm, and a second round of research effort was prepared.

The main improvements of that second round had to do with bringing in some nationals to those third countries to the initial stages of the development of the research so that some country peculiarities could be introduced in the research design. At the same time, researchers began to expand the number of countries surveyed, including distant countries (mostly Japan). Questionnaires were then improved, and culture was introduced as a control variable along with the other dependent and independent variables. The result was that many of those studies could identify that something different went on in different countries, but the nature of the phenomenon was not completely clear. Logically, little or no advice could be given in terms of how to manage the phenomenon beyond the need to increase the prudence of practitioners. The main assumption behind this approach was that a given situation could be compared across cultures (for instance, leadership behaviors) and that country differences could be identified within common behavior constructs, similar to different people enjoying different flavors of ice cream. What this research was not ready to solve was the issue of the nature of the construct itself (the specific leadership behaviors).

Researchers had been too quick in their assuming that they were dealing with the same phenomenon only across different cultures. But, as the discussion above on the commitment differences in Japan and the US illustrated, there is a point where the assumption of sameness of the phenomenon can no be longer maintained. Attachment to the organization according to American practise—our common concept of commitment—simply does not apply in Japan. The Japanese hold such a different view of the duties toward their organizations that transplanting an American commitment concept will not help capture the Japanese attachment phenomenon. People across countries may no longer be favoring different ice cream flavors; they may prefer different types of dessert altogether.

In other words, culture is not like another variable missing in previous efforts that careful research has to introduce into the research design. Culture is, if anything, a meta-variable that helps determine the rest of variables. This means that we need to look beyond single explanations of what is at work in a given situation (higher or lower levels of commitment, for instance) and move towards a deeper understanding of the whole pattern of events and responses in a given context. The whole research design needs to be framed and thought through in terms of how the questions make more or less sense in different cultural contexts, and all the research apparatus can then just follow. In order to do so, however, the researchers themselves need to be fluent in the different cultural traditions, and research teams have to include researchers with multiple cultural backgrounds and expertise. This explains why this type of research is much more expensive and time-consuming than standard research. We cannot avoid this type of research if we are to make progress in the management of global organizations, because this is not only a research design issue. In fact, those approaches to culture bring us substantially differentiated brands of knowledge on leadership across cultures.

The first approaches ignored the cultural element. Tacitly, they espoused a universal approach in that effective leadership was not sensitive to cultural distance. In so doing, they provided some sort of baseline for future studies that focussed on culture as another independent variable. Departures from that baseline constituted the phenomena with which culture was likely to be interacting. This helped experts begin to isolate some of those phenomena, but the knowledge so derived mostly referred to a local, mostly American reality. Comparative studies were launched, and differences in the cultural domain could be traced to specific cultural dimensions. We learned that where countries lay in terms of their extent of individualism-collectivism, and power distance, for instance, could help us understand that leadership behaviors had more to do with the work tasks than personal relations, or that leader traits centered on being independent, forceful, and assertive. Alternatively, in more collectivist cultures, leaders tended to focus on personal interactions (even becoming paternalistic), emphasized face-saving, and displayed values of interdependence, collaboration, and humility (Gelfand, Bhawuk, Nishii, and Bechtold, 2004). Later-generation studies (like those of the GLOBE program) began to show that the very definition of the organizational phenomena is dependent on the culture of the country. Therefore, one also needed to attend to intra-cultural differences, realizing that, in the end, humans within a given culture hold much in common but they also behave differently. With this, the field began to achieve a needed balance between the cultural context and the particularities of each person, and more realistic and pragmatic approaches to leadership management could emerge.

To understand the managerial implications of this state of things, consider the best practise approaches that many strategy and people management textbooks spouse. The fundamental idea behind this approach is that after careful benchmarking of managerial practise in a given industry, one can isolate those practises championed by the best performers and diffuse them across firms in the industry. This is not the place to dwell on this matter, but a cursory review of textbooks—as well as the dominant advice from strategy and people management consultants—shows that those compilations of best practises very rarely introduce cultural considerations at all, implicitly assuming levels of cultural homogeneity that are not realistic. We need to reconsider this situation, as firms compete in increasingly diverse environments.

Cross-cultural leadership: Current approaches and limitations

Peter Drucker has stressed that the organization of the future will not survive on the assumption that leadership was some sort of innate trait that firms needed to identify among their current or potential personnel. Some leaders might be born but, if at all, they are too few to solve the leadership needs of global companies (Drucker, 1996). Leadership skills, most management experts conclude, improve with formal educational programs. Differences appear on how to approach leadership so that local managers may become global leaders. Different authors present three main alternatives to do so.[4]

The first alternative, which we call the *universal approach* to cross-cultural leadership, considers leadership as fully standard across boundaries, regardless of the culture of the location. This assumes that leadership traits and behaviors are constant and universal. Once the best approach to leading an organization has been identified and developed, its applicability across cultures should not be problematic and organizational performance should follow. This is how most Western leadership theories evolved. The literature on transformational leadership is a clear example of this line of thought. In this view, leaders are to create a universally accepted vision for the future or the organization, and all resources are then to be marshaled to fulfill that vision. Research, however, has shown that these universal models do not travel well, especially when leaving Western countries (Kase, Slocum, and Zhang, 2011).

The second alternative, what we call the *normative approach*, focusses on the enduring personal knowledge, skills, and abilities that characterize global leaders. These are prescriptive models advising how to behave in different settings. What this approach does is to elaborate a view of global leadership from the standpoint of global realities, whereas the universal approach simply generalized findings from local (Western) settings to the global arena. It is in a way similar to the universal approach in that its advice travels equally across borders, but it is already born from the experience of sophisticated managers in borderless, global organizations. This is the approach behind most models emphasizing the need for a global mindset and cultural intelligence. Successful global leaders in this view exhibit cosmopolitanism, cognitive complexity, honesty, humility, and personal resilience. Research, however, still needs to support these claims, and doubts arise among experts on whether those global traits can actually be equally effective in all parts of the world. When analyzing the communication patterns of successful leaders, for instance, different cultures favor and require different mediated cognitions (including language and language structures, selective perception, cognitive evaluation, and cultural logic) and communication protocols (that is, appropriate logics, message formatting, conversational pragmatics, and acceptable behaviors). Those mediated cognitions and communication protocols depend on the cultural context, and it is not clear that a single normative approach addresses the issue for all cultures under a global agenda (Nardon, Steers, and Sanchez-Runde, 2011).

Finally, the third alternative, which we name the *contingent approach*, assumes that there are no universal, prescriptive models, either developed at the local or global scale, that work effectively regardless of culture. This view takes leadership as culturally embedded, and that successful leaders need to attune their skills and behaviors according to cultural expectations and demands. This is a major finding from the GLOBE research program mentioned earlier. Leadership is culturally contingent. Successful leaders in one country tend to score higher in some dimensions (like assertiveness, person or task orientation, or individualism, to name a few) and lower in others. Successful American managers, for instance, are mostly assertive, performance-oriented, and individualist. Chinese leaders, in contrast, tend to score higher than Americans in power distance and uncertainty avoidance.

While we sympathize with this contingent approach, we do not feel comfortable in strongly adhering to one alternative to the complete exclusion of the others. We can gain a lot from a thoughtful balancing of these approaches. Take, for instance, the issue of ethical leadership across cultures. GLOBE researchers studied the endorsement of ethical leadership across cultures, and found some convergence, among theorists, on several key attributes of ethical leaders, including the following five: character and integrity; ethical awareness; community and people orientation; motivating, empowering and encouraging people; and ethical accountability. Using their own empirical data from more than 60 cultures, those researchers derived four factors that matched four of those five attributes mentioned. The results showed that all cultures endorsed those factors (what would seem like support for universalist and normative approaches), but that the endorsement differed significantly across cultures (as a contingent approach would predict) (for a more elaborate analysis, see Steers, Sanchez-Runde, and Nardon, 2010: 372–3).

Once recognized that leadership is fundamentally a cultural construct, we think that is it key to focus on the local expectations produced at the location where leaders need to act. The rationale for this is deeply anchored in the psychology of leadership learning behaviors, which are mostly local by definition. Let us summarize the environments in which these leadership behaviors first take place and we will better understand the challenges of functioning in transplanted environments, away from our own original ground.

Individual leadership patterns follow role behaviors learned from early ages. The influence of family, school, and first work environments are crucial for self-understanding and relating to others. Authoritarian paternal roles and disciplinarian schooling, for instance, breed command-and-control, non-participative management attitudes toward performance and work relationships (Fiske, 1992; González-Simancas, 1992; Kohn, 1993). The lasting influence of the management style of an individual's first boss is well documented in the organizational behavior literature (Gerstner, 1994). It is only natural that individuals grow up taking their experiences as the only alternatives available, and the realization that a broader range of possibilities exists requires having experienced some of those alternatives. Of course, those early educational experiences typically take part in local environments (Triandis, 1994). It is true that diversity is increasingly present in most social settings in many countries, but their long-term effect on future behaviors still needs to be assessed (Heine, 2008). Interestingly, most leadership development typically remains silent about the personal, educational background individuals experience and rather focusses on forward-looking initiatives, like coaching and mentoring.

Initial experiences at home, school, and work present some notes that make them significantly different from newer experiences for managers, including the development and training remedial programs at companies or business schools in which managers and expatriates usually engage.

Firstly, initial learning experiences (including leader and follower roles and situations) are just about learning, in the sense that small children and young adults experience them with a blank background, in a vacuum of prior experiences. The influence of those experiences is deep and lasting. Leaders working in one culture who need to lead in a different culture have to learn new approaches that will coexist with their prior ones, and this creates cognitive complexity and inconsistencies. This learning is therefore not simple and straightforward, and their effects are more volatile and superficial. Internalizing this newer, secondary cultural learning is then likely to take longer and may not proceed as easily. Second, initial experiences, because they are the first ones the person acquires, become absolute, and cannot be related to other experiences, thus remaining unreferenced and unconditioned. Newer learning, to the contrary, operates against a background of initial experiences that become a referent, a comparison node, for incoming ones. At times, in case of conflicting initial and new experiences, some de-learning needs to take place, something that was never the case when the initial experiences happened. This makes, again, for a more complex, problematic, and fragile acquisition of newer leading-following roles. At this point, however, we lack empirical research that supports the educational and training approaches that resolve these issues.

Another difference in the development of leadership roles relates to the strength of the cultural environment in which the learning takes place. Home and school tend to constitute very strong environments in the sense that the values espoused are extremely salient and homogeneous. The work environment tends to be culturally weaker in that value congruence is not usually as strong owing to the presence of more diverse viewpoints and backgrounds. It is true that smaller and local firms tend to be more culturally homogeneous and consistent than larger and multinational companies. But the cultural environments in both types of organizations are still weaker than those of single homes and schools. The roles learned in stronger culture environments (home, school) are generally likely to hold a more profound influence on the individual and, again, those environments are usually local, and less diverse than standard work environments. Learning newer roles, which might become a better fit to changing cultural conditions and geographies, meet more serious challenges than learning the original roles met.

In sum, cross-cultural leadership models, regardless of whether they are universal, normative, or contingent, need to account for the individual learning processes through which global leaders need advance, as well as relate those processes to the strength of the work context in which they will operate. Unless this issue is seriously addressed, we will not advance beyond the basic, general principles.

In the next section, we illustrate the effects of culture on the concept and practise of leadership in China, against the background of current Western approaches.

Leadership in context: The example of China

Some international companies operating in China portray the behavior of Chinese employees as passive, uncertain, and ambiguous. Issues then arise as to how leaders should manage their Chinese personnel, but mostly in a way that takes Western management principles and practises as given, rather than questioning whether those principles and practises are appropriate across cultures. What may seem like neutral, value-free tools and systems, however, are always embedded within a given set of cultural values, and even what merely look like technical alternatives should be understood within their cultural contexts (Steers, Meyer, and Sanchez-Runde, 2008).

An adequate understanding of the Chinese context should trace the different historical and ideological traditions in China and the West (Jullien, 2002). The Western tradition begins with the culture, beliefs, and traditions of ancient Greece. The Greeks evolved the concept of *eîdos* as the ideal form that humans should pursue and achieve as *télos* or goal. The task of leaders then consists of bridging the gap between the ideal and reality. By contrast, this concept of ideal form or archetype never developed in ancient China. Instead, reality was understood as a process emanating from the interaction between opposing principle—yin and yang. Equilibrium and order would not follow from achieving some ideal state (a goal-oriented approach, so typical in the Western tradition), but from the natural propensity of things, with which humans should not interfere (here, the concept of *wu-wei* or no action that we mentioned before). Because the Chinese emphasize specific processes rather than ideal concepts and states, their thinking and practise tends to be more pragmatic, whereas Western approaches linger on abstraction. Leaders in the Chinese tradition need to locate themselves in the flow of reality in what appears, under Western reflection, like a passive mode, so that the natural flow and evolution of events is not disturbed. Each situation presents itself full of potential to be exploited, rather than in a blank slate mode requiring inspiring vision and ideals to be pursued actively. Therefore, the Chinese tradition ignores the task of leadership as defining action plans properly executed. There is not a sense of a goal or specific finality to be achieved, but the need to assess the situation so that favorable effects can be appropriated from the natural evolution of events. Chinese leaders then excel at patience and humility (beyond the grandness of heroic action, as in Greek drama), and things look as though they simply happened rather than people achieving some final states of events.

By contrast, Western management is based on the idea of results attained from minimizing the gap between goal and achievement, the planned and the attained. Action becomes an external disruption of the natural order of things (which only a fool would try to accomplish under traditional Chinese eyes). Western action is seen by the Chinese as extemporaneous, direct and costly, while Chinese activity is slow, indirect, progressive and natural, imposing itself without resistance (see Table 11).

Traditional thinking turns into particular ways of managing people. Following the Sino-American comparison, differences can be traced to multiple areas, and we will now briefly mention the fundamental leadership area of team dynamics and the bases for collaboration and compliance (for a more detailed description and application in a specific company, see Sanchez-Runde, Nardon, and Steers, 2011).

American management traditionally follows a functionalist model in which leader excellence is viewed in terms of task accomplishment that is instrumental for success. By contrast, the Chinese approach is more personal in nature. The personal integrity of each leader is the key requirement for organizational success. In this way, the Chinese manager wins the trust and respect of his collaborators, while the American would value job competence and technical expertise on the tasks at hand. This begins to explain the enormous importance that the Chinese give to personal relationships (guanxi) where American rather emphasize strict professionalism. Formal behavior by Americans (rather than emphasis on personal relationships) is seen as professionalism.

Table 11: East–West foundations of leadership

	Western traditions	Chinese traditions
Leadership beliefs	Seek to achieve ideal end states (*eîdos* and *télos*)	Seek to balance countervailing forces (*yin* and *yang*)
Leadership goals	Establish and pursue aspirational goals; manage the results	Create conditions conducive to success; manage the process
Leadership logic	Logic of application; articulate objectives and determine reasonable means to desired ends	Logic of exploitation; place oneself in a position to exploit opportunities as they emerge
Leadership bias	Bias for action; capture the initiative	Bias for patience; let events come to you

This leads to reliance on formal, impersonal rules and policies. The Chinese regard this as somewhat naïve, in that reality is too complex to be subsumed under strict rules and policies, and the personal touch becomes inescapable. Because these dynamics operate at the center of all organizational action, the implications go beyond interpersonal exchanges between leaders and followers. One can see the influence beyond individual matters, for instance, in the differential structuring arrangements typical of American and Chinese firms, as well as their effects on decision-making (we cannot examine this process here; the interested reader can find a more detailed description, with applications to the organizational structures in eight countries, in Steers, Nardon, and Sanchez-Runde, 2009).

Naturally, these different decision-making approaches are not completely deterministic. American management has spread its influence well beyond Western borders, and Asian countries have adopted many aspects of Western practise. This means that it will become increasingly common to find hybrid approaches around the world, particularly in Asia. Asian approaches, however, have not been so widely adopted outside Asian borders—at least not yet. In a way, this unbalanced pattern of foreign practise adoption enriches Asian management by enlarging its own behavioral repertoire and might eventually become a source of advantage. This is similar to what has happened in other fields, such as medicine and the health sciences, where Asian countries have added Western practises to their own traditional ones while the West lags behind in benefiting from alternative approaches.

Concluding comments

We cannot afford to discard culture as a key element in the development of global leadership. Naturally, this makes for a more difficult approach to leadership, for several reasons. First, because different cultures require, to some extent at least, different leader behaviors, leadership development becomes a never-ending endeavor. Second, because it is not clear that what works in one culture will also prove effective in another, global leaders always move across borders as novices, never as experts. One knows what to expect and can cut corners when feeling completely at home, as an expert. When moving to another country, the leadership learning process begins again, rather than merely continuing from prior assignments. Global leaders, in a sense, never completely become experts, and always need to be alert to all the facts and dynamism in the new country with which they are not completely aware. This is why global leadership requires continuous prudence and humility. This is why, so far at least, the research literature has not been able to assign a significant weight to the impact of experience at previous leadership assignments as a predictor of future successes. Of course, this is different from what happens within our natural environments, and makes for complex learning challenges.

The challenges go beyond personal attitudes and behaviors on the part of global leaders. Educational institutions, and international business schools particularly, need to rethink the curriculum of their programs to introduce the cultural variable. Most of what business schools teach was thought and developed in—and for—Western environments. Very few programs introduce, in any systematic way, cross-cultural courses and approaches to assess the generalization of findings across cultures. Because some of those programs are actually quite diverse in terms of country of origin of participant members, some informal cross-cultural exchanges may actually take place. But school and program development needs to take a more direct and conscious approach to prepare global leaders who will work effectively across cultures.

NOTES

1 For a basic review of the challenges derived from the ambiguity of the basic concepts for people management, see Sanchez-Runde (2004).

2 The first cross-cultural, international, and comparative studies began to appear, in a non-systematic and rather exceptional way, during the 1980s and 1990s, mostly following the work by Geert Hofstede (1980). It has not been until very recently,

with the GLOBE study of 62 societies led by Robert House (2004) that a more comprehensive, major take on the subject has actually happened. Of course, there have been many other smaller-scale studies, but we still face a substantial deficit in the field. Let us add, parenthetically, that this situation is not peculiar to leadership studies but rather common to all management disciplines.

3 The team of researchers of the INNFORM Program studied innovative organizations in the United States, Europe, and Japan between 1995 and 2005, with participating teams from the University of Warwick, IESE Business School, Oxford University, University of Saint Gallen, Jönköping University, ESSEC, Erasmus University, Hitotsubashi University, and Duke University. This effort still constitutes the leading study of innovating organizations.

4 Here we follow some of our previous work on cross-cultural leadership (Sanchez-Runde, Nardon, and Steers, 2011). A more elaborated view can be found in the authors' introduction to the "Special Issue on Cross-Cultural Leadership" to appear by the end of 2012 in the *Journal of World Business* (Steers, Sanchez-Runde, and Nardon, in press).

REFERENCES

Cyert, R. and March, J. (1992) *A Behavioral Theory of the Firm* (Oxford: Blackwell).

Drucker, P. (1996) "Not Enough Generals Were Killed." Foreword to F. Hesselbein, M. Glodsmith, and R. Beckhard (eds) *The Leader of the Future* (San Francisco, CA: Jossey-Bass): xi–xv.

Evans, P. and Doz, Y. (1992) "Dualities: A Paradigm for Human Resource and Organizational Development in Complex Multinationals." In V. Pucik, N. Tichy, and C. Barnett (eds) *Globalizing Management: Creating and Leading the Competitive Organization* (New York, NY: Wiley): 85–106.

Fiske, E. (1992) *Smart Schools, Smart Kids* (New York, NY: Touchstone).

Gelfand, M., Bhawuk, D., Nishii, L., and Bechtold, D. (2004) "Individualism and Collectivism." In R. House, P. Hanges, M. Javidan, and P. Dorfman (eds) *Culture, Leadership and Organizations: The GLOBE Study of 62 Societies* (Thousand Oaks, CA: Sage): 437–512.

Gerstner, L. (1994) *Reinventing Education: Entrepreneurship in America's Public Schools* (New York, NY: Dutton).

González-Simancas, J. (1992) *Educación: Libertad y Compromiso* (Pamplona: EUNSA).

Hampden-Turner, C. (1990) *Charting the Corporate Mind: From Dilemma to Strategy* (Oxford: Blackwell).

Handy, C. (1994) *The Age of Paradox* (Boston, MA: Harvard Business School Press).

Heine, S. (2008) *Cultural Psychology* (New York, NY: Norton).

Hofstede, G. (1980) *Culture's Consequences: International Differences in Work-Related Values* (Newbury Park, CA: Sage).

House, R., Hanges, P., Javidan, M., Dorfman, P., and Gupta, V. (eds) (1994) *Culture, Leadership and Organizations: The GLOBE Study of 62 Societies* (Thousand Oaks, CA: Sage).

Jullien, F. (1992) *Penser d'un Dehors (la Chine): Entretiens d'Extrême Occident* (Paris: Seuil).

Jullien, F. (1996) *Traité de l'Efficacité* (Paris: Éditions Grasset & Fasquelle).

Kanungo, R. and Mendonca, M. (1994) *Work Motivation: Models for Developing Countries* (New Delhi: Sage).

Kase, K., Slocum, A., and Zhang, Y. (2011) *Asian versus Western Management Thinking: Its Culture-Bound Nature* (New York, NY: Palgrave Macmillan).

Kohn, A. (1993) *Punished by Rewards* (Boston, MA: Houghton Mifflin).

Lincoln, J. and Kalleberg, A. (1990) *Culture, Control, and Commitment: A Study of Work Organization and Work Attitudes in the United States and Japan* (Cambridge: Cambridge University Press).

Mittroff I. and Linstone, H. (1993) *The Unbounded Mind: Breaking the Chains of Traditional Business Thinking* (Oxford: Oxford University Press).

Mowday, R., Porter, L., and Steers, R. (1982) *Organizational Linkages: The Psychology of Commitment, Absenteeism, and Turnover* (San Diego, CA: Academic Press).

Nardon, L., Steers, R., and Sanchez-Runde, C. (2011) "Seeking Common Ground: Strategies for Enhancing Multicultural Communication." *Organizational Dynamics* 40: 85–95.

Pettigrew, A. and Fenton, E. (eds) (2000) *The Innovating Organization* (London: Sage).

Sanchez-Runde, C. (2004) "Changing Foundations of People Management." In S. Chowdhury (ed.) *Next Generation Business Handbook* (Hoboken, NJ: Wiley): 872–883.

Sanchez-Runde, C. and Pettigrew, A. (2003) "Managing Dualities." In A. Pettigrew, R. Whittington, L. Melin, C. Sanchez-Runde, F. van den Bosch, W. Ruigrok, and T. Numagami (eds) *Innovative Forms of Organizing: International Perspectives* (London: Sage): 243–250.

Sanchez-Runde, C., Massini, S., and Quintanilla, J. (2003) "People Management Dualities." In A. Pettigrew, R. Whittington, L. Melin, C. Sanchez-Runde, F. van den Bosch, W. Ruigrok, and T. Numagami (eds) *Innovative Forms of Organizing: International Perspectives* (London: Sage): 251–276.

Sanchez-Runde, C., Nardon, L., and Steers, R. (2011) "Looking Beyond Western Leadership Models: Implications for Global Managers." *Organizational Dynamics* 40: 207–213.

Schumaker, J. (1997) "Religious Motivation Across Cultures." in D. Munro, J. Schumaker, and S. Carr (eds) *Motivation and Culture* (New York, NY: Routledge): 193–208.

Steers, R., Meyer, A., and Sanchez-Runde, C. (2008) "National Culture and the Adoption of New Technologies." *Journal of World Business* 43: 255–260.

Steers, R., Nardon, L., and Sanchez-Runde, C. (2009) "Culture and Organizational Design: Strategy, Structure, and Decision-making." In R. Bhagat and R. Steers (eds) *Culture, Organizations and Work* (Cambridge: Cambridge University Press): 71–117.

Steers, R., Sanchez-Runde, C., and Nardon, L. (2010) *Management Across Cultures: Challenges and Strategies* (Cambridge: Cambridge University Press).

Steers, R., Sanchez-Runde, C., and Nardon, L. (in press) "Leadership in a Global Context: New Directions in Research and Theory Development." *Journal of World Business* 47.

Triandis, H. (1994) *Culture and Social Behavior* (New York, NY: McGraw-Hill).

Index